EZRA TAFT BENSON

STATESMAN, PATRIOT, PROPHET OF GOD

FRANCIS M. GIBBONS

DESERET BOOK COMPANY
SALT LAKE CITY, UTAH

Visit us at DeseretBook.com

First printing in hardbound 1996.
First printing in paperbound 2009.

Library of Congress Cataloging-in-Publication Data

Gibbons, Francis M., 1921–
    Ezra Taft Benson : statesman, patriot, prophet of God / Francis M. Gibbons
      p.   cm.
    Includes bibliographical references and index.
    ISBN-10 1-57345-148-7 (hardbound)
    ISBN-13 978-1-60641-219-0 (paperbound)
    1. Benson, Ezra Taft.   2. The Church of Jesus Christ of Latter-day Saints—Presidents—Biography.   3. Mormon Church—Presidents—Biography.   I. Title
BX8695.B38G52   1996
289.3'092—dc20
[B]   96-27336
           CIP

Printed in the United States of America

10 9 8 7 6 5 4 3 2 1

To Helen

Contents

Acknowledgments   ix

1   Roots   1

2   The Boy   14

3   The Boy Matures   29

4   The Missionary   46

5   From Student to Married Man   66

6   Professional and Personal Growth   80

7   To Boise, to Berkeley, and Back   91

8   To Washington   108

9   Called to the Twelve   124

10   Shepherding the Saints in Europe   145

11   Apostolic Initiatives   159

12   Into the Maelstrom   175

13   The Battle over Subsidies   193

14   The Battle against Surpluses   202

15   Global Salesman   213

Contents

16 The Transition 234

17 Presidential Overtures 244

18 Major Changes 263

19 President of the Twelve 270

20 President of the Church 295

Epilogue 319

Bibliography 323

Index 329

Acknowledgments

Thanks go to members of the staff of the Historical Department of the Church; to Ruth Stoneman for research assistance; to members of the Benson family, especially Reed Benson, who was very helpful; to many friends and associates at Church headquarters who worked with President Benson; and, as always, to the Mentor.

Chapter 1

Roots

When the baby was named Ezra Taft Benson at his birth on August 4, 1899, the name was famous already. His great-grandfather, who bore the same name and was a member of the Council of the Twelve Apostles of The Church of Jesus Christ of Latter-day Saints, had given the name distinction. This ancestor never used the full middle name, however, preferring only the initial "T," thus providing a convenient way to differentiate the two.

Other differences between them became more apparent as the great-grandson matured and as his innate qualities and drives were reflected in his achievements. The crowning achievement that distinguished him from his namesake and, indeed, from all save a small handful of men, was his elevation to the prophetic office when he became the thirteenth President of The Church of Jesus Christ of Latter-day Saints.

Although the working careers of this pair were different due to the contrasting environments in which they lived, they were alike in their attitudes, their methods, and their basic qualities of character. Both were energetic, prayerful, spiritually minded, zealous, patriotic, and self-disciplined; they were men who were filled with faith and determination, who worked hard, who were concerned more with issues and principles than with personalities, who were whole-souled, and who had a driving desire for self-improvement. Also, they possessed a deep sense of love and loyalty, especially toward their families. It was said of the Bensons that if you challenged one of them, you should be prepared to contest with all of them. When a member of the family was challenged and in difficulty, the others presented a united front of active support.

These qualities derived mainly from heredity. John Benson, the first family ancestor in America, arrived in Boston from London aboard the *Confidence* in April 1638. In the new land he became a farmer. He operated farms at Hingham and then at Hull, Massachusetts. With some exceptions, his descendants have farmed in America for more than three centuries. It is an occupation that teaches independence, faith in God, family unity, honesty, frugality, and industry. From the time of John Benson's arrival in America in 1638 until February 22, 1811, when the first Ezra Taft Benson was born in Mendon, Worcester County, the family played a vital role in the development of Massachusetts and in the struggle for independence from England.

It was in the Mendon area that Ezra T.'s father, John, met and married Chloe Taft. The first Taft on Chloe's line to come to America was Robert Taft, who arrived in 1667. He was one of the first settlers in Mendon. His name, along with thirty-eight others, appears on a bronze plaque in Mendon's Memorial Park. Other families from this area related to the Bensons or to the Tafts are the Aldriches, the Thayers, the Whites, and the Holbrooks.

Robert Taft was a housewright, an occupation equivalent to that of contractor and builder today. His descendants followed various business and professional occupations while retaining close touch with the land. The influence of his Benson and Taft ancestors explains in part the career path Ezra T. Benson followed. As a youth, he farmed with his father near Uxbridge, Massachusetts. John had moved his family there when Ezra T. was six years old. When he was fifteen, Ezra moved into town, where he worked for three years as an assistant in a little hotel owned by his brother-in-law Calvin Rawson. After operating his grandmother's farm for a year when she became widowed, he purchased his brother-in-law's interest in the hotel, which he managed profitably for two years. Meanwhile, he married Pamelia Andrus (sometimes called Andrews).

In 1835 Ezra T. Benson moved his family to Holland, Massachusetts, where he and a brother-in-law, Orrin C. Andrus, leased and operated a cotton factory. Caught in a spiral of falling prices, the factory suffered severe losses, and the business had to be abandoned. Ezra T. then cared for his family by operating another small leased hotel and by serving as the town postmaster. The Bensons later moved to Salem, New Jersey, where Ezra T. made a living buying and selling goods.

In the spring of 1837, the Bensons moved to St. Louis, Missouri. Ezra T. had wanted to go west for several years. Indeed, he had an urgent feeling to go there, without knowing the reason why or precisely where in the West he should go. As he matured, such feelings or promptings became more frequent and compelling, especially after he became a member of The Church of Jesus Christ of Latter-day Saints.

In St. Louis, Ezra T. revealed his entrepreneurial skills again. He became associated in business with a Mr. Trowbridge, whom he had not known before. Provided with a stock of goods by his partner, Ezra T. began working along the Illinois River, north of St. Louis, selling and bartering. Later, he and another partner, Isaac Hill, laid out a town site on the Illinois River named Pike, not far from Lexington, Illinois. Here he dealt in real estate and built a home. He also built a warehouse in which he stowed cut cordwood for sale to passing steamboats. Then, seeking better opportunities in a place he considered to be healthier, he moved to Quincy, Illinois, on the Mississippi River, south of Commerce City, later renamed Nauvoo.

When Ezra T. arrived in Quincy in the fall of 1838, events were maturing in neighboring Missouri across the river that would result in the forcible expulsion of the Mormons. Joseph and Hyrum Smith and other Church leaders were then imprisoned in the jail at Liberty, Missouri. While they were there, Missouri governor Lilburn W. Boggs issued his cruel extermination order against the Latter-day Saints. Under the direction of Brigham Young, President of the Twelve, the refugees streamed out of Missouri, crossing the Mississippi into Illinois. Most of them established temporary quarters near Quincy. The scene was chaotic; they lived in wagons, tents, or hurriedly erected lean-to shelters. A skimpy diet, poor sanitation facilities, and exposure brought on an epidemic of intestinal illnesses. This was Ezra T. Benson's first personal introduction to the Mormon Church and its members.

He had heard reports about the Latter-day Saints before. These were garbled and uncomplimentary, portraying the Mormons as fanatics, unreasoning and belligerent, even murderous. He could not reconcile these stories with the character of the people whom he met near Quincy. Not only were they intelligent and humble, but they were buoyant and optimistic in their adversity. He saw no evidence of fanaticism among them. In their meetings, he saw none of the wild, uncontrolled emotionalism that had been reported. And he found a refreshing friendliness and camaraderie that made him feel at home among them. He decided these people and their beliefs had been grossly misrepresented. His changed attitudes led him into a serious study of the Mormon Church and its doctrine.

There was an aspect of the Mormon story that seemed peculiar to Ezra T. and that presented something of a stumbling block. This was the belief that Joseph Smith had seen and conversed with the Father and the Son and that the gift of prophecy and the other gifts of the Spirit were evident in the Church. Though he had never openly affiliated with a church, Ezra T. held the common sectarian belief that the canon of scripture was full and that there were to be no further revelations from God or heavenly appearances to the earth. His search, therefore, was impeded by this basic doubt regarding the fundamental premise of the Mormon Church—that God continually reveals himself to those who have faith in Him. Undoubtedly this impediment was a major factor that delayed his baptism into the Church.

There were several milestones along the path of Ezra T. Benson's conversion. The first was his friendship with a Mormon family named Gordon, who had left Missouri in advance of the main exodus and had established a home near Quincy. Thomas Gordon, the husband, impressed with Ezra T.'s appearance and conduct, invited him to stay in the Gordon home until he could prepare a place for his family. This gave Ezra T. an intimate view of a Mormon family and of the impact of Mormon teachings upon personal conduct. It also opened the door to Mormon meetings to which the Gordons invited him as their guest.

The first Latter-day Saint meetings he attended did not impress him. At one of them, for instance, the speaker spoke so long and uninterestingly that Ezra T. left before the meeting ended. However, he was exposed favorably to Latter-day Saint literature in the home, which he was at liberty to read in his leisure. Meanwhile, he acquired a tract of land near Quincy from another member of the Church, Dr. Ells. He built a house there, enclosed the two-acre tract with close paling, and planted a variety of fruit trees and some ornamental trees. It became the family home of the Bensons until they moved north to Nauvoo.

When Pamelia arrived in Quincy, she was introduced to Ezra's Mormon friends and began to attend Mormon meetings with him. Her keen interest in the Church was kindled immediately. But her husband was only lukewarm toward it until they attended a series of meetings in the summer of 1840. The first was held in July in a Baptist church in Quincy, where Sidney Rigdon was scheduled to discuss the claims of the Mormon Church with a Baptist minister, Dr. Nelson. When Elder Rigdon was unable to attend, his place was filled by Ezra's friend, Dr. Ells. Joseph Smith attended the meeting and sat on the stand, but he did not speak. Ezra T. seemed as much interested in this fact as he was in the two talks. Also he was interested in the Prophet's composure and his friendly, benign countenance while Dr. Nelson bluntly attacked his character and motives and ridiculed his teachings. It occurred to Ezra that Joseph Smith's conduct was the opposite of what one might expect of a charlatan. At the same time, he was impressed that Dr. Nelson's talk advanced no evidence or authority to counter the claims of Dr. Ells, but relied solely on bitter denunciation of Joseph Smith and the Mormon Church.

Another meeting was held in the afternoon at a grove outside Quincy. Again Joseph Smith attended and did not speak. An Elder Cairns was appointed to answer Dr. Nelson, who continued his attacks. This time he scoffed at the idea of people speaking in tongues. He illustrated by using an exaggerated gibberish, asking what tongue he was speaking in. Answering, Elder Cairns quoted 2 Peter 3:3, suggesting the scripture characterized Dr. Nelson. Ezra was impressed that it did. He was confirmed in this belief when Dr. Nelson had a kind of fit on the stand and would have fallen had not others sprung to steady him.

There is little doubt these meetings convinced Ezra T. Benson that Joseph Smith was a prophet. It seems ironic because the Prophet Joseph, noted for his eloquence and persuasiveness, said nothing. He let his disciples and the impressive body of religious literature he had translated or authored speak for him. He merely sat and listened with poise and self-confidence, obviously assured that nothing Dr. Nelson could say would undermine him or his teachings.

The process begun with these meetings reached fruition

later in the summer when Ezra and Pamelia attended two more Mormon meetings in Quincy. They were held by Orson Hyde and John E. Page, members of the Twelve who had been called to go to the Holy Land to dedicate it. The Apostles delivered impressive sermons on the gathering of the Jews, the rebuilding of Jerusalem, and the gathering of the Ten Tribes, all supported by relevant scriptures. At the end of the meeting, Pamelia, with tears in her eyes, asked Ezra if he had given money to help these men on their mission as they had requested. Ezra said he had given them fifty cents, all the money he had. Pamelia replied that she would have given money to them too if she had had any, because the two Apostles were deserving of it.

Soon after these meetings, Pamelia told Ezra she was converted and wanted to be baptized. He had reached the same conclusion but asked her to wait a week to enable him to resolve a private matter. So on a Sunday afternoon, July 19, 1840, following a sacrament service in the Quincy Branch, Ezra T. Benson and Pamelia Andrus Benson were baptized in the Mississippi River by Daniel Stanton. A large crowd watched from the riverbank.

An incident at the sacrament meeting preceding the baptisms suggests the depth of the Bensons' conversion. During the service a loud dispute arose between two men at the sacrament table. Afterward, Pamelia asked Ezra what he thought of it. He said such a display of personal weakness was irrelevant to the eternal truths taught by the Church. This spiritual maturity was recognized a few months after his baptism when Ezra T. Benson was called as the second counselor in the Quincy Stake presidency by Hyrum Smith, who had been assigned to create the new stake. Hyrum Smith ordained Ezra T. a high priest at the time he set him apart.

Although Ezra T. Benson was only twenty-nine years old when he was baptized, he was a man of wide experience. For almost half of his life he had been engaged in various business enterprises. He had shown resiliency and initiative in conducting them, especially when faced with temporary setbacks. And he had shown a knack of forming profitable and lasting friendships in new localities where he settled. These qualities would be valuable to his new church that was building a modern city at Nauvoo and was engaged in an international missionary effort.

Directing this ambitious work was the dynamic young leader, Joseph Smith, who was six years older than Ezra. From the time he first saw the Prophet in Quincy before his baptism, Ezra seemed magnetically drawn to him. There was something about Joseph Smith that inspired loyalty and a sense of discipleship in able, spiritually sensitive young men like Ezra T. Benson. So pronounced was this in Ezra that only a few months after his call to the stake presidency, he felt impressed to gather with the Saints in Nauvoo, where he would be under the direct influence of this man. However, before acting on that impression, Ezra, because of his leadership responsibilities in Quincy, sought the Prophet's counsel. Joseph received him graciously. After listening to Ezra's plans, the Prophet told him he should do what he was impressed to do and that if he decided to come he would be welcome.

In the spring of 1841, Ezra T. disposed of his interests in Quincy, loaded his belongings in a wagon, and with his family traveled to Nauvoo, arriving the first week in April. He went first to the home of Bishop Vinson Knight, whose house was located a block north of the Prophet's home and adjacent to the home of Brigham Young. The bishop invited the Bensons to stay with him and his wife, Martha McBride Knight, and their family until Ezra could find a place to rent. The bishop also invited the newcomers to accompany his family to the general conference then in progress. When Ezra asked about the safety of his wagon and personal effects, the bishop assured him they would be safe and that in any event he would be responsible for anything taken. Nothing was touched.

A special feature of this conference was the laying of the cornerstones of the Nauvoo Temple, a structure on which

Ezra T. Benson would perform many hours of labor. Located on the bluff overlooking the burgeoning residential neighborhoods below, the temple site afforded a sweeping view of the Mississippi River as it curled around the promontory that once was swampland but that had been reclaimed for prime residential sites. During the ceremony, the Prophet explained baptism for the dead, a doctrine known of old but lost through the Apostasy.

Ezra T. Benson arrived in Nauvoo at a time of critical transition. During that month, the Prophet Joseph Smith took his first plural wife. Rumors of polygamy in the Church had circulated for years. They sprang from a revelation Joseph received in the early 1830s. Not until April 1841, however, did he teach and practice it. Ezra learned about this later when he was inducted into a small circle of men directed to practice the principle.

Ezra's arrival in Nauvoo also coincided with a conspiracy against the Prophet by some of his closest associates who sought his death. This occurred while most of the Twelve Apostles were abroad on missions. They returned a few weeks after the April general conference, and at a special meeting held on August 16, 1841, the Prophet announced the time had come for the Twelve "to stand in their place next to the First Presidency, and attend to the settling of emigrants and the business of the Church at the stakes, and assist to bear off the kingdom victoriously to the nations" (*History of the Church*, 4:403). This change strengthened the role of the Twelve in Church government, paving the way for the transfer of prophetic authority at the death of the President of the Church. Soon after their return from abroad, Ezra aligned himself closely with members of the Twelve while maintaining his first allegiance to the Prophet Joseph Smith. These relationships were an important factor in Ezra T. Benson's later call to the Twelve.

A man with Ezra T. Benson's experience and skills had little difficulty making his way in Nauvoo. He soon purchased a lot, fenced it, built a log cabin on it, and beautified it with plants. He later built a brick home on the lot. Ezra became involved in various enterprises in town and associated with some of the leading brethren. One of them was Heber C. Kimball, to whom Ezra confided his willingness and desire to serve a mission for the Church. In June 1842 this desire was realized when he was called to the eastern states. Later he was called to the Nauvoo high council and was one of the 340 men who campaigned for Joseph Smith in his bid for the presidency of the United States. After the Prophet's martyrdom, Ezra was called on another mission to the eastern states, where he served as president of the Boston Massachusetts Conference. Meanwhile, at the suggestion of the Brethren, he entered into plural marriage, being sealed to Pamelia's sister, Adeline Andrus.

In early February 1846, Ezra T. Benson, his two wives, and two children crossed the Mississippi River to join the Latter-day Saint exodus. They left their comfortable home and furnishings behind. There were no complaints or recriminations even though both wives were expecting children. Pamelia gave birth to a little girl, Isabella, on March 15 while they were on the trail. Later at Garden Grove, a Mormon way station, Adeline gave birth to a son while lying in a wagon box. He was named George Taft Benson, the grandfather of Ezra Taft Benson. A few weeks later, on July 16, 1846, while at Council Bluffs, Iowa, Ezra T. Benson was ordained an Apostle and set apart as a member of the Council of the Twelve.

Ezra T. played a key role in preparing the pioneer company, counseling with Brigham Young and helping recruit members for it. He served as the captain of the second company of ten during the trek from Winter Quarters to the Salt Lake Valley. After moving his family to the valley, he built a gracious two-story home at the corner of South Temple and Main Street and became actively involved in developing the city and surrounding areas. Among other enterprises, he promoted the construction of a grist mill in Tooele Valley, west of Salt Lake City, in 1852. Remains of the mill still stand.

Following the so-called Utah War of 1857, President Brigham Young called Ezra T. Benson to preside over the Saints in northern Utah's Cache Valley. This furthered a plan of colonization that had seen other members of the Twelve called to preside in outlying areas. George A. Smith and Erastus Snow, for instance, had been sent to southern Utah; Lorenzo Snow to Brigham City, Utah; Orson Hyde to Carson Valley, Nevada, and then to Sanpete Valley, Utah; Charles C. Rich to San Bernardino, California, and later to the Bear Lake region of Utah and Idaho; and Franklin D. Richards to Ogden, Utah. When President Young extended the call to Ezra T., he casually suggested that Ezra sell his Salt Lake City home to Daniel H. Wells, a counselor in the First Presidency. With no hesitancy, Ezra accepted the call, sold his home to President Wells, and moved his family to Cache Valley. Soon after, he built a rustic cabin on a lot in Logan, Utah, now identified as 139 East First North Street.

Elder Benson's stoical acceptance of this change was mirrored in the attitudes of his wives. None of them complained about leaving their pleasant home in the heart of Salt Lake City and moving to an undeveloped area where, for some time, they would live in primitive conditions. The incident reveals a Benson family characteristic of subordinating personal interests to the overriding interests of the Church.

Elder Benson first saw Cache Valley in November 1859. In company with Elder Orson Hyde, he went there to organize the 150 families living in six small communities: Logan, Maughan's Fort, Spring Creek, Summit Creek, Cut Creek, and North Settlement. All except Logan were given new names: Maughan's Fort became Wellsville (named in honor of Daniel H. Wells, to whom Ezra T. had sold his Salt Lake home), Spring Creek became Providence, Summit Creek became Smithfield, Cut Creek became Richmond, and

11

North Settlement became Mendon (named in honor of Ezra T.'s ancestral home in Massachusetts).

Elder Benson soon brought his organizational skills to bear in the development of Cache Valley. The work load was divided among the little communities, so some were responsible for plowing and planting, some for building, some for digging ditches and canals, and some for making furniture and fixtures for the homes. Meanwhile, he constructed a mill as he had done in Tooele and joined with others to construct a private canal to carry water from the Little Logan River. He also was one of the principals in organizing a cooperative and was instrumental in establishing public schools. Later he became involved in constructing the transcontinental railroad and represented his area in the territorial legislature. Amid all this he was the spiritual leader of the Latter-day Saints in the valley, directing the work of the bishops. And occasionally he filled special apostolic assignments, as he did in 1864 when he accompanied Elder Lorenzo Snow to the Hawaiian Islands to settle a controversy created by the apostate Walter Murray Gibson.

After the exodus, Ezra T. Benson was sealed to Eliza Ann Perry, Olive Mary Knight, Elizabeth Golliher, and Mary Larsen. These four women, with Pamelia and Adeline Andrus Benson, his first two wives, bore him thirty-eight sons and daughters. Many of these children married and settled in Cache Valley. One of them, George Taft Benson, Adeline's son who was born in Garden Grove during the exodus, married Louisa A. Ballif, the daughter of converts from Switzerland. George T. and Louisa played a prominent role in colonizing the northern part of Cache Valley, located in what became part of the state of Idaho. Settling in a small rural community south of Preston, Idaho, they were the parents of thirteen children. One of these children, George Taft Benson Jr., married Sarah Dunkley. Like his father, George T. Jr. was active in Church affairs, serving successively as a member of a bishopric, a member of the stake high council, and a member of the Franklin Stake presidency. He also was active in promoting civic improvements and served for several years as a county commissioner.

George Taft Benson Jr. and Sarah Dunkley were the parents of eleven children. The oldest was a son whom they named Ezra Taft Benson in honor of his great-grandfather. What follows is the life story of this son, who was endowed at birth with the solid qualities of his ancestors and with a distinguished name that would be a constant motivation to him.

Chapter 2

The Boy

Whitney, Idaho, the birthplace of Ezra Taft Benson, is so small that it is not shown on some maps. A cluster of farms in Cache Valley near the Utah border was organized as a community when the Mormon ward in Preston to the north was divided. The name Whitney was suggested by George Taft Benson Sr., the bishop of the new unit. It honors Orson F. Whitney, the longtime bishop of the Eighteenth Ward in Salt Lake City, whom George Taft Benson admired for his character and his writings. The town's namesake, who later became a member of the Twelve, played key roles in the life of Ezra Taft Benson, serving as his mission president in Great Britain and performing his temple sealing to Flora Amussen. So the name Whitney was reminiscent of more than home to the man who became the thirteenth President of The Church of Jesus Christ of Latter-day Saints.

The surroundings, the inhabitants, and the ruling principles of Whitney were conducive to the growth of good people. The fertile valley, originally called Willow Valley by

the early trappers, yielded flourishing crops of fruits, vegetables, and grains. A tributary of the Bear River that flowed
through the valley provided water for irrigation, and the
abundant forest on the mountains to the east, some of
whose peaks towered to ten thousand feet, provided ample
timber for building. The name Cache, later used to identify
the valley, derived from the practice of early trappers to
cache their beaver pelts there. Jim Bridger and some of his
friends trapped the tributaries of the Bear River as early as
1824 and 1825. Bridger is reputed to have been the first
Anglo-Saxon to see the Great Salt Lake. He built a boat in
Willow Valley and floated down the Bear River to its outlet
on the Great Salt Lake. Floating far enough into the lake to
detect that the water was saline, Jim Bridger at first thought
the lake was an arm of the Pacific Ocean.

At the time of the birth of Ezra Taft Benson on August 4,
1899, the Latter-day Saints had been developing Cache
Valley for several decades. As already noted, they had cultivated the soil; had built homes, mills, and roads; had
established schools; and had been organized into ecclesiastical units for worship purposes and to provide the mechanism for cooperative efforts and for the teaching and
perpetuation of Mormon doctrines.

The Mormon religion is like a seamless garment. There
is no line to separate temporal and spiritual affairs, nor to
differentiate between Sabbath and weekday conduct and
responsibilities. The ideal and the goal is that a Latter-day
Saint will be a Saint at all times and in all places, constantly
led by the whisperings of the Holy Ghost. This aim is fostered by regular teaching and exhortation in formal group
meetings; by teaching in the homes by assigned priesthood
brethren and Relief Society sisters; and by regular family
prayers, devotionals, and scripture study. And on an individual basis, Latter-day Saints are admonished to have a
prayer always in their hearts so they will be enlightened and
guided constantly by spiritual promptings.

George T. Benson Jr., the father of President Ezra Taft

Benson, was of the third generation of Bensons to live in Cache Valley and to be molded and motivated by those concepts. The direct example of his father, who served as bishop of the Whitney Ward for twenty-three years, and the reputation of his grandfather, Ezra T. Benson of the Twelve, who died several years before George Jr. was born, provided a special impetus for him to adopt their values. And when he married Sarah Dunkley, he had an even stronger incentive to do so.

Sarah's father, Joseph Dunkley, was converted in England and migrated to Utah in 1854 with his wife, Margaret Leach, who was childless. He later married Mary Ann Hobbs, who died in childbirth, and Margaret Wright, who gave birth to thirteen children—eight sons and five daughters. Sarah, child number six, was born in Franklin, Idaho, south of Whitney near the Idaho-Utah border, in 1878, twenty years after her father was called by Brigham Young to help settle the area.

The normal difficulties of farming a new land were aggravated by occasional friction with the Indians, whose ancestors had roamed the area for generations. Understandably upset by intrusions on their hunting grounds, the Indians, though not warlike, were prone to take what they wanted from the possessions of the settlers, especially their horses and cattle. To avoid open conflict, the farmers carefully guarded their stock, while never retaliating when something was taken. This wise policy, formulated by Brigham Young, minimized the friction between the Indians and the Mormon settlers. Learning of the peaceful attitudes of the Latter-day Saints, and apparently anxious to reduce the chance of armed conflict, the Indians often would come openly to ask for things they wanted. A legend in the Dunkley family reveals the way this standoff played out between the two groups and the spunky character of Sarah Dunkley's mother: An Indian appeared at the Dunkley house one day while Margaret was alone and asked for flour. She complied without any question, as she did when

16

he asked for sugar. But when he asked for more flour, she refused because she doubted there would be enough for the family. At that the Indian left peacefully. When Margaret told Joseph about the incident, he expressed concern that she had not given the Indian what he had asked for. That night a horse was stolen from Joseph's barn.

Sarah Dunkley inherited the sturdy characteristics of her parents. She grew into a beautiful young woman, dark eyed with luxuriant black hair, who was spirited and independent and who knew how to work. She also was fun loving and liked to tease. These and other qualities of character later found their way into her famous son.

George met his future bride through one of his sisters who was Sarah's friend. Because Sarah was three years his junior, George at first paid scant attention to the little Dunkley girl from Franklin. Later, as she began to blossom into womanhood, he noticed her. Indeed, he became infatuated with her. Eventually George T. Benson became convinced he wanted to marry Sarah Dunkley. He pursued her persistently, regularly traveling to Franklin in the family buggy he was allowed to use once a week. Their courtship followed the customary pattern of the day, with visiting in the family parlor or "front room," attendance at Church meetings, group socials and dances, picnics, and buggy rides into the nearby mountains. When George found that his feelings toward Sarah were returned, they decided on marriage but delayed it until they had prepared a home. It was a two-room, stuccoed frame house with a lean-to in back set on a forty-acre farm near Whitney. In time the farm was expanded to include 120 acres. George obtained timber from the nearby forest and, though aided by his family and neighbors, did much of the work of building the house. He also worked part-time on the railroad to acquire means to purchase needed materials. Meanwhile Sarah, an expert seamstress, helped by her mother, made curtains, quilts, towels, and other accessories. When all was ready, they traveled to Logan, Utah, where they were married in the temple on October 19, 1898.

Sarah conceived soon after the marriage. Two relatives, Lulu Parkinson and Louise Alder, also were carrying babies when the three of them went to the Logan Temple to receive prenatal blessings, a common practice at the time. Each of them bore sons, great-grandsons of Ezra T. Benson. Since Sarah's child was born before the other two, he became the first great-grandson of the Apostle and was given his full name, Ezra Taft Benson. Soon this was shortened to "T," the name by which he would be called by his family and close friends during much of his life. As the inheritor of this famous name, the child also received mementos of his namesake: a blade with his great-grandfather's name engraved on it, a scabbard that his great-grandfather had received as a member of the Nauvoo Legion, and a cane. These became Ezra's valued possessions and important reminders of his distinguished roots.

It is difficult to assess the impact that Ezra's name had on him. Surely it was a strong inducement toward good conduct. Raised in an orthodox Latter-day Saint home and told of the character and achievements of his namesake, Ezra had a strong incentive to avoid anything that would dishonor the name. Moreover, he seems to have sought to add luster to it. The principle at work here is illustrated in the Book of Mormon by the sons of Helaman, Nephi and Lehi. Their father said he had named them after their first parents so that when they considered the significance of their own names, they would remember the first Nephi and Lehi and their good works and would seek to emulate them (see Helaman 5:5–7).

Ezra Taft Benson did not enter the world with ease. Because her baby weighed more than eleven pounds, Sarah had difficulty giving birth to him. After a long, painful struggle, aggravated by the use of instruments, she lay exhausted on the bed; and the baby lay on a sideboard, not breathing and seemingly without life. The doctor turned

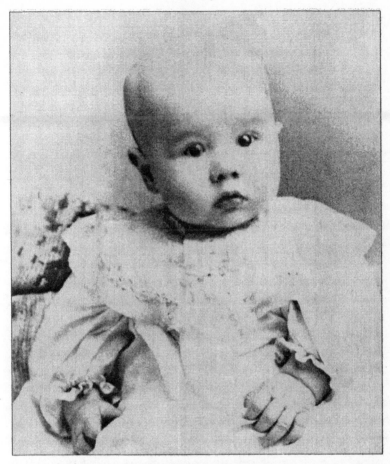

Ezra Taft Benson as a baby

first to the mother, assuming the baby had not survived. The two grandmothers who hovered nearby, seeing the emergency, stepped in to use practical skills they had learned during years of childbearing and midwifery. They hurriedly took the infant into the other room, where they alternately dipped him into basins of warm and cold water. The bracing effect of these dunkings soon brought the baby to life, wiggling and crying. It was a welcome sound to all, especially to the mother, whose exertions were rewarded with what she wanted most—a live, healthy baby. Though aware

19

of the discomfort, the inconvenience, the uncertainty, and the pain connected with childbirth, Sarah Benson endured this agonizing experience ten more times, putting herself at risk to give life to the eleven Benson children.

There was a feeling in the family from the beginning that there was something special about Sarah Benson's oldest child and that his life had been preserved at birth by divine intervention. His grandmother Louisa Benson, for instance, was heard to say that while she loved and admired all of her grandchildren, there was something unique about Ezra, whose achievements would be a source of pride to the entire family. She therefore admonished everyone to avoid making derogatory remarks about him. And the boy's uncle, Serge Benson, who ran the local store, confided to his children that Ezra was an exceptional young man who had a singular mission to perform. When someone commented on Ezra's upright bearing, Serge said it was no wonder, as he was the only boy he knew who had done nothing shameful.

Comments like this, noised about in the family, hardly could have failed to reach Ezra's ears. Nor is it unreasonable to suppose that as he grew, the boy received spiritual promptings, even though vague, about his identity and his life's work. Knowing now what he became, we must assume that Ezra Taft Benson was among that select group of leaders seen by Father Abraham and was chosen for his prophetic office before the foundations of the world (see Abraham 3:22–23). The process of piercing the veil of forgetfulness that descends on all at mortal birth was shown in the life of the Savior: He learned obedience from His sufferings (see Hebrews 5:8–9), He gained in wisdom and stature and in favor with God and man as He matured (see Luke 2:52), and He came to know who He was and why He had been sent to earth. As President Benson's life unfolded, did he go through a similar maturing process?

The Benson home in which Ezra was raised was clean and comfortable but spartan. It lacked the amenities we take for granted today—hot and cold running water, bathroom facilities, electricity, and central heating. Although in time many conveniences and even luxuries were added, during Ezra's early years they were missing. Sarah cooked on a wood-burning stove, the heat from which warmed the two-room house. Water was hauled at first, then was pumped when a well was dug, and finally was piped into the house. A washtub, set on the kitchen floor, was used for baths. The outdoor toilet stood some distance from the house. The little home was lighted by kerosene or gas lamps until the arrival of electricity.

Yet there was coziness and a sense of security and well-being not found in many homes. That feeling was enhanced by the spirit of love, prayer, and faith that pervaded the home. George and Sarah Benson believed in the teachings of the Mormon Church. They believed literally that God was their spiritual parent who loved them, knew them by name, was anxious for their happiness and success, and would respond to their earnest prayers. Therefore, prayer and love for God, shown in an anxious desire to keep His commandments, formed the foundation of their home. Some of Ezra Taft Benson's earliest recollections were of kneeling in prayer with his family.

George Benson taught his son that wherever he went or whatever he did, he was never alone, that his Heavenly Father was always near, and that he could reach out and receive help through prayer in any circumstance. "This is prized above any other advice I have ever received," reported a mature Ezra Taft Benson. "It has become an integral part of me, an anchor, a constant source of strength" (quoted in Frederick W. Babbel, *On Wings of Faith* [Salt Lake City: Bookcraft, 1972], p. 85). As President of the Twelve, he sought to teach missionaries at the training center how to obtain heavenly blessings through prayer. This was his formula: "A person must be clean, then he must strive to obtain the Spirit by the prayer of faith, with sincerity and real intent. Your prayers must be asked with the same fervor and intent as the prayer of Enos in the Book of Mormon. Enos was spiritually healed. Through his mighty supplications to the Lord God, he experienced what the faithful of any dispensation can, do, and must experience if they are to see God and be filled with His spirit" (*Church News*, June 23, 1979).

President Benson's firm handshake, which was evident into old age, was a legacy of his years of labor on the farm. Because farming at that day was particularly labor-intensive, George was anxious to involve Ezra, and the six sons who followed him, in the operation of the farm as soon as possible. By age five, Ezra was able to drive a team of horses. Other farm duties soon gravitated to him like filings to a magnet. There were potatoes to dig, grain to shock, hay to harvest and haul, sugar beets to thin, crops to irrigate, and cows to milk. It was this last activity, more than the others, that developed President Benson's powerful handshake. In time, George acquired a herd of seventeen holsteins that had to be milked twice daily. It was an activity that could not be postponed, nor could one fake it. Milking had to be done regularly, and it had to be done thoroughly. Failure on either score would be reflected immediately in the worsened condition of the cows, one of the farm's most valuable assets.

The regular performance of these farm duties over a period of years toughened Ezra's physique, gave him feelings of competence and self-worth, and taught him discipline and dependability. Whatever success he attained in life, President Benson attributed it chiefly to his capacity for hard, sustained work, which he learned first on his father's farm. His father also taught him to work with intelligence. George Benson was widely regarded as one of the most progressive and successful farmers in Cache Valley. He applied the principles of good farm management, crop rotation, soil preservation and enrichment, insect control, and wise irrigation. Later Ezra, applying these principles and others he learned at college, lifted farming in Cache Valley to a new level of expertise. As we shall see, one of the major innovations he introduced was in the creative marketing of farm products, an innovation that marked his work as county agent, as agricultural economist with the University of Idaho extension division, as agricultural cooperative executive in Washington, D.C., and as U.S. secretary of agriculture.

There are many farm boys who learn how to work and how to work intelligently. But Ezra Taft Benson brought a special quality to the task that others lacked, and this set him apart. He liked farm work. Indeed, he loved to work on the farm. And in his formative years he never had any ambition other than to be a farmer—and a good one. Because of this, he brought an unusual zest and enthusiasm to the job. This is reflected in an incident President Benson enjoyed retelling: At age sixteen, a neighboring farmer hired Ezra to thin an acre of beets, thinking it would take him two days to do the job. It was arduous work that had to be done in a stooped position, using a wide-bladed hoe on an eight-inch handle. Starting at sunup, he worked steadily through the day, finishing at sundown. His employer was so astonished that he paid Ezra two five-dollar gold pieces and two silver dollars. "Never before, nor since, have I felt quite so wealthy," reported a mature Ezra Taft Benson, "nor quite so sure that I was the physical equal of any living man."

While the lesson of hard, intelligent, zestful work was vital to Ezra's success later in life, he learned other valuable lessons from his parents. It was they who introduced him to the scriptures. The Book of Mormon was a favorite. It was read frequently as a family, especially on Sundays and holidays and during long winter evenings. The parents also encouraged the children to read other good books during their leisure. Among the books that exerted a strong influence on Ezra were Leo Tolstoy's *What Men Live By* and John Bunyan's *Pilgrim's Progress*. The success stories of Horatio Alger were motivational, as were biographies of George Washington and Abraham Lincoln. When graduating from the eighth grade, he received as a gift a two-volume set of

Orison Marden's *Little Visits with Great Americans*, which he read over and over, treasuring up the examples of those who had achieved notable things, sometimes against great odds.

Without radio, television, or movie houses and without nearby neighbors, the Bensons had to provide their own entertainment. As the children grew up, they learned to play a variety of musical instruments. Ezra learned to play the trombone and for a while took piano lessons. He also sang well, either in solo or with groups. On long winter nights, the Bensons enjoyed sharing their musical talents.

The family home grew as the number of Benson children multiplied. Rooms were added as necessary to accommodate the new arrivals. Being the oldest, Ezra not only carried an increasingly heavy load of outdoor work but also was expected to help supervise the younger children. When his parents began to sing in the ward choir, for instance, he was placed in charge on Wednesday nights while George and Sarah went to choir practice. And he also was responsible for the children when the parents attended sessions in the Logan Temple. As an adult, President Benson remembered his mother's elaborate preparations for a temple session and her happiness as she carefully cleaned and pressed the sacred clothing. Her reverential attitude and her obvious enjoyment in going to the temple created a compelling desire in her son Ezra to share the experience.

Of all the family joys shared by the Benson family, none was more exciting or more filled with eager anticipation than Christmas. The celebration began with a trip to the mountains to cut the Christmas tree. The children always insisted that it be tall enough to touch the ceiling in the living room. The homemade decorations, each one with a history of its own, were then brought out from their storage place and carefully arranged on the tree. Often there was caroling on Christmas Eve. Using the bobsleigh and with bells on the horses, the carolers—muffled warmly, rosy cheeked, and exhilarated by the crisp air and the starry, clear sky—serenaded their neighbors with the favorite songs of Christmas.

The ritual on Christmas morning was undeviating. The children were required to have a glass of milk and some bread before going to the living room to see what Santa had brought. Invariably they each found stockings filled with candy, nuts, fruit, and a personal gift. President Benson commented that as a boy he had found a Santa suit while rummaging in a trunk and, correctly conjecturing why his father was never around when Santa appeared, made a careful canvass of the farm shortly before the following Christmas with his younger brothers. They found several gifts buried in the wheat in the granary. This revelation seems not to have diminished their excitement at Christmastime, but only to have heightened the mystery of where the gifts were hidden and, presumably, to have sharpened their skill in keeping from their parents the fact they knew all about Santa Claus.

On Christmas morning, after opening gifts and having breakfast, the family would pile into the sleigh for the traditional visit to the grandparents' homes. There they would eat goodies amid a chorus of childish chatter, interspersed with singing, recitations, and story telling. And at the Dunkley home, Grandma Dunkley, a bonny Scottish lass, often would entertain the family with her version of the lively Highland fling, a Scottish folk dance.

It hardly needs to be said that the deportment of the Benson children did not always coincide with this picture-perfect portrayal. They were spirited, independent children who held different views, had different interests, and were known occasionally to quarrel and squabble. Once while a sister was on a stepladder decorating the Christmas tree, "T," a notorious tease, gently shook the ladder. Startled, the sister playfully tossed to her brother a dustpan, which accidentally caught him on the lip. When the small cut healed, it left a scar that was a constant reminder to Ezra of the hazards of teasing.

But the incident did not cure him. He continued throughout his juvenile years to tease in a good-natured way and to play practical jokes. He was at his best at Halloween, when he joined with others in mild forms of harassment, shifting privies or moving wagons, for instance. And a nighttime foray into a neighbor's watermelon patch provided the grist for amused reflections as an adult. Hearing the marauders in his watermelon patch, the neighbor fired his shotgun into the air to frighten them away. One of the boys who had a pistol responded by firing it into the air. The neighbor, a little nervous now, called out to tell the boys to fire their weapon into the air because that was what he was doing! It was a standoff. We are left to speculate whether or not the boys got a melon that night, by appropriation or gift.

Ezra was not averse to fighting as a boy, if provoked. The most conspicuous example of his fisticuffs involved a cousin, George Parkinson. While walking home from school, George harassed Ezra's young brother Joe. Ezra told George to stop, but George ignored him. Ezra warned that if he didn't stop, he would make him stop. George continued, so Ezra attacked. When Ezra had bloodied his cousin's nose, skinning his own knuckles in the process, George stopped the harassment and went home. So did Ezra and Joe. At home Sarah, after hearing her son's explanation about the blood on his shirt and the skinned knuckles, hit on a motherly scheme to restore peace between the cousins. She instructed Ezra to go to Aunt Lulu's, George's mother, for a start of yeast. Because of the fight, Ezra protested vigorously—that was the last place in the world he wanted to go at the moment. However, Sarah was adamant. She told Ezra that while it was commendable that he had protected Joe, it was no excuse for fighting. So Ezra went. When Aunt Lulu saw Ezra at the door asking for a start of yeast, she instantly perceived Sarah's strategy. Seizing the opportunity, she brought the cousins together, face-to-face, and delivered an impromptu discourse on forbearance and family unity. It was effective. George never harassed Joe again, and Ezra gave up fisticuffs for good.

As Ezra matured, his sports were basketball and softball, not boxing. He became proficient in both, basketball especially. The attributes he brought to the sport were physical strength, quickness, endurance, and an extraordinary desire to win. Ezra Benson was a determined competitor. It was an attribute he carried into every aspect of life. In more sedentary activities, the trait was muted to an extent and hardly noticeable to some. But it was always there, beneath the surface, a constant, driving force that impelled him along. Who can fail to see this characteristic in Ezra Taft Benson's role as secretary of agriculture? He was prepared to take on, and did take on, the powerful special interest groups entrenched in Congress who were determined to preserve the status quo of high government subsidies for agriculture. Far from deterring him, their opposition merely acted as a spur to more determined efforts to change the system. And occasional defeats or setbacks never altered his fixed objective. He came back to the fray, again and again, fighting, scrapping, and driving toward his goal.

It was the same on the basketball court, of course. But his competitive drives were tempered by a scrupulous insistence to play by the rules. Ezra never played dirty. But he played hard, and he played to win. We gather that this characteristic mirrored qualities deep inside his father, George Benson. The father was inordinately confident of the athletic skills of his sons and once announced in the local newspaper that the Benson boys could defeat any basketball team around. He was an avid fan, seldom missing a game in which Ezra or any of his other sons played. And he was vocal, shouting instructions or encouragement to his boys on the floor. At one tense game between the Oneida Academy, Ezra's team, and Brigham Young College at Logan, with the score tied near the end of the game, George Benson was heard to shout in exasperation, "Hell, 'T,' put it in!" It was the only known time George Benson used an

George T. Benson Jr. (right) and his seven sons; Ezra is next to his father

expletive. He insisted that his boys not swear, and he would not tolerate vulgarities or profanity in his presence.

The Oneida Academy team on which Ezra was a star played teams throughout southeastern Idaho and northern Utah. They seldom lost. One victory especially rewarding to "T" Benson was over Ricks College at Rexburg, Idaho. It was a hard-fought game, won by Oneida in the last seconds. One of the players on the Ricks team was Marion G. Romney, who became an associate of Elder Benson in the Quorum of the Twelve Apostles. More than a half century later, Ezra was still savoring this victory, more than once mentioning it in the presence of Elder Romney—who obviously did not enjoy being reminded of it.

Chapter 3

The Boy Matures

Before enrolling at the Oneida Stake Academy, Ezra attended a small school in Whitney. Because scheduling was arranged around the demands of the farming cycle, the students were excused in the spring to help plant the crops and in the autumn to help harvest them. Despite these interruptions, Ezra completed the prescribed studies in six years.

Ezra was an interested and diligent student. Like many students of that day, he became a skilled penman. His distinctive signature with its intricate swirls and loops reflected that. He also studied mathematics, civics, history, and geography, acquiring factual knowledge from his teachers that increased his understanding of the world and provided tools for his life's work. One teacher, however, a great-aunt, taught him much more than useful facts. In a way Ezra could never explain, this teacher imbued him with an appreciation for learning and with a desire to seek higher education. Her influence was a major factor that motivated him to pursue graduate studies after receiving his undergraduate degree from Brigham Young University. And his graduate studies at Iowa State University at Ames and the University of California at Berkeley provided him with the knowledge, tools, expertise, and academic stature that were essential to his success as a farm cooperative executive in Washington, D.C., and as the U.S. secretary of agriculture. As one searches for milestones on Ezra Taft Benson's journey to eminence, the influence of the selfless teacher in that humble rural school stands out as one of the most prominent.

During his school years, Ezra experienced a spiritual awakening and received a priesthood blessing that would have a significant effect on his future. While he had always had a spiritual orientation, the boy now began to seek for personal, spiritual guidance. Occasionally he went alone into the mountains. There he would walk among the towering trees, pondering and praying. These solitary interludes revitalized his spirit and provided insights into life's meaning and his earthly mission.

From childhood, Ezra had a compelling desire to fill a full-time mission for the Church. Often he had heard young elders report their missions. Despite their stories of hardships and privations, Ezra looked forward to the day he would be called to serve. One Sunday evening at sacrament meeting when Ezra was sixteen, that desire was rekindled when he heard two returned missionaries give their reports. At the time there also came to him a desire to receive a patriarchal blessing. He immediately went to his father to ask how he could receive one. Being told he needed the bishop's approval, he went to his grandfather, who after careful questioning gave him a recommend. Ezra then went to the patriarch, John Edward Dalley, a benign, white-haired man who gave him the blessing. It was all Ezra had hoped and prayed for. He was promised that he would fill a mission to the nations of the earth, raising his voice in testimony; that he would be protected in his travels; that he would grow in favor with his Heavenly Father; and that many would bless his name. It is safe to assume that Ezra read and reread this blessing, practically committing it to memory. While the mission call would not come for several years, he had confidence it was only a matter of time. Meanwhile, his task was to prepare for that day by living worthily and by learning the principles he would teach.

Before that time came, however, Ezra gained special insight into the impact of missionary service on a family. On a Sunday in the spring of 1912, the Benson children did not attend Church services to avoid exposure to chicken pox, which was prevalent in the community. When their parents returned home, the children were troubled to see both had been crying. The parents explained that George had received a letter from President Joseph F. Smith calling him to serve in the Northern States Mission for two years. However, the tears were not caused by the call. Indeed, both were happy about that and about the fact that George was deemed worthy to serve. They were sad only because they would be separated, especially since Sarah was carrying her eighth child. There was never a question about accepting the call. That was assumed by everyone. All personal considerations were put aside in deference to the summons from President Smith.

The uncomplaining, willing way in which George and Sarah accepted this sudden intrusion into their personal lives made a profound impression on Ezra and the other children. It was the most striking example of faith in the Church and obedience to the direction of the prophet they had seen. It taught them as nothing else could have done that the expressed convictions of their parents about the Church were genuine. It also demonstrated where their priorities lay, especially when it became necessary for their father to sell part of his farm to raise the money necessary to keep him in the mission field and to provide a financial cushion for the family in his absence. And in time the incident demonstrated the truth of the principle that it is not possible to make a sacrifice for the Church, given the rich spiritual and temporal rewards the members of the Benson

31

Sarah Benson and her first seven children (she is also pregnant with the eighth) at the time of her husband's 1912 mission call; Ezra, the eldest and tallest, stands behind his mother

family received in the years ahead that were traceable to the father's willing acceptance of this call. Moreover, the selfless example of the parents instilled a commitment to missionary work in all the children, reflected in the fact that they each later accepted mission calls and helped finance missions for their own children and grandchildren.

Necessary help to operate the farm was obtained when James Chadwick agreed to work the forty-acre row-crop acreage on shares. For convenience, he and his new bride moved into part of the Benson home. Meanwhile, Ezra became responsible for the dairy herd and care of the pasture land. And as the oldest child, he assumed a more important role in the family. Under the burden of these duties, Ezra matured rapidly beyond his years, playing the role of a man while in his early teens. By selling milk, cream, and butter; trading eggs for groceries; using produce from the family garden and orchard, fresh or bottled; and drawing as needed from the little nest egg George had provided, the family survived very well, though frugally. And in case of an emergency, there was a host of Benson and Dunkley relatives nearby.

A smallpox epidemic struck Whitney while George was in the mission field. It afflicted the entire Benson family and caused the house to be quarantined. Because of Sarah's pregnancy, the doctor urgently recommended that George return home. Sarah demurred, insisting that he remain in the field to complete his mission. Despite intense pressure from the doctor, she remained adamant. Because of the conditions under which the baby son was born, he was weak and underweight. In time he grew into a robust, healthy baby. He was given the name of his father, George Taft Benson, and was the third lineal descendant so named.

The father's letters from the mission field brought excitement and joy to the family. Each one was avidly read and reread. They were filled with reports about his work, descriptions of the areas where he served, expressions of love, and inquiries about conditions at home. Notably absent were any criticisms, complaints, or censures. George Benson was always positive in his attitudes, preferring to carry his own burdens, so the difficulties he encountered in the field were kept to himself. At home, Sarah practiced the same philosophy. She shielded from her husband any problems she had so he would be free of worry and able to concentrate on his work. These characteristics found their way into the lives of Ezra Benson and the other children, who kept their own counsel, carried their own load, and, as far as humanly possible, solved their own problems.

George performed most of his missionary labors in Iowa and Illinois. The work consisted of tracting, street meetings, cottage meetings, and supervising local Church units. One of his experiences became a legend in the family: He and his companion rented a room in a nonmember home where other elders had lived. George was surprised to learn that though previous missionaries had lived there over a period of ten years, none of them had challenged the owners to study the doctrines of the Church. Soon after moving in, George was asked to offer a prayer at the end of a discussion. In it he challenged them to read the Book of Mormon in its entirety. Later, he and his companion taught them, and ultimately the family was baptized. The circle was closed forty years later when Elder Ezra Taft Benson, then a member of the Twelve, performed the temple marriage for a member of this family.

The Book of Mormon, the centerpiece of his family's religious instruction, was also George T. Benson's key missionary tool. Ezra later said the Book of Mormon was read in the family home on almost a daily basis. It was there he acquired a love for the book and a determination to study it diligently throughout his life. After Ezra became President of the Church, that love was translated into a vast effort to flood the earth with the Book of Mormon and to motivate the members of the Church to study it each day.

When George T. Benson returned from his mission, he was thirty-nine years old and the father of eight children. He immediately assumed the reins of family leadership, relieving Ezra of much of the responsibility he had shouldered while his father was away. Carrying that responsibility, if only for a relatively short time, gave the son an increased appreciation for the role his father had played in the family, and in Ezra's personal life, over the years. And the growing commitment and enthusiasm toward the Church that George felt as a result of his missionary labors doubtless strengthened Ezra's own loyalties and increased the admiration he had for his father.

Ezra always considered his father to be a man of unrivaled character. From earliest childhood, he had looked up to him and had sought to be like him. A crucial evidence of that admiration was the son's ambition to be a farmer just like his father. And that ambition remained fixed even after he had been out in the world as a missionary to Great Britain and as a university student living away from home. The sophistications of the world and the condescending attitudes some have toward farmers in no way altered his objective. Nor was he deterred by the thought of taking the beautiful city-bred girl he fell in love with to Whitney to live in the rural environment where he had been raised.

Ezra knew his father was a happy man, contented with his lot in life, when he heard him singing the songs of Zion as he milked the cows. So often did this happen that Ezra learned the words to many favorite Latter-day Saint hymns merely by hearing his father sing them over and over. That zestful attitude toward farm work seemed to seep into his very being. He liked the independence farm work offered; and notwithstanding the occasional uncertainties created by vagaries in the weather or market prices, he liked the security farming provided, the security of owning the assets and the tools to create wealth and to contribute to the general prosperity. He also liked the healthful lifestyle of the farm and the regular periods between harvesting and planting when the work demands were reduced so as to allow for activities of self-improvement. And finally, being aware of the trials and temptations facing young people in urban centers, Ezra undoubtedly wanted to provide his children with the advantages he had enjoyed of growing up in a rural farm setting where Latter-day Saints predominated.

Aside from all this, there well may have been two other factors at work here that magnetically drew Ezra Taft Benson to a career in farming: heredity and destiny. With three centuries of American farmers in his background, the vocation may have been in his blood. Who can infallibly account for the tendency in many families to perpetuate an occupation from generation to generation? When John Benson received that land grant in the Massachusetts Bay Colony in 1638 and began to farm it, did he commence an American agricultural dynasty whose influences subtly swayed one of its princes three centuries later? Whatever brought it about, when Ezra began his schooling at the Oneida Stake Academy in 1914, he knew precisely what he wanted to become.

The academy, part of the Church's secondary school system, was first located in Franklin, Idaho. It remained there until 1898, the year before Ezra was born, and was then moved to Preston, where a new two-story, cut-stone building was erected for its use. Nine years later, a second building was added; and during the years Ezra attended the school, a well-equipped gymnasium was constructed. These buildings, along with the nearby playing fields, were the campus of the academy. Because of interruptions to attend a military training camp at the college in Logan during World War I, and to give his father emergency assistance on the farm, Ezra would not graduate from the academy until the spring of 1919.

During his early career at Oneida, Ezra rode his horse to and from the academy each school day. On the way home in the afternoons, he often would stop at Warm Creek to check his string of muskrat traps. The pelts he harvested, after they had been stretched, shaped, and dried, were sold to a furrier in Chicago to help defray the cost of Ezra's education.

The principal of the academy when Ezra first enrolled was J. Robert Robinson. He was replaced a year later by Joseph A. Geddes, who served during the remaining time Ezra attended there. The curriculum at the academy included all of the basic courses taught in high school—science, mathematics, biology, business, history, and physical education—but also offered special courses in domestic science, agriculture, vocational training, carpentry, music, and missionary work. Because the school was owned and directed by the Church, the secular courses were interspersed with religious instruction and devotionals. While Ezra was interested in his studies, and did well in all of them, he gave special emphasis to those courses that better equipped him to succeed as a farmer. He also took special pride in the carpentry skills he learned at the school and in specimens of his work—an oak desk with matched shelving, a hat rack, a cupboard, and a table.

The academic courses opened a new world of thought and reflection for the student from Whitney whose interests, until then, had been severely restricted by the isolated environment in which he had been raised. For example, he now acquired a taste for good literature (other than the scriptures), to which he was introduced by a favorite teacher, Harrison R. Merrill.

Ezra also was motivated and challenged by the larger student body, which was drawn from a wide area. One of his new acquaintances was young Harold B. Lee (called Hal by his friends), who came from Clifton on the west side of the valley. When this pair of ruddy Idaho farm boys—born only five months and a few miles apart—met at the Oneida Stake Academy, no one among their schoolmates could have imagined, even in their wildest flights of fancy, that each of them, in turn, would become the prophet and President of The Church of Jesus Christ of Latter-day Saints. The paths they would take to that office were widely divergent, as were their main interests while they studied at the academy. Ezra's predominant interest in agricultural and manual arts courses and in basketball has already been mentioned. Harold, on the other hand, was on the debate team, managed the school's athletic teams when they were on the road, and worked on the school paper. He aspired to be a teacher. Both he and Ezra, however, sang together in choruses and played together in the band, Ezra on the trombone and Harold on the alto horn.

While Oneida was much larger, better equipped, and better staffed and administered than the Whitney school, it was still a very small, rural school. Almost the entire student body consisted of young Latter-day Saints, most of whom came from a farming background. All the teachers were orthodox members of the Church, and their duty was to teach not only secular subjects but also Mormon doctrine and Mormon ethics. This included close instruction in the Latter-day Saints' dietary laws, which prohibited the use of tea, coffee, tobacco, and alcohol. And the teachings of morality applied equally to boys and girls, there being no double standard. Moreover, the teachers were strict with the students, insisting on careful preparation and on precise observance of the rules of classroom procedure.

Evidence of the effectiveness of this small rural school is seen not only in the lives of its two most distinguished alumni, Harold Lee and Ezra Benson, but also in the solid achievements of hundreds of other students who attended there and who imbibed the spirit of the school. That spirit was generated in large part by the doctrines of The Church of Jesus Christ of Latter-day Saints, which were repeatedly emphasized to the students at Oneida. These young, impressionable students were taught that they were literal spirit children of Deity and therefore had the seeds of godhood in them; that the purpose of earth life was to take bodies and prove themselves; that the glory of God is intelligence; and that the knowledge and experience one gained in mortality would be valuable and helpful in the hereafter. These seminal ideas provided a powerful incentive for the students to achieve; and the impetus of their experience at Oneida carried over to exert a profound, positive influence throughout their lives.

Once Ezra was wrongly accused of violating a rule at Oneida. The unpleasant experience proved to be very stressful for him. It occurred when his pencil lead broke during an examination. As he leaned over to ask a classmate for his knife, the teacher mistakenly thought he was cheating, took his papers, and reported him to the principal. Despite Ezra's emphatic denials of guilt, the principal accepted the teacher's version of what had happened and as punishment forbade him to play in the next basketball game. Ezra was crushed, not so much because of the punishment, but because of the humiliating reflection on his character and on his family. That his parents believed him and that ultimately he was permitted to play did not remove the stigma nor the hurt that always remained with him. However, the emotional scar left by the incident was a constant reminder for him to avoid any situation that would reflect adversely on him or on his family.

Another incident at the academy involved Ezra in controversy. It occurred in connection with the founders' day celebration in 1916. The senior class, of which Harold Lee was a member, celebrated by fixing their class flag to the academy's flagpole. Then each of them climbed the pole to kiss the flag as a symbol of class unity and loyalty. After singing together and giving the class yell, they retired in a jovial mood. Their mood turned to anger the next morning when they discovered that the underclassmen, which included Ezra Benson, had removed the flag. The uproar that ensued was quieted only when Preston's small, underworked police force intervened. We can be assured that this meaningless fracas afforded Harold Lee and Ezra Benson with moments of amused nostalgia in the years ahead.

During this period, Ezra first began to show the qualities of leadership that would be so evident later in his career. He was appointed secretary of the Young Men's Mutual Improvement Association (YMMIA) in the Whitney Ward, assistant Scoutmaster, and later Scoutmaster. There were twenty-four boys in the troop, ranging in age from twelve to sixteen. The oldest Scouts were only two or three years younger than Ezra, so there was great camaraderie among them.

At this time Scouting had been part of the Church youth program for only a few years. It included overnight camping, cookouts, hiking, and work on merit badges, all of which was underlain by an emphasis on faith in God and loyalty to country. However, the structure of the Church lent itself to stake and regional troop competitions in singing and other activities. Because of his interest in music, Ezra organized a chorus of Scouts in the Whitney Ward troop, and they easily won a stake competition. The chorus was then invited to compete in regional finals scheduled in the Logan Tabernacle. To give his Scouts an edge, Ezra promised them a hike from Whitney to Bear Lake if they won. He did not know what effect his promise had on the singers. He did know, however, they had never sung better than at Logan when they won first place in the regional finals.

At a meeting to plan the hike, a young Scout who clearly was oblivious to girls suggested they get crew cuts to simplify grooming on the trail. Although the older boys showed little enthusiasm, the suggestion was approved. And when Ezra was confronted, he yielded and agreed to join them.

They descended on the barbershop in high good humor. After several boys had received their crew cuts, Ezra got in the chair. There, in front of his troop, the barber played a sly trick on the Scoutmaster. He offered to barber the rest of the boys free of charge if Ezra would allow him to shave his head! Urged on by his boisterous troop, Ezra agreed. The next day twenty-four lively Boy Scouts with new crew cuts, guided by their bald leader, walked eastward from Whitney toward the mountain. Twenty miles beyond was their destination, Bear Lake. This trek, through mountainous country of rare beauty, helped forge a lasting bond between Ezra Taft Benson and his troop of boys. They met occasionally during the years that followed, always with mutual delight and with a cordial remembrance of their Scouting experiences, which included (according to Harold Maughan, one of the Scouts) games of "Run-my-sheepie-run" played on horseback and especially the stay at Bear Lake.

The last known encounter President Benson had with any of these Scouts occurred at a fireside in the Salt Lake Tabernacle, reported by the *Church News* on February 20, 1988: "In the fireside's most poignant moment, President Monson introduced members of the Whitney Ward scout troop of which President Benson was called to be scoutmaster nearly 70 years ago. The Prophet beamed and gestured triumphantly as several members of the troop, now men in their 70s and 80s, stood in the congregation to acknowledge their former scoutmaster."

Ezra's work as Scoutmaster in Whitney was the beginning of a lifetime of activity with the Boy Scouts of America.

At Preston when he and Flora lived there, he became the leader of the senior Scouts. At Boise he served as a Scout commissioner for three years. In 1943, after his call to the Twelve, he was elected to the National Committee on Rural Scouting and served in that capacity for many years. In recognition of that service, he was awarded the Silver Antelope on April 24, 1951, Scouting's highest regional award. Through the years, he attended numerous Scout encampments, including national jamborees, as he did in 1977 when he attended the national Scout jamboree in Moraine Park, Pennsylvania. On these occasions he would stand for hours shaking hands with Scouts from all over the country, expressing his encouragement and support. And it was not uncommon at Scout encampments for him to recount the story of his famous hike over the mountain to Bear Lake, with shaven head and with twenty-four raucous, crew-cutted Scouts in tow.

After the United States entered the war in 1917, Ezra had a strong desire to become involved. He was then eighteen years old and a man in every sense of the word—tall, muscular, and handsome (his sister Margaret said the girls "swooned" over her brother). Ezra's patriotism was shared by his family, and after discussion with his parents, it was decided he would withdraw from the Oneida Academy temporarily to enroll in a military training program at the Utah Agricultural College in Logan, Utah. There he lived in a barracks with other recruits and received both field and classwork training in military history, tactics, and discipline.

In the autumn of 1918, farmers in Cache Valley urgently needed help to harvest their crops because so many men were away in the service. The directors of the training camp in Logan were persuaded to give their recruits a two-week leave to help with the harvest. The day before the recruits were scheduled to leave for home, Ezra had a compelling urge to go home immediately. When the prompting was repeated a second and then a third time, Ezra was convinced of the need to act. He went to his superiors, obtained permission to leave early, caught a ride to Whitney, and was home by noon. Later in the day, he developed a high fever that made him delirious. He drifted in and out of consciousness for three days. In a rational moment he heard the doctor say that only the power of God could save him. Invoking heavenly power through their priesthood, Ezra's father and grandfather joined to bless him. As a result of this blessing and his mother's solicitous care, Ezra's fever broke and he gradually recovered.

He felt doubly blessed by the incident because of the spiritual prompting that got him out of the barracks and home early and because of the priesthood administration. He learned later that a flu epidemic had struck his barracks after he had left and that many of his classmates had died, including the two friends who bunked on either side of him. One of them was his cousin, George B. Parkinson. Ezra always believed that he too would have died had he remained in the barracks, and also that the Lord had preserved his life for a purpose. He still had work to do.

The armistice in November 1918 ended both the war and the need for Ezra to continue his military training. He left Logan and returned to the Oneida Academy, from which he graduated in the spring of 1919. It is inferred that Ezra felt a sense of exhilaration upon returning to the academy. His life had been spared, the war was over, and a promising future lay ahead. That same sense also seemed to dominate his life during the eighteen months following his graduation from the academy. Ezra was living at home, working with his father on the farm, and enjoying his service in the ward and an active social life with his many friends. His father still had the Dodge he had purchased several years before, and Ezra was allowed to use it on special occasions. This privilege seemed to be in jeopardy when he reported he had driven it fifty-one miles an hour on the stretch of paved road between Smithfield and Logan, the only paved road in the valley. His mother was aghast, protesting he could have been killed. His father was surprised the car could go that fast. We gather that Ezra was allowed to use the car in the future on condition he hold down the speed.

In the autumn of 1920, Ezra began preparations to enroll at the agricultural college in Logan for the winter quarter. To this end, he traveled there to spend a few days with friends. Housing, curriculum, and employment possibilities were much on his mind. Ironically, the subject of matrimony was suddenly injected into his thinking in a way that would always be a source of amazement and gratitude to him and to the woman who became his wife, Flora Amussen. At the couple's sixtieth wedding anniversary, President Benson recounted the circumstances surrounding this unexpected development. "We were out near the dairy barns," he explained to the press, "when a young woman, very attractive and beautiful, drove by in her little car on her way to the dairy to get some milk. As the boys waved at her, she waved back. I said, 'Who is that girl?' They said, 'That's Flora Amussen.' I told them, 'You know, I've just had the impression I'm going to marry her. When I come down this winter, I'm going to step her'" (*Church News*, Sept. 14, 1986).

His friends ridiculed the idea, explaining that Flora was one of the most popular and attractive girls on the campus. The list of her attainments at the college was intimidating. She was the student body vice president; a member of the Periwig Club, the national dramatic society; a member of Sorosis, a social club; chairman of the junior prom committee; president of the girls' athletic club; and a skilled tennis player. In addition to all this, she lived in a large home with her mother, drove her own sporty car, and was accustomed to a rich, urban lifestyle wholly foreign to Ezra's experience. All this was irrelevant to the self-confident young man from Whitney. He told his friends that the status and achievements of this fascinating young woman would only make the quest more interesting.

Ezra was surprised not long afterward when Flora, the weekend guest of his cousin, Ann Dunkley, appeared at Sunday School in Whitney. And he could hardly believe his good fortune when his uncle Joseph, Ann's father, asked if Ezra could drive the girls to Lava Hot Springs in the afternoon. He seized the chance, making hurried arrangements for someone to do his milking.

Flora Amussen ostensibly was as much intrigued with Ezra Benson as he was infatuated with her. There was a strength and virility about him that, coupled with a natural self-confidence and outgoing friendliness, caused the girls to like him. It is not likely that Flora was immune to these attractions. Given these circumstances, the trip to Lava Hot Springs and back was an enjoyable one of mutual discovery and appraisal. For Ezra, it was gratifying to learn that Flora's wealth and her prominence on the campus had not given her an exaggerated sense of self-importance. She was friendly, exuberant, and openly appreciative of any courtesies shown to her. Aside from Ezra's physical attractions, Flora was impressed by his wholesomeness and honesty. And his attitude and conduct conveyed the impression he could be trusted. It is unclear whether, in this early stage of their acquaintance, Flora was convinced that Ezra was to be her husband. If not, Ezra's certainty was sufficient for both. Meanwhile, the hours they spent together demonstrated that they were compatible and that there was a foundation of mutual respect and admiration upon which a more permanent relationship could be built.

When Ezra enrolled for winter quarter, the aim of strengthening his relationship with Flora undoubtedly stood high on his list of priorities. Yet he did not press his suit immediately; he was content to let the relationship mature slowly. In this delicate maneuver, he showed commendable restraint, waiting until the time was ripe before asking her for a date.

Ezra and his sister Margaret lived with their grandmother Benson in Logan while attending the college. When feasible, they went to and from the campus together and sometimes went to parties and dances together. Because the student body was relatively small, Ezra occasionally saw

Flora on campus or at these social functions that made it possible to visit with her informally and to keep the acquaintance alive. However, when he learned that Margaret had a date for a dance, he decided to make his move. He called Flora and invited her to go to the dance with him. She hesitated because, as a student body officer, she had to help award athletic sweaters to members of the football team at intermission. For that reason, she had declined other invitations to the dance. When Ezra persisted and assured her he would accommodate himself to her duties, she accepted.

Ezra was nervous when he approached Flora's home, an impressive three-story building that looked like a mansion to him. He had learned that Flora's mother had acquired her wealth from her husband, Carl Christian Amussen, a deceased Salt Lake jeweler. He found that the mother shared Flora's gentle, cordial personality. While her daughter was finishing her preparations, the mother, Barbara Amussen, engaged Ezra in conversation, inquiring about Whitney and about his family. His name was not unfamiliar to her, for she, as well as most other residents of Cache Valley, was well acquainted with the reputation and achievements of his namesake, his great-grandfather Ezra T. Benson. No doubt Barbara Amussen, an astute judge of character, was pleased with what she heard from this young man and what she saw in him. A lasting bond of friendship and mutual admiration seems to have been formed between Flora's mother and her future son-in-law from the very beginning.

Chapter 4

The Missionary

zra's courtship of Flora Amussen, which began with their date to the college dance mentioned in the preceding chapter, extended over more than five years. But there were two lengthy periods when they were apart. The first separation began in the summer of 1921 and was triggered by a letter from 47 East South Temple Street in Salt Lake City, Utah. In the letter, Heber J. Grant, the President of the Church, called Ezra to serve in the British Mission with headquarters in Liverpool, England. The excitement created by the long-anticipated call was heightened by the location of his field of labor. Ezra's roots extended into both England and Scotland. The thought of laboring in the lands of his ancestors was intriguing, as was the idea of traveling overseas to see the historic culture from which his own culture had sprung.

There were many details to handle before he could leave, including arrangements for wardrobe, luggage, passport, and inoculations. Then there was the usual round of farewells and parties in his honor. The most unique of these was one hosted by Flora. To add intrigue to his voyage, she invited the guests to write letters to him that were sealed and numbered consecutively, with instructions to Ezra to open one each day while at sea. These reminded him of friends and home, but especially of the one who originated the novel idea. It was typical of Flora. She was never content to do things in an ordinary way, but insisted on stamping everything she did with the flair of her own personality.

There were special family gatherings where the missionary received counsel and blessings from his parents. At one of these, on July 13, 1921, Ezra was ordained an elder by his father. The next day, George and Sarah accompanied him to the Logan Temple, where he received his endowment. Then, in company with Flora, they traveled with him to Salt Lake City. There he was set apart for his mission by Elder Seymour B. Young of the First Council of the Seventy. And on the evening of July 16, he boarded the train at the Salt Lake City Depot, after final embraces from his parents and whispered words of love and admonition.

Flora boarded the train also and rode with Ezra as far as Ogden, Utah. There were some last things to be said in private before they parted. While the subject of their conversation remained confidential, their later conduct implies they then affirmed an "understanding" they had that, though not a formal engagement, created a special bond between them. Their good-bye at Ogden, according to Ezra's account, was "quick and snappy."

In company with several other missionaries destined for their fields of labor, Elder Benson traveled to Montreal, Canada. Before boarding their English ship, the *Victorian*, on July 22, the missionaries were treated to a concert in the park conducted by the famous band leader John Philip Sousa.

Because of the long voyage down the St. Lawrence River to the ocean, Ezra was unable to test his sea legs immediately, nor to open the first of his special letters. The North Atlantic crossing was typical, marked by intermittent high winds, heavy seas, and some seasickness. After the first day, however, when the turbulence was especially pronounced as the ship breasted the heavy ground swells off the Newfoundland coast, Ezra suffered only occasional discomfort. This enabled him to experience fully the novelty of a sea voyage with the excitement of marine life sightings, the vague concern about icebergs that had sunk the *Titanic* only nine years before on this same route, and the vastness and the ever-changing face of the ocean that stretched to the horizon all around. The rising and setting of the sun was a special fascination, as the sun seemed to emerge from the water at dawn, then to return there at dusk like a huge red fireball from which steam might be expected to rise as it disappeared into the sea.

Imbued with the spirit of their calling, the missionaries tried to engage other passengers and the crew in conversation, hoping to lead into gospel discussions. The results were negligible, although the effort doubtless eased any guilt feelings caused by the elders' enforced inactivity and surely helped prepare them for the widespread indifference and even hostility they would encounter once they actually commenced their work ashore. Yet, who knows for certain what silent, unmeasurable impact an earnest, clean-cut, and handsome missionary like Ezra Taft Benson might have had on those whom he met during this memorable voyage?

As the *Victorian* eased its way up the Mersey River toward the Liverpool pierhead, Elder Benson was treated for the first time to the sights, the sounds, and the smells of an ancient seaport. For centuries ships of every size and description had sailed in and out of this harbor, unloading or picking up passengers or cargo. For instance, every President of the Church until that time, except the Prophet Joseph Smith, had stepped ashore at Liverpool, ready to undertake the same work for which Ezra had been sent there. Presidents Brigham Young, John Taylor, Wilford Woodruff, Lorenzo Snow, Joseph F. Smith, and Heber J. Grant had walked on Liverpool's docks and had cleared

*Ezra Taft Benson at
the time of his mission
to England*

customs there before beginning their ministries in Great
Britain. Moreover, future Presidents of the Church—George
Albert Smith, David O. McKay, and Joseph Fielding Smith,
who were then members of the Twelve—had done the same.
When Elder Ezra Taft Benson arrived at this same Liverpool
dock on August 21, 1921, could he have had vague stirrings
that he would follow in that distinguished line more than
sixty years later?

Although it was past midnight when the missionaries
stepped ashore at Liverpool's Mersey River Pierhead, there
were members of the mission staff there to greet them, to
shepherd them through customs, and to help them retrieve
their luggage. They were then driven to the mission home
and office, called Durham House, at 295 Edge Lane, where
they were allowed to sleep for several hours before being

briefed about mission procedures and goals and before receiving their field assignments.

Ezra's mission president, Elder Orson F. Whitney of the Twelve, presided over not only the British Mission to which he had been assigned but also the European Mission, which included eight separate, subordinate missions—the Swiss-German, French, Swedish, Norwegian, Danish, Netherlands, Armenian, and South African Missions. Elder Benson first met his distinguished, overworked mission president the following day. President Whitney, who was then sixty-six years old, had been a member of the Council of the Twelve for fifteen years. He was widely regarded as perhaps the most literate General Authority the Church had produced. He had authored, among other literary works, a history of Utah, a definitive biography of his grandfather Heber C. Kimball, and an epic poem titled "Elias," which sketched, in the most lofty language, the plan of salvation from the premortal existence through the dispensations of the earth. He also had good administrative skills, attested by his long service as bishop of the Eighteenth Ward in Salt Lake City, the ward whose membership at first was composed almost entirely of members of the families of Brigham Young, Heber C. Kimball, and Newell K. Whitney. Ezra would learn, undoubtedly with some surprise, that after his call as bishop, President Whitney also was called as a missionary to Great Britain, although he was not released as the bishop of the Eighteenth Ward. His counselors in the bishopric merely carried on while he was away.

Ezra served under President Whitney for sixteen months. The impact the Apostle had on the young elder was compelling and lasting. Especially because of President Whitney's apostolic calling, Elder Benson listened intently to everything he said, and he performed with alacrity everything his mission president told him to do. He was especially impressed by the experiences President Whitney shared with the missionaries as he met with them in training and report meetings. One of these, which Ezra heard

President Whitney relate several times, touched him profoundly. The incident occurred while Orson F. Whitney served as a young missionary in Pennsylvania. In a vivid dream or vision, Orson saw the Savior in the Garden of Gethsemane. With the Savior were Peter, James, and John. "I saw Him as plainly as I have seen anyone," Elder Whitney reported, referring to the Savior. "He was of noble stature and majestic mien, not at all the weak, effeminate being that some painters have portrayed; but the very God that He was and is" (as quoted in Bryant S. Hinckley, *The Faith of Our Pioneer Fathers* [Salt Lake City: Bookcraft, 1974], pp. 211–12). Such a testimony, borne by a mature, honorable man who was precise in using words, made a lasting impression on Elder Benson. It also infused him with an extraordinary enthusiasm for the work and a commitment that was reflected in all that he did.

Following his first meeting with President Whitney, Elder Benson was assigned to labor at Carlisle in the Newcastle Conference, the northernmost conference in England. He traveled there by train with a companion, Elder Russell Hodgson, arriving the first week in August. En route, the young elders passed some significant places in the history of the Church in the British Isles: Preston, where the first baptisms in England were performed in the River Ribble; Milnthorpe, where President John Taylor was born; and Penrith, where, as a teenager, President Taylor learned the turner's trade as an apprentice. Located between the Cumbrian and Pennine Mountains, in a valley called the Vale of Eden, Penrith, a short distance south of Carlisle, is near the Lake District, one of the most beautiful and picturesque areas in England. From this area came the so-called Lake Poets: William Wordsworth, Robert Southey, and Samuel Taylor Coleridge, who were contemporaries of John Taylor. One may infer that the poetic language found in many of Elder Taylor's sermons and writings was inspired in part by the images he absorbed during the five years he lived in Penrith.

Carlisle, where Elder Benson first labored as a missionary, is the capital of Cumberland County. It lies near the mouth of the Eden River, eight miles from the Solway Firth, and eight miles from the Scottish border. It is one of the oldest cities of England and was important during the Roman occupation, being near the western end of Hadrian's eighty-mile wall constructed across northern England in the second century A.D. to protect Roman Britain from northern invaders. While physical evidence of the Roman occupation did not exist in Carlisle when Ezra labored there, other features of the city attested to its antiquity. Most prominent among these was the massive Norman castle built in 1092, less than three decades after the Norman invasion of England. One can imagine the culture shock Elder Benson experienced upon his arrival to find that the past history of the city was counted in centuries and millennia instead of in decades, as was true of the history of Cache Valley.

He also found that the ancient character of Carlisle's buildings and streets was mirrored in the attitudes of its people. Most of them were bound by the rigid traditions of their ancestors and were suspicious of those who challenged them. This intrinsic resistance to change was magnified as it applied to the Latter-day Saints because of a pervasive campaign of vilification that had been directed toward the Church for several decades. The British press often attacked the Mormons, printing distorted stories about them that were usually based on half-truths or flagrant lies. Headlines such as "Assassins Who Carry Out Orders of Utah Saints" and "Women in Chains of Slavery" were not uncommon. And a militant woman named Winifred Graham seemed to regard abusive attacks on the Church as her life's work. In a letter to the First Presidency after he became president of the British Mission, David O. McKay reported, "Winifred Graham and her . . . associates have opened the flood gates of hell and are deluging England with the vilest slander that impure minds can imagine." He also wrote that he hoped "the Lord would take her in hand," because he hated to fight a woman (letter of Feb. 27, 1924, David O. McKay Papers, Church Historical Department).

In such a climate, missionary work was difficult and baptisms were few. It was especially hard for handsome, virile young men like Ezra because of false reports that the missionaries sought to trap young women into the Church in order to take them to Utah to live lives of debauchery. Despite these handicaps, Elder Benson began his work in Carlisle with enthusiasm and determination.

His first companion in Carlisle was Elder Ralph S. Gray, with whom he did some of his best missionary work. Their usual routines included tracting, cottage meetings, street meetings, and some administrative and teaching duties at the Carlisle Branch. The street meetings were the most difficult for Ezra, yet the most exhilarating, at least after they ended. In time he came to look forward to them.

The elders traveled around Carlisle on bicycles, their "iron horses." When tracting, they would ride to the neighborhood selected, park their bicycles, and work the doors. The results varied. Typically they had more success in lower-class neighborhoods. These people, who lived on the economic edge, were inclined to be more humble and more receptive to the elders' message. It was from this economic class that most of the converts came, people whom Ezra called "the best."

September 29, 1921, was a beacon day in Elder Benson's missionary life. On that day, he and Elder Gray baptized and confirmed three new converts, a fact duly reported in the *Millennial Star,* the British Mission's official publication edited at that time by President Orson F. Whitney. He traced his editorial lineage through eighty years to the first editor, Parley P. Pratt, whose first issue of the *Star,* published in Liverpool in the early 1840s, had on its cover Elder Pratt's well-known poem "The Morning Breaks, the Shadows Flee." Elder Benson, like all British missionaries, looked forward to the issues of this historic paper that kept them informed of what was going on throughout the mission, motivated them to keep up with the pacesetters, and contained important instructions from the mission president and other mission leaders.

The entry in Elder Benson's journal on January 1, 1922, "Make it a banner year," tells much about the enthusiasm and the energy he brought to the work. Elder Gray later provided good insight into Ezra's personality and drive as a missionary in a congratulatory letter he wrote on August 2, 1943, following Elder Benson's call to the Twelve. Wrote he: "True to your pattern, as I knew you in England, you have continued on with the same energy and loyalty to self and church that characterized your Mission Field Activities."

Later in January, the Carlisle elders encountered unusually strong opposition. It was generated in part by a lurid film, *Trapped by the Mormons,* which was based on one of Winifred Graham's scandalous books about the Latter-day Saints. When their identity was known, people refused to talk to the elders. They were forcibly ejected from one home, and the women in one neighborhood were highly agitated from fear they were there to kidnap them and take them to Utah. The depth of the ignorance and bigotry that prevailed is well illustrated by one irate naval veteran who denounced the elders because his ship's crew was not allowed to go ashore when they made port at Salt Lake City!

Such rejection had a wearing effect on the missionaries. To encounter it day after day tended to blunt their enthusiasm. But there were antidotes. A chief one was the upbeat letters from home. Ezra's parents wrote almost weekly. His father's letters were especially helpful, because George knew precisely what Ezra was experiencing and knew how to give good counsel. His mother's letters were filled with expressions of love and support and news about the family. Flora's letters were less frequent, usually one a month. This did not reflect a lack of interest but an agreement she and Ezra had made. Both realized that frequent correspondence would distract Ezra from his work. Moreover, they agreed the letters would be strictly platonic, devoid of "mush." But

Flora's inventive nature enabled her to pour into her monthly letters such a variety of news and motivational snippets, all so cleverly phrased, that Ezra was constantly buoyed up as he thought about them and reread them.

The most important antidote to discouragement that Elder Benson found, however, was the strength he derived from fasting and prayer. It was in the mission field that he first began really to test these spiritual tools he had been taught about from infancy. Although his life in Whitney had not been easy and free from challenge, neither had it been unduly difficult. Even during the time his father was in the mission field, when such heavy responsibility had been placed upon him as the oldest child, life had been relatively secure and free from undue upset. He had been in the midst of his family, surrounded by caring relatives and Church members, and cushioned against dire want by the nest egg his father had provided. In these sheltered circumstances, he did not often have compelling needs of the kind experienced in the mission field.

In the distant land of his mission, far from home, among unfriendly people, and subjected to ridicule or even threatened by physical assault, Ezra undoubtedly felt very much alone at times and perhaps even frightened. Any fears would have arisen not only from physical sources but also from unseen, spiritual forces as well. He had been taught about the continual warfare between good and evil, and about satanic powers aimed at thwarting God's work—not imaginary powers, but real and frightening powers like those brought to bear against the Prophet Joseph Smith in the Sacred Grove at the very inception of the latter-day work. Though not to the extent experienced by Joseph Smith, Ezra most likely had felt the impact of these hostile powers and had seen the effect of them in the bitterly false attacks made on the Church by the likes of Winifred Graham. And he had been taught that they could be controlled through the intervention of God's power, invoked by fervent prayer as Joseph Smith had done in the Sacred

Grove. It is inferred, therefore, that the counsel about prayer which Elder Benson gave many years later to the missionaries at the Missionary Training Center was based on his own experiences as a missionary when he prayed with fervency, wrestling to control adverse influences and to achieve success in his work. As we shall see, he used the tools of fasting and prayer, honed first during his missionary service in Great Britain, to solve the complex problems he faced throughout life.

Frequent reliance upon prayer in performing his missionary work had a pronounced effect on the growth of Elder Benson's character. He became more spiritually minded, more sensitive to the whisperings of the Spirit, and more positive in exercising his priesthood authority. One day a spiritual impulse told him that his grandmother Louisa Benson had passed away. Ten days later he learned through the mail that she had died about the time the whispering came to him. The experience sharpened his watchfulness for those inner impressions and his discipline in relying upon them.

In May 1922 Elder Benson was called as clerk of the Newcastle Conference and as president of the Sunderland Branch. This entailed a move to the east coast of England, on the North Sea. There he was at the other end of Hadrian's famous wall and in the heart of a major mining, shipbuilding, manufacturing, and shipping center.

In Sunderland, ten miles southeast of Newcastle, Ezra labored with the conference president, Elder James T. Palmer. Ezra's clerical duties entailed compiling reports of both missionary work and work in the conference branches, handling funds funneled through the office, answering correspondence from Liverpool and from missionaries or members in the conference, and routing letters and Church publications to the missionaries. As branch president, he had the administrative responsibility to direct all the branch activities, to counsel with the members, to bless them, and to correct them when necessary. He also spent much time trying to locate members of record who had moved without leaving a forwarding address. This was tedious, unrewarding work except when, after much sleuthing, a lost one was found. Elder Benson also was occasionally required to act for the conference president when the latter was away from headquarters. These myriad duties introduced Ezra to Church functions he had not fully understood before and provided him with important training for future duties, both in the mission field and later.

What time was left after Elder Benson had finished his clerical and branch duties was devoted to regular missionary work of the kind he had performed at Carlisle. Although there was less time for this work, Ezra's experience and increased spiritual depth made it more effective. He and Elder Palmer shared many rare teaching experiences, one of which neither would ever forget. At a special meeting arranged by branch leaders at nearby South Shields, Elder Benson was to speak about the Apostasy. He had prepared accordingly; yet when he stood, he spoke only of the Book of Mormon, ignoring his assigned subject. Later he could not reconstruct what he had said. He knew only that he had spoken with a freedom he had never enjoyed before. Elder Palmer referred to it as "a strong and impressive discourse" about the truthfulness of the Book of Mormon. Afterward, several people in attendance commented that during Elder Benson's sermon, the Spirit had borne witness to them that the Book of Mormon is true.

The experience taught Ezra an important lesson: that it was not his words that brought conviction to his hearers, but rather the Spirit's influence accompanying his words. He had no control over that influence; he could only, through his faith, conduct, and words, help create an environment in which it could function. The result was reminiscent of Paul's dictum "I have planted, Apollos watered; but God gave the increase" (1 Corinthians 3:6). It is probable that this experience, and others like it, inspired Elder Benson's oft-repeated statement after his elevation to the apostleship: "It's the Spirit that counts." The experience also foreshadowed a long tradition of emphasis and reliance on the Book of Mormon, a subject that Ezra never tired of speaking or writing about. When he became President of the Church more than sixty years later, the Book of Mormon would become the centerpiece of his prophetic ministry. Very likely, his persistent advocacy of that sacred record will be what future generations will remember most about him.

In November 1922 Elder David O. McKay succeeded Elder Orson F. Whitney as president of the British Mission. Both had been ordained to the apostleship on the same day, April 9, 1906. However, because Elder Whitney was the older of the two, he had seniority over Elder McKay in the Quorum of the Twelve. They had sat side by side in quorum meetings since their ordination, and aside from the apostolic creed that bound them together, they had much in common in their shared love for good literature.

Only a few months before succeeding Elder Whitney, Elder McKay had stopped in Liverpool on the way to Salt Lake City, following his round-the-world trip with Hugh J. Cannon. When Elder Whitney saw Elder McKay off at the Liverpool dock, little did either of them realize that only a few months later Elder McKay would return with his family to take up residence in Durham House, replacing Elder Whitney as president of the British and the European Missions. Because Elder McKay had been away from Salt Lake City for one year, conventional wisdom would have suggested he be allowed to remain at home for a while before being given another overseas assignment. The two Apostles and their families probably were not surprised, however, considering the unconventional demands the Church had always made upon those called to the apostleship. The future apostle and prophet then laboring in Sunderland would learn all about that "imperious mandate" soon enough.

Elder Benson did not meet his new mission president until two months after Elder McKay replaced Elder

Whitney. On January 8, 1923, Elder McKay and his wife, Emma Ray, arrived in Sunderland for meetings with the missionaries of the Newcastle Conference and with the local Saints. Ezra was attracted immediately to this tall, handsome, self-confident man who would play such an important role in his future life. As an apparent remedy for the humiliating attacks the British press had made against the missionaries, Elder McKay sought from the beginning to instill in them a sense of dignity and self-worth. "He said for us to hold our own and fear no man," Ezra quoted him as saying. "Go with head up, we have nothing to be ashamed of." A final piece of advice from the new mission president could serve as the credo to describe the attitude Ezra Taft Benson carried with him through the remainder of his life: "The world steps aside for the man that knows where he is going" (journal of Ezra Taft Benson).

It seems clear that Ezra's high regard for his new mission president was reciprocated. Only a few days after returning to Liverpool, Elder McKay wrote to Elder Benson, calling him as president of the Newcastle Conference. Ezra was overwhelmed. He seemed to have had no premonition that the call was coming. And when he stopped to reflect on his new duties, he was even more anxious. He would be responsible for all Church affairs in Northern England, whether with missionaries, local leaders, or members. Within the conference were eight branches, about six hundred members, and eleven missionaries. Moreover, he was responsible to oversee the work of his conference clerk, who would serve as his companion and assistant.

Elder Benson's opportunities to speak and counsel were noticeably increased. He made regular visits to the eight branches to review the work of the branch leaders, to give them necessary counsel and direction, and to speak at branch meetings. He also met regularly with the missionaries, giving them guidance about their work, encouraging those who were despondent, and correcting those who were dilatory or disobedient.

Such was Ezra's performance as conference president that members acquired a proprietary attitude toward him, referring to him as "Our Benson." His open, friendly, whole-souled attitude endeared him to the northern British Saints. In addition, his labors among them provided important training for his future service in Church leadership. Being a conference president at that time, in an area where there were no organized stakes, was the equivalent of serving simultaneously as a stake president and as a mission president. Not only did he have delegated authority for all Church matters in northern England, whether in proselyting or administration, but also he was the Church spokesman to all who were not members of the Church. That he served without counselors amplified the significance of his role and intensified the pressures under which he worked.

An initiative that President McKay launched shortly before Ezra's call as conference president gave added stimulus to missionary work in the British Isles. He had announced that the mission goal for 1923 was for each member to bring at least one other person to a knowledge of the gospel during the year. This provided Ezra and the other conference presidents with an effective tool to coordinate the efforts of missionaries and members in pursuit of a common proselyting goal. So successful was this initiative in Great Britain that President McKay was inspired to announce it as a goal for members worldwide when he became President of the Church. One of the Apostles who helped implement the prophet's global vision was his former Newcastle Conference president, Elder Ezra Taft Benson.

Opposition to the Church seemed to grow apace with advances in proselyting techniques. The filth stirred up by Winifred Graham and her confederates complicated Ezra's leadership role. Rude receptions at the doors, hecklers at street meetings, and vicious rumors about Mormon intentions thrived in an atmosphere of hatred. The opposition became so intense that President McKay directed that street meetings and some tracting be discontinued temporarily. He also instructed the missionaries to avoid any conduct that could be misinterpreted and to leave the young ladies alone "absolutely."

When the street-meeting ban was announced, Elder Benson had already scheduled one to be held on a Sunday evening near the Sunderland railway station. Rationalizing that a prearranged meeting did not fall within the ban, Ezra and his companion went ahead with it. A boisterous crowd of longshoremen, miners, and others gathered, many of whom had been drinking in the pubs nearby. They were in no mood to listen to sermons, especially if preached by the Mormons. The crowd, pushing ever nearer to the elders, grew morose and threatening. Sensing the danger, Ezra stopped speaking and began to pray silently for help. At the moment of peril, a tall, muscular man pushed his way through the crowd to Ezra's side and, looking him in the eye, said he believed Ezra's words. The appearance of the stranger, which Elder Benson felt was a direct answer to his fervent prayers, temporarily stayed the crowd. Meanwhile a British bobby appeared to disperse the people and to instruct Elder Benson to return to his digs. He did so, but because he and his companion had become separated in the fracas, Ezra donned a disguise and went to search for him. On the street, Ezra heard that his companion had suffered a head injury; and as Ezra frantically looked for him, he again encountered the bobby, who said he had helped the companion to his quarters. Returning, Ezra found his companion putting on a disguise to go look for him. Relieved there had been no serious injuries, they embraced each other, then kneeled in a prayer of thanksgiving.

As there was rich food for thought here, Elder Benson often reflected on this incident. Using a rationalization for an excuse, he had deliberately disobeyed the direction of his priesthood leader. No good came from it, other than the hard lesson he learned not to disobey again. Indeed, there had been much negative fallout: his companion had been injured, Ezra had lost credibility as a leader by ignoring the direction of his superior, and the Church had been held up to ridicule by the unruly mob that attacked them. On the other hand, the experience affirmed Ezra's deep conviction that God would come to his aid in an extremity if he prayed fervently and with faith.

Though he likely did not recognize it at the time, Elder Benson served in Great Britain at a crucial time in Church history. During almost a century of proselyting, the Church's admonition to new converts was to gather to Zion, the land of America. The effect of this policy eventually became counterproductive, for it deprived local congregations of vital leadership, making them overdependent on missionary guidance and stunting their growth. David O. McKay, with his special view of the international character of the Church gained from his recent world tour, was in the vanguard of Church leaders who began to change the strategy. With the change, the admonition to new converts was to remain in their home countries to help build up the Church locally. Later, as a member of the Twelve, Elder Benson played an important role in this transition under the direction of President David O. McKay; and because of his worldwide travels as U.S. secretary of agriculture during eight years, he perhaps gained a view of the global potential of the Church that was clearer than that of any of his brethren.

Ezra received his honorable release as a missionary on November 2, 1923, with competing emotions. He regretted leaving the work and the people whom he had come to love. Yet he longed to rejoin his family and the appealing young woman from Logan who had been in his thoughts often.

Honored by the Saints in Sunderland at a farewell party, he was lauded for his service and was given many thoughtful gifts. Always appreciative of courtesies shown to him and sensitive in his feelings, "Our Benson" could not suppress the tears, even had he wanted to.

At President McKay's invitation, Ezra joined his mission

president for a conference in Sheffield and then accompanied him to Liverpool by automobile. After staying overnight at Durham House and receiving final counsel from President McKay, he took the train to London and then flew to Paris with two companions. It was Ezra's first flight. The airsickness caused by heavy turbulence, which all but the pilot suffered, may have caused him to question whether it was the transportation of the future.

At that day missionaries often were authorized, if not encouraged, to tour foreign lands near their fields of labor before returning home. It was thought that the exposure to foreign cultures would expand their horizons of thought and sympathy, better equipping them to live more useful and more satisfying lives afterward. However, the proliferation of missionaries and missions since then have made that practice infeasible. So today, missionaries are instructed to make a beeline for home when their service has been completed.

Ezra and a companion spent a month touring on the Continent. In France, Belgium, and Germany they saw some of the scars left by the recent conflict—fields and farms lacerated by grinding trench warfare, and buildings shattered by artillery fire. These grim sights stood as stark reminders of war's insanity. And the terror of the battlefield was still mirrored in the faces of some, or in the empty sleeve or pant leg of a veteran seen on the street or on the train. The talk of a war to end all wars, current at the time, makes incredible the visit Ezra Taft Benson made to these same countries less than a quarter of a century later when, as an Apostle of mercy, he saw even greater devastation caused by still another war.

However, the glitter of Europe's major cities, Paris, Berlin, and Brussels, somewhat masked the wounds of the war and opened up a new field of reflection for Elder Benson. On every hand were evidences of great antiquity and intelligence. The ancient churches, the libraries, the museums, and the art galleries doubtless aroused feelings of admiration in the young elder from Whitney, and perhaps even a sense of cultural backwardness not uncommon among American tourists in Europe. Yet it is assumed that none of these grand sights could quite measure up in his estimation to the charm of the little rock chapel at home, nor to the imposing temple atop the hill in Logan.

His visit to Switzerland was doubly rewarding. In Lausanne he was reminded of his Ballif ancestors, especially of his great-grandfather who had lived and preached there before he was converted to the Mormon Church. And there in a beautiful Alpine setting reminiscent of home, he was happy to greet one of his uncles, Serge Ballif, who then presided over the Swiss Mission.

Elder Benson and his companion boarded their ship, the *Merita*, for the return voyage on December 2, 1923. Ezra found a winter crossing of the North Atlantic to be an experience one would not want to repeat if it could be avoided. The wild turbulence of the sea during most of the voyage nullified all activities except the mere act of nauseous survival. One could hardly imagine how the ship remained intact in the midst of such violence.

This rough crossing made his arrival on American soil all the more appreciated. On the way home, he stopped in Salt Lake City to report his mission. While at Church headquarters, Ezra made arrangements to receive a second patriarchal blessing, this one from the Patriarch to the Church, Hyrum Gibbs Smith. Ezra's experiences in the mission field caused him to feel the need for additional spiritual insights into his future life and work. Among other things, Patriarch Smith promised that Ezra's name would be held in honorable remembrance throughout time and that he would live to "a goodly age" to complete his earthly mission. He also was admonished to be true to his convictions, to be humble, not to shrink from duty "when it's made known," and to "keep thy trust in the Lord."

Ezra arrived in Whitney on Christmas Eve in time to help his parents retrieve and arrange the gifts for his younger brothers and sisters. It was a choice experience for all to be reunited to share the traditional Christmas festivities. And in the days that followed, the family enjoyed listening to Ezra's detailed account of his missionary experiences.

Chapter 5

From Student to Married Man

When Ezra returned from England, he had two immediate goals in mind—more education and marriage. His relationship with Orson F. Whitney and David O. McKay, both men of intellect and education, and his exposure to the cultures in Great Britain and Europe had broadened his horizons and imbued him with the desire to develop his inherent powers through higher education. In addition, he wanted to build on the relationship he had with Flora Amussen, to determine whether it might bloom into marriage. He took a step toward both goals when he registered for the winter semester at the Utah Agricultural College in Logan.

He found Flora engaged in the same whirl of activities at the college as when he first met her. There was an unusual aura about this young woman that intrigued Ezra. It seemed to be a combination of physical charm, intelligence, self-confidence, and a certain sense of preeminence traceable to the trappings of wealth in which she had been raised.

Flora's father, Carl Christian Amussen, a dedicated

convert to the Church, owned a prosperous Salt Lake City jewelry business whose fashionable shop was located on Main Street a half block from Temple Square. It was the place where the elite of the city purchased their jewelry. The location is still marked by a facade built into the wall of a bank that now stands on the site. Barbara Smith Amussen, Flora's mother and Carl's second polygamous wife, bore him seven children. Flora, the youngest of these, and the last child fathered by Carl Amussen, was born July 1, 1901. Her father died fifteen months later. At the time of Flora's birth, Barbara and her sister Martha, Carl's first polygamous wife, and their children lived in a fourteen-room home in Logan, which Carl had purchased for them after the Manifesto. Following Carl's death, proceeds from his estate enabled Barbara and her children to live comfortably in the Logan home, with surpluses sufficient to provide for the education of the children and to purchase luxurious extras like Flora's sports car.

After Ezra enrolled at the Logan college in early 1924, he and Flora began to date, though not exclusively with each other. She had a set of friends she had known from childhood and with whom she socialized; and there were other girls whom Ezra had dated, one especially who had written regularly while he was in England. So their dating was sporadic, especially because of Flora's many commitments at school. It was during this period, for instance, that she played the lead role of Viola in Shakespeare's *Twelfth Night*, with its numerous memorization sessions and frequent rehearsals.

As Flora and Ezra resumed their dating, a subtle change was introduced into their relationship. Before his mission, Ezra lacked the social polish of his college peers who came from an urban background. Flora, therefore, perhaps unconsciously, seemed to have a somewhat condescending attitude toward him, looking upon him as one who, though handsome and intelligent, needed someone like her to lead him from his rural ways into genteel society. However, the refining experiences of two and a half years abroad had made immense changes. Ezra had learned to excel in a society more sophisticated than anything Flora had seen, and he had traveled extensively in continental Europe. More important, perhaps, he had served in a notable leadership position, had become more spiritually attuned, and had associated on a personal basis with some of the high leaders of the Church. This had given him a new social refinement, a broader view of the world and the Church, and a desire to develop his innate talents. Having imbibed the counsel of Elder McKay, Ezra knew where he wanted to go and expected the world would make way for him.

These changes in Ezra's status and perceptions could not have failed to make a deep impression on Flora. Indeed, it seems that now, perhaps for the first time, she began to catch a glimpse of the unusual qualities of this man and of the high status for which he was destined. With this realization came a desire to be of help to him.

Although Ezra had not proposed marriage, Flora felt it was likely he would do so. Acting on that assumption, she fasted and prayed that the Lord would inspire her to do what was best for Ezra. She sensed that immediate marriage might interfere with his plans for more education and might even destroy them. This prompted her to inquire about serving a mission. With no assurance Ezra would wait for her, Flora submitted a missionary application through her bishop and soon received a call from President Heber J. Grant to serve in Hawaii. Ezra was surprised when he heard about it, because Flora had not consulted with him. But as they discussed it, both agreed it was the best thing to do under the circumstances. Not the least of the advantages was that Flora would learn firsthand about missionary work, providing insight into what Ezra had done in England. Moreover, as can be seen in retrospect, Flora's missionary service would help her achieve the spiritual maturity he had attained and would help qualify her in important ways to become the wife of one foreordained to be a prophet.

Flora boarded the train in Salt Lake City on August 26, 1924, with Honolulu as her ultimate destination. Repeating what they had done when Ezra left for England, he got on the train with her, riding as far as Tooele, thirty miles to the west. There were more private things to discuss, including, we assume, an affirmation of the "understanding" they had about their future relationship.

Meanwhile, Ezra had decided to transfer from the Agricultural College in Logan to Brigham Young University in Provo. He seemed to feel there was a superior faculty at BYU, and he welcomed the pervasive influence of the Church found in Provo. He spent part of the summer at BYU's Alpine School in Provo Canyon, where the students lived in tents, enjoying the magnificence of the mountains while pursuing their studies. One of the favorite professors was Dr. Adam S. Bennion, superintendent of the Church Department of Education and a future Apostle who, though thirteen years older than Ezra, would not be called to the Twelve until 1953, ten years after Ezra's call to that quorum.

Ezra enrolled at BYU at a crucial time in its history. Shortly before, there had been a serious debate among its trustees about whether the school should be discontinued, together with other Church-financed schools, with the Church restricting its financial involvement in education to Church seminaries. Twelve of the stake academies already had been closed, and plans were in progress to close others. Ezra's mission president, Elder David O. McKay, was in the forefront of those trustees who opposed closure of BYU. An incident that occurred on August 6, 1924, shortly before Flora left on her mission, hinted that the views of Elder McKay and his associates predominated. On that day the Church General Board of Education appropriated $125,000 for the planning and construction of a new library on the BYU campus, the heart of any good university. Named after President Heber J. Grant, this library was dedicated in 1925 on the fiftieth anniversary of the school's founding. That same year, the university was organized into five colleges, three divisions, and thirty-four departments, all of which created the initial framework for the growth of BYU into a major university. Years later, Ezra Taft Benson would play a leading role in the further development of the university as a member, and later as the chairman, of its board of trustees.

Ezra found an air of excitement and progress on the campus of his new school as he began his studies in the autumn of 1924. Now a twenty-five-year-old returned missionary accustomed to hard work, faced with the prospect of marriage within a few years, and motivated by the challenges of his mission presidents, Ezra Benson was prepared to be a diligent and focused student. His intensity was increased by a commitment he had made to his brother Orval. After purchasing their father's farm in Whitney, they had agreed that Ezra would finish school first, then would run the farm while Orval filled a mission and completed school. Ezra's plan to graduate in two years required that he take an average of twenty credit hours a quarter, a crushing academic load. Given his ambition to farm, it is not surprising that Ezra's major at BYU was in animal husbandry with a minor in agronomy. He also took classes in science, mathematics, history, philosophy, and sociology, all of which enlarged his perspectives of life and the world around him.

Ezra did not allow his primary emphasis on academics to restrict his social life and extracurricular activities. His maturity and discipline enabled him to provide time for everything. He was elected president of the men's glee club, president of the Agriculture Club, a member of the Mask Club, and chairman of the senior entertainment committee. He attended student-body dances, plays, lectures, canyon parties, snow carnivals, and other social functions, sometimes dating and sometimes going alone or in groups. Indeed, because of his enthusiastic involvement in every aspect of university life, he was voted "Most Popular Man on Campus" in his senior year and the "Man Most Likely to Succeed."

In all this Flora was not forgotten. They had agreed, as they did when Ezra went to England, that their correspondence would be limited to one letter each month so that Flora could devote herself to missionary work. And because there was no formal engagement, Ezra was free, as Flora had been in Logan, to engage fully in university life.

Ezra graduated with honors from Brigham Young University in the spring of 1926. His scholastic record earned him a research scholarship in agricultural economics at Iowa State College in Ames, Iowa. The scholarship carried a monthly cash stipend of seventy dollars in addition to tuition and books. While it was not a lavish amount, it was sufficient to enable a young couple to live frugally while Ezra worked toward a master's degree. It was a financial windfall he would always appreciate. As graduate degrees were uncommon in those days, it would be the means of lifting him to a level few of his peers would attain. It also would open doors to opportunities he could not then foresee.

With an assured income and with the excitement of graduate studies beckoning, the only missing piece in the puzzle was a wife with whom to share the adventure. Actually, it was not a puzzle at all. From the moment he first saw Flora driving her little sports car, he knew by spiritual means they were destined to be married. During the intervening years, he had dated other girls; but although they were beautiful and talented, none of them was *the* girl.

When he informed Flora of the scholarship, Ezra hinted broadly that he would like to take her to Ames as his wife. Nothing final was decided, however, until she returned home from Hawaii in mid-June. In less than a month of serious dating, during which time Ezra monopolized most of Flora's time while figuratively wearing out the road between Whitney and Logan, they both came to know in special, intimate ways that they were deeply in love and

71

*Flora Amussen at the
time she married
Ezra Taft Benson in
September 1926*

wanted to be joined in marriage. On July 12, 1926, they announced their engagement and their plans to be married on September 10.

Viewed in retrospect, there is a remarkable symmetry in the paths that brought this couple together from radically different backgrounds. They enjoyed similar, pivotal experiences in the security of well-ordered homes, college training, missions, and the opportunity to test their talents and skills in competition with others. Both were competitive, as evidenced by the way they gravitated to positions of prominence at college and in the mission field. That they both were spiritually sensitive is indicated by Ezra's impression that Flora was to be his wife and by the whispering to Flora of the need to assist Ezra. Both had faith in their future together, as shown by the confidence with which they planned to leave for Ames, there to live on a shoestring for a year while Ezra attended graduate school. They knew where they were going. As Elder McKay had promised Ezra, the world would stand aside for them.

The quiet, impressive marriage ceremony was performed in the Salt Lake Temple at 9:30 A.M. on September 10, 1926, by Elder Orson F. Whitney of the Twelve. Afterward, a wedding breakfast was held in the President's Suite of the Hotel Utah, a building now named the Joseph Smith Memorial Building. In that suite today hangs a portrait of Ezra Taft Benson, the thirteenth President of The Church of Jesus Christ of Latter-day Saints, along with portraits of his twelve predecessors and those who have succeeded him.

Two days before the ceremony, Ezra carefully packed in his Model T Ford pickup all their things, which included camping equipment and a tent that would serve as a bridal suite during their eight nights on the road. As soon as the wedding breakfast was over and good-byes had been said, they hurriedly changed their clothes, cranked up the Model T, climbed in, and were on their way. Ahead of them was a trip of more than a thousand miles over mostly dirt roads through the states of Utah, Wyoming, Nebraska, and Iowa. Any inconvenience of either travel or sleeping accommodations was swallowed up in the joy of their new marital relationship and in the excitement of the adventure that lay ahead.

The trip itself was a major adventure. It was less than a quarter of a century since the first automobile trip had been made across the United States. In 1903, Dr. H. Nelson Jackson drove his Winton across the continent from New York to San Francisco in sixty-three days. In 1909, when Henry Joy, president of the Packard Motor Company, wanted to drive west from Omaha, he asked somebody in Omaha how to get to the road going west. He was told there wasn't one. Asking what he should do, he was taken westward until they came to a wire fence. "Just take down the fence and drive on and when you come to the next fence, take that down and go on again," he was told. "A little further," Joy said, "there were no fences, no fields, nothing but

73

two ruts across the prairie." (See Helen B. Gibbons, "Horseless, Helpless Carriages: The 3 M.P.H. Adventure," *Deseret News,* May 8, 1980.) Now, seventeen years later, many improvements had been made; but long-distance automobile travel was still in its infancy and required careful preparation and mechanical skill to do it safely.

With his tools and know-how, Ezra had prepared for every contingency, except for an unexpected breakdown in Iowa when a magnet from the flywheel came loose and flew through the casing. Hailing a passerby, Ezra arranged for a tow to the nearest town, where, fortunately, there was a mechanic. It was a day's job to repair the damage. That night as they camped near a stream, a torrential rain leaked water into the tent, soaking their bedding. And when the Ford wouldn't start the next day, they needed another tow. Ezra was embarrassed he had subjected his bride to such inconvenience on their honeymoon, and he was fearful she would take cold. He need not have feared, for he found that Flora was durable and resilient despite her genteel upbringing. This episode, perhaps as much as anything else, convinced Ezra that his new bride would be a true partner in what he thought at the time would be a life on the farm.

Aside from the novelty of the trip and the thrill of the honeymoon, Ezra was excited because their journey paralleled the route of the Mormon pioneer trek west and took them through some of the most fertile farmland in America. Occasionally Ezra would stop to question farmers about their crops and herds and to make comparisons with farming in Whitney. Especially in eastern Nebraska and in Iowa, he was impressed with the picturesque appearance of the farms with their well-tilled fields and their white houses and barns enclosed in white fences. On reaching Council Bluffs, Iowa, and then in traveling on to Ames, Ezra doubtless was reminded about his pioneer heritage in a special way. It was at Council Bluffs on July 16, 1846, that his great-grandfather and namesake, Ezra T. Benson, was ordained to the apostleship by President Brigham Young. About thirty miles south of Ames lay Des Moines, where his father had worked as a missionary; and about thirty miles south of Des Moines lay the site of Garden Grove, where his grandfather George T. Benson was born in a wagon box. And now a fourth-generation Benson had come to Iowa to pursue his dream of higher education, a dream neither his father, grandfather, or great-grandfather had any hope of realizing, in part because of the insistent demands on their time made by their families and the Church.

The official name of the school in which Ezra enrolled in the autumn of 1926 was the Iowa State College of Agriculture and Mechanic Arts, later to be named the Iowa State University of Science and Technology. Its campus occupied a one-thousand-acre tract landscaped into a naturalistic park within the city. The campus also included an additional eight thousand acres operated as experimental farms near Ames and in other parts of the state. The graduate school in which Ezra enrolled was considered to be the nation's best one specializing in agricultural science. Its reputation had attracted a faculty of note, in part because of the large percentage of the school's operating budget allocated to agricultural research. Moreover, the quality of the student body matched the faculty because it was composed of the top graduates of colleges throughout the country. Here Ezra would be able to acquire knowledge and skills from his professors and through his own research, as well as test his discipline and motivation against the best students in the country in his field.

Ezra and Flora found an apartment only a block from the campus. The quarters consisted of a small combination living room/bedroom and a tiny kitchen. Down the hall were bathroom facilities that they shared with three other couples. The humid climate spawned cockroaches in abundance, and Flora battled these pests throughout their stay with an arsenal of insecticides and a determined ingenuity. It was a battle she would never win, though a cockroach entered the Benson apartment at its peril, as Flora took no prisoners.

This apartment represented the acid test of Flora's dedication to her husband and his career. A more stark contrast between the living accommodations in the gracious fourteen-room home in which she had been reared and this miniature, bug-infested apartment would be difficult to find. But she adjusted to the change willingly, even joyfully, determined to support and assist her husband in any way possible. So she went about her household duties with a happy enthusiasm. Because she was anxious that whatever she and Ezra achieved would be done together as a team, she relinquished to her mother an allowance she had received from her father's estate, being determined to live on Ezra's monthly stipend of seventy dollars. After paying for housing, food, and tithing, only twenty dollars remained each month for all the other items in their family budget. It was tight, but they managed.

Their food budget was augmented by vegetables they were allowed to glean from the experimental farm and by buttermilk given free of charge to graduate students. They drove the Model T only when absolutely necessary, and they took full advantage of the events on campus that were free of charge. Unfortunately, their budget did not include Big Eight football games, admission to which was four dollars, an amount the Bensons simply could not afford.

The Bensons' spartan lifestyle did not inhibit them socially. They entertained in their little apartment without any sense of inferiority or deprivation. Flora, trained well by her dignified mother, did the best she could with what she had, welcoming guests with aplomb to share their simple fare. We gather that a chief source of social satisfaction for her at Ames was the evening they hosted Dr. C. L. Holmes, dean of the department of agricultural economics, serving dinner on a makeshift table without apology or explanation. The pattern set here in the Bensons' first home would be followed throughout their lives. They made no pretensions.

Their guests saw the Bensons as they really were—open, friendly, down-to-earth, and comfortable with themselves and their status, whatever that might be. Twenty-five years later this family characteristic would be revealed on a national stage when Flora, assisted by her daughters, would act as hostess in her home to the cream of official Washington society, treating them to typical Benson hospitality.

Ezra and Flora also enjoyed socializing and worshipping with five other Latter-day Saint families then living in Ames. There being no Mormon chapel or rented facility in town, they rotated in gathering together twice monthly in each other's apartments to worship. On alternate weekends, they often carpooled to attend services in organized branches in nearby Des Moines and Boone. Perpetuating the traditions learned in their homes as they grew up, Ezra and Flora always had their personal and family prayers in the privacy of their apartment and often studied the scriptures together. As expected, the Book of Mormon received special attention.

Academically and professionally, the year Ezra spent in Ames was perhaps the most significant and productive of his career. Especially important was his exposure to the theories of agricultural economics. Crop rotations, cultivation, pest and disease controls, fertilization, financing, breeding, and cost controls were, of course, traditional subjects the well-trained farmer always emphasized. But Ezra felt that training in agricultural economics and marketing skills were the things most needed by farmers at that time. Consequently, while at Ames he gave special attention to these subjects. They were subjects he stressed later—whether as a farmer, as an agricultural agent, as a national farm executive, as U.S. secretary of agriculture, or as chairman of the board of directors of the Church's large ranch in Florida.

This critical period in the lives of Ezra and Flora Benson passed pleasantly and quickly. Almost without their realizing it, the school year drew toward a rapid close in May 1927. Ezra was busily occupied in preparing for his oral exams and in finishing his thesis. His nervous anticipation of the orals was more stressful than the fact, for he passed them very smoothly. His careful preparation and the verbal skills and poise under pressure he had developed in England were crucial to his success. Such was his standing among his peers that he graduated with honors and was inducted into Gamma Sigma Delta, the national honor society of agriculture. Moreover, Dr. Holmes offered him a teaching position for the coming year, an opportunity that Ezra declined with thanks. There were urgent duties at home that beckoned him, including his commitments to Orval and the obligations to his father in the purchase of the farm. Besides, he wanted to begin the career for which he had made such long preparation in both theory and practice.

The graduation ceremonies were held on June 13, 1927, and Ezra was awarded his master's degree. This event, the culmination of the uncounted hours of study, lectures, recitation, and exams that comprised his college education, elevated him to a select circle of excellence. That he had been inducted into the prestigious national honor society of agriculture added even more luster to his achievement. These insignia would follow him throughout life, marking him as someone who, through intelligence and industry, had attained a distinction in his field reserved for only a favored few. Upon returning to Whitney, a place where no one before him had received a master's degree, he would find that his accomplishment was magnified beyond imagination.

Ezra and Flora decided to return home via St. Paul and across the northern states of Minnesota, North Dakota, and Montana. It is suspected that this decision was based not only upon a desire to see new country and to broaden their knowledge of the United States, but also upon the connection to Ezra's master's thesis: "The Beef Cattle Situation in the Northern Range Area in Its Relation to the Iowa Feeder." St. Paul, the capital of Minnesota, is the commercial, industrial, and transportation center for a large agricultural region in the northern states. Its meat-packing industry ranks second in the United States both in livestock sales and in cattle, calf, and hog slaughter. It is assumed that Ezra wanted to visit the northern range area about which he had written and the St. Paul market through which most of the livestock sales from that area are funneled. This was typical of Ezra Benson, the agricultural expert who was always more interested in learning firsthand about conditions in the field than depending on the analysis of reports and statistics.

But there was much more than St. Paul's meat-packing industry for Ezra to see and learn about by traveling this northern route. He was anxious to see the farms along the way and to question the owners about their soils, their crops, their problems, and their methods of operation. We can be assured he made mental or written notes of anything he learned through these interrogations that would be useful when he commenced again to operate the Whitney farm.

The travelers found the roads on this northern route to be more rough and rutted than those through Nebraska and western Iowa. This was troubling because they learned shortly before leaving Ames that Flora was expecting their first child. To give her some respite from the constant bumping of their car, she boarded a train at Cleveland, North Dakota, and rode it to Dickinson, North Dakota, a distance of more than two hundred miles. Ezra came later in the car to pick her up. Driving through what later became part of the Theodore Roosevelt National Memorial Park in the Dakota Badlands, the Bensons traveled into Montana and thence southwesterly across Wyoming into Utah. Two weeks after leaving Ames, they arrived safely in Whitney, tired and dusty but happy and anxious to join in the traditional July Fourth celebration, where they were greeted by family and friends.

Chapter 6

Professional and Personal Growth

E zra and Flora settled into the Benson family home
on the Whitney farm, which Ezra and Orval had
purchased. While it was not up to the standards of
the Logan home in which Flora had been raised, it
was a vast improvement over the cramped apartment in
Ames. Very soon Flora fixed the imprint of her personality
on the house by using knickknacks, pictures, curtains, and
flowers to add a touch of beauty, scouring and waxing the
floors, and recovering or polishing furniture. Once she had
done everything possible to spruce up the house and make
it more attractive, she accepted it without complaint and, as
she had done in Ames, received visitors to the home without apology or explanation. She also contributed signifi-
cantly to the work on the farm, especially in the dairy and
in feeding the threshers at harvest time.

Meanwhile, Ezra devoted himself to making the farm a
showplace where he could apply and illustrate what he had
learned about scientific farming. For the first few months,
Orval worked with him prior to his departure for the

The Benson family farm in Whitney, Idaho

Danish Mission. Then his brother Valdo moved into the house to help with the work, being chiefly responsible for the delivery of milk bottled on the farm. As a marketing device, the brothers had coined the motto "You can whip our cream, but you can't beat our milk." It seemed to typify the positive, aggressive attitude the Bensons brought to their enterprise. They were determined to compete and to succeed, but in doing so to be absolutely aboveboard and honest, friendly, and open to all.

Ezra was proud of his herd of holsteins and began immediately to take steps to upgrade it through more scientific care and breeding. He also analyzed the acreage included in the farm, deciding what changes to make in the crop rotation cycles and the methods of fertilization so as to ensure maximum yields while preserving the soil. And he monitored the health and the production of his flock of chickens, whose eggs yielded another source of ready cash or a commodity for barter. Some hogs were raised on the farm, either for sale or consumption by the family; and horses were raised too, either for farm work or for recreational uses.

In addition to money crops (sugar beets and grain) and

alfalfa for livestock feed, the farm included a truck garden that provided vegetables for the family table, to be eaten fresh or to be bottled for out-of-season use. Fruits from the orchard provided other table food, whether fresh or bottled.

Ezra looked on a farm as a self-contained economic unit that, if properly managed, would provide a good livelihood for the owner and his family while contributing to the health and wealth of the community. It was an exciting and rewarding, even a creative, process that he enjoyed managing and observing. It seems apparent that Ezra Taft Benson could have lived out his life on the Whitney farm, totally content with his lot, while rearing a good family and contributing to his church and his community. But if that were his aim, he should have known it was never intended to be, for a man of his intelligence and drive, an honors graduate with a master's degree from the most prestigious agricultural college in the nation, could not forever remain on a small farm in remote Whitney, Idaho. As we shall see, his credentials and character would act like a magnet, powerfully drawing to him unforeseen opportunities and responsibilities that would take him away from the farm.

There were factors beyond prudent, scientific management upon which the success of Ezra's farm depended. These included factors over which he had no control, factors like market prices, demand, and government restrictions. At the time Ezra took over the management of the Benson farm, agriculture in the United States had been in gradual decline for several years. This decline was caused chiefly by a loss of foreign markets as the production of wheat and cotton increased in other countries, by a reduction in domestic consumption through changes in dietary and clothing styles, and by lower prices due to agricultural surpluses. Moreover, the farmer was handicapped by the need to sell his products in the open market while he purchased his farm machinery and tools in a protected market. This put the squeeze on the farmer's buying power and his profits.

These conditions were aggravated in the months ahead

by an orgy of speculation in the stock market. Many investors, confident about the future of the economy, made large purchases on margin, believing that as stock prices rose, they could make a killing by acquiring stock at the lower margin price and selling at the higher current price. In order to put a brake on this inflationary spiral, the Federal Reserve Board raised its discount rate in the summer of 1929. This automatically produced an increase in interest rates by member banks, creating anxiety among those who had bought on margin and among those, like most farmers, who operated on borrowed funds.

Anxiety turned to fear when Great Britain also raised its discount rate, which helped bring on a worldwide market crisis. This resulted in the collapse of the American economy, beginning with the stock market crash in October 1929. These ruinous events, which came to a head shortly after Ezra was appointed county agent, introduced him to the complex way in which farm economics were intertwined with government regulations, and they demonstrated that all he had learned about scientific farming would fail to create a dependable farm economy unless order were created in the government sector. A desire to help bring that about doubtless was a key factor impelling Ezra to accept the offer of government service when it was extended to him many years later by President Dwight D. Eisenhower.

Meanwhile, an event that occurred on January 2, 1928, radically altered the perceptions that Ezra and Flora had toward life and rendered unimportant any concerns about farm economics. On that day their first child was born, a son whom they named Reed Amussen Benson. As the first of six children who would be born into this family, Reed would always occupy a place of special importance in the eyes of his parents, especially his father. When Reed grew to maturity, his father came to rely on his counsel with as much confidence as upon the counsel of almost anyone else. This was apparent during the Eisenhower years, as it was in the decade afterward when Reed was affiliated with the John

Birch Society. During the Washington years, Reed worked for a while on his father's staff and later worked for another government agency in the capital. This made it convenient for Ezra to use him as a sounding board or intermediary or, in some instances, as a substitute for himself to fulfill speaking and other assignments. It was well known that if one wished to get access to Secretary Benson, one of the surest ways was through his son Reed.

Yet the other five children played equally important roles with their father at different times and in different ways. He took all of them into his confidence as they reached the age of understanding, often giving them documents he had written or was studying, asking the children to read them and give their opinion. Nor was it uncommon for the father to discuss issues of importance with the children, drawing out their views and suggestions.

Ezra's practice of sharing documents carried over into his daily work, whether as an agricultural executive or as a General Authority of the Church. The practice seemed to have a twofold purpose: to elicit ideas from others and to educate the recipients about circumstances or issues that Ezra considered important. So at Church headquarters, he often sent copies of articles and speeches about things that interested him to fellow General Authorities and others. It was a means of mutual education, of trying to build a consensus, and perhaps of kindling an interest that would lead the recipients to independent study and reflection and, hopefully, to a shared understanding with him.

In all this, Flora participated with her husband as a full partner. A woman of deep spirituality who seemed to sense instinctively that her husband was destined for greatness, she subordinated her personal interests to his interests and the interests of her children. From the inception of their family life, the children were taught that God lives and that He hears and answers prayers. They were also taught that when any member of the family, and especially the father, was faced with a special challenge, they were to join together in praying for his success. A notable example of this occurred in the Salt Lake Tabernacle when a friend of one of the girls was seated on the row with the Benson family. When it was announced that Elder Benson would be the next speaker, the one seated on the end whispered to the next one, "Pray for Dad." That message was passed on from one to another, including the friend, until it reached the one on the other end of the row. They were all joined in silent prayer for Elder Benson, including the friend, who was astonished at the unity of purpose in the family and the commitment to prayer the incident demonstrated.

During the twenty-two months Ezra operated the Benson farm in Whitney, he and Flora were active in the Church as they always had been and always would be. He served on the stake board of the YMMIA while Flora was sustained as president of the Whitney Ward YWMIA. Also, Ezra was ordained a seventy during this period by Elder Melvin J. Ballard of the Twelve. As such, Ezra became involved in missionary work in the stake. At this time, no full-time missionaries worked within organized stakes, so all missionary work in the Franklin Stake was performed by the local seventies. While he did not have the enormous pool of nonmembers to work with that he had had in England, Ezra prized the opportunity to continue with the Church work he valued so highly, even though it was on a greatly reduced scale.

As suggested, it was beyond reason that Ezra Benson would continue for long to operate the small farm in Whitney when his training and character portended work within a larger arena. The Franklin County commissioners began the process that uprooted him from the family farm and set him on the path that led to the highest position in agriculture in America. Knowing about Ezra's academic credentials, his practical knowledge of farming, and his reputation for industry and integrity, they invited him to become the county agricultural agent at $150 a month. Financed jointly by the county, the state of Idaho, and the U.S.

Department of Agriculture, the position was tied to the University of Idaho extension service for scientific support and counseling. At first, the university opposed the appointment because of a policy that forbade a county agent from living in the county he served. Soon, however, the university was willing not only to make an exception to the policy but also to authorize Ezra to continue to live on the farm and operate it. The change in the university's position seems to have occurred promptly after it studied the candidate's qualifications. The reviewers obviously were loath to lose the services of one with such impressive credentials simply because of a policy of questionable utility.

With that change, Ezra accepted the offer with Flora's consent and support. He also eased the concerns of the university about the exception to the policy by deciding to relinquish the direct management of the farm to Kenneth Olverson and to move his family to Preston, the county seat. This arrangement helped minimize the concerns of farmers in the county who might have felt reluctant to accept counsel from a competitor, and it helped to insulate him against conflict-of-interest charges. Moreover, it simplified the administration of his work by being nearer to the county commission offices and USDA representatives.

This was not an easy decision for Ezra Taft Benson to make. It meant turning his back on a dream he had cherished all his life. Although there was a chance he might return to the farm, it was doubtful because of the decision made at the same time to buy and furnish a home in Preston. His involvement with county, state, and federal agencies and university officials clearly would lead him away from the practicalities to the theories of farming and would immerse him in the complex relationships between the practicing farmer and the several layers of government bureaucracy with which the farmer had to deal.

The red brick home Ezra purchased in Preston was only partially finished. He helped reduce the cost by doing some of the carpentry work himself. The house included a basement apartment that could be rented out or occupied by the family as it grew. When the deal to buy the home was closed, family growth was imminent since Flora was expecting again. She gave birth to her second child on May 2, 1929, a son whom she and Ezra named Mark Amussen Benson. Of the many distinctions this son would achieve, none would be more satisfying to him and his parents than his service in the presidency of the stake in which his parents resided at the time his father became President of the Church.

The Bensons moved into their new home near the first of July in 1929, almost two years to the day after Ezra and Flora returned from Ames. The seeming permanency of their new situation was deceiving. They would call Preston home for less than two years. Not knowing that, however, they proceeded to act as if they intended to stay there the rest of their lives.

Ezra and Flora Benson were a lustrous addition to Preston, Idaho. There were many in town who remembered Ezra's exploits on the basketball court when he was a student at the Oneida Academy. Also, news of his scholastic achievements at Provo and Ames had filtered into the community. Because the population was predominantly Mormon, the name Ezra Taft Benson itself was enough to endow him with a certain celebrity status. As for Flora, her reputation as a wealthy debutante from Logan seems to have been well known in town. Her moving into a new home with a new baby and a toddler while she was still in her twenties, with a promising husband who occupied a position of prestige, elevated her to a place of rank among her peers. Besides these trappings, Ezra and Flora's favored position in Preston was enhanced by a complex network of family relationships. Here and in the surrounding area could be found numerous Benson, Ballif, and Dunkley relatives.

So the Bensons settled into their new home and community with ease and confidence. They were members of the Preston First Ward, where the two returned missionaries were welcomed with enthusiasm. Very soon they were integrated into the activities of the ward and the stake. When Flora was appointed to the stake YWMIA board, her skills in dramatics and dance found ample opportunity for expression. Because Ezra's reputation as a Scouter had preceded him, he soon found himself leading a group of senior Scouts. He also continued with his work as a seventy.

Meanwhile, Ezra plunged enthusiastically into his work as the county agricultural agent. Here was a challenge that stretched his mind and his endurance. There were hundreds of farmers in the county, all of whom needed help of some kind to improve their condition. The onset of the Great Depression multiplied those needs. Because needs varied from farm to farm, Ezra decided from the beginning that his principal work would entail one-on-one counseling with farmers in the field, where individual problems could be studied and personalized remedies prescribed. This strategy made Ezra's office in Preston little more than a way station where he dropped in occasionally to check the mail, fill out reports, and touch base with the county commissioners. The rest of his working hours were spent traveling around the county, visiting with farmers and instructing them in modern methods of farming.

What he found in the field coincided with his view that the farmer's greatest need was improved skill in marketing his products. Toward this end, he championed the organization of the Franklin County Grain Growers' Association and the erection of their own flour mill. Through this cooperative effort, the farmers eliminated intermediate handling costs and increased their bargaining power by controlling the flow of their products into the market when prices were most favorable. Ezra also demonstrated the value of cooperation by collecting hogs into a common pool, grading them according to size and quality, and then selling them in quantity in an out-of-state market.

He also emphasized the need for careful budgeting and cost controls. This also entailed instructions in accounting and in negotiating bank loans since, as already noted, most farmers financed their operations on borrowed money. The increase in interest rates that took effect about the time Ezra began his work as county agent impacted heavily on the farmers of Franklin County, as it did elsewhere. In time the squeeze would cause some farmers to lose their farms through mortgage foreclosures.

In the meantime, Ezra did all he could to share his knowledge and expertise with the farmers in Franklin County. He taught them about crop rotation, pest and weed control, and fertilization. He conducted demonstration seminars where farmers gathered on different farms to see personally how certain procedures worked successfully, or unsuccessfully. Occasionally he would invite specialists from the University of Idaho at Moscow to give instructions and counsel.

Disturbed about the large numbers of youth who were leaving the farms, Ezra aggressively promoted the 4–H program as a means of reversing the trend. A main purpose was to portray farm life in a more positive light. Through the skillful use of awards, competitions, social events, and publicity, much was done to change the image of the farmer from one of a grinding drudge to that of an intelligent, well-trained scientist-entrepreneur. While he never said it in words, what Ezra seemed to have in mind was that the future farmers of Franklin County would follow the path he had blazed—would develop a genuine pride in their vocation, pursue higher education, and apply scientific methods to the management of a farm and the marketing of its products.

The personal image Ezra projected and his attitudes were as important as what he said in changing the image of a farmer in the minds of youth. When he went into the field to train and motivate, he didn't wear ill-fitting and grubby-looking coveralls and unsightly clodhoppers. He wore jodhpur pants, laced knee-high boots, khaki shirt with a tie, a vest, and a western-style hat. And he moved with alacrity, usually with a pleasant expression on his face, acting as if he knew exactly where he was going and what he intended to do when he got there. Everything about him—how he looked and acted and what he said—conveyed the idea that Ezra Taft Benson enjoyed being a farmer and was proud to be a farmer. There can be little doubt that his example changed the perceptions of many of the youth about farmers and, quite possibly, elevated the self-esteem of his peers.

Obviously it did not take the administrators at the University of Idaho very long to discover that a remarkable man was at work in Franklin County. News of the laudable things taking place there regularly reached Moscow. Nor did it take them long to decide they wanted to utilize his skills in a wider arena. So on October 15, 1930, they offered him the position of agricultural economist and specialist with the University of Idaho Extension Division in Boise.

Though it meant uprooting his family after less than two years in Preston, and though it meant moving, perhaps permanently, from the area where he had been born and raised, the decision to accept the offer was not a difficult one to make. His creative work in Franklin County seems to have convinced Ezra that his professional future did not lie in operating a farm but rather in training and motivating others in how to farm efficiently and profitably. This kind of work was more congenial to his nature, which seemed to be actuated by a desire to serve and to help others. So when Flora enthusiastically concurred in her husband's feelings, he accepted the offer.

By this time, Orval had returned from his mission and had taken over the management of the farm. In consultation, the brothers decided to dissolve their partnership in view of Ezra's decision to accept the offer that would take him and his family to Boise. Orval's acquisition of his brother's interest in the farm meant Ezra's final severance from his lifelong dream. Never again would he return to active farming. And in the future, his visits to Whitney and the scenes of his childhood would only be sporadic and of short duration. Ezra Taft Benson was on his way to the destiny marked out for him.

Chapter 7

To Boise, to Berkeley, and Back

Excitement and anticipation marked the Benson family's move to Boise in the autumn of 1930. It was not unlike the move from the Whitney farm to Preston several months earlier. Two main purposes dominated Ezra's thinking: to settle his family in a comfortable, secure place and to tackle the challenges of his new duties.

Once a suitable house was found, Flora soon transformed it into a home as she had done at Ames, Whitney, and Preston. She was determined to make it a place of culture and refinement where the children would find support and solace and where her busy husband would find a refuge from the daily pressures he would encounter on the job. The family transition was smoothed by the presence of a strong, active stake in Boise. This, and the friendly ward into which they moved, provided a ready-made circle of friends who enriched the Bensons' spiritual and social lives.

Because of their background in the Church, it is not surprising that very soon both Ezra and Flora again found themselves active in the MIA, he serving on the YMMIA stake board and she on the YWMIA stake board. At the same time, Ezra was appointed as a Scout commissioner. Later he became the stake superintendent of the YMMIA. These roles enabled the Bensons to exert a strong, positive influence on the young Latter-day Saints in Boise. Determined to provide the Mormon youth with a program of quality activities, they became intimately involved in planning and directing youth dances, athletic events, and camp-outs. While Flora's home duties restricted her involvement in the execution of these programs, Ezra played an active, enthusiastic role. He joined in the field sports and was a fierce and vocal competitor as he had been at the Oneida Academy. On the camp-outs he had a repertoire of songs, stories, and poems that never failed of an appreciative audience.

Ezra did his work out of a basement office in the Idaho state capitol building. As at Preston, the office got comparatively little use. He spent most of his time in the field, counseling with farmers throughout the state. Because the state embodied a diversity of climate and topography, there was no fixed counsel he gave the farmers whom he visited. His recommendations were tailored to fit special needs.

However, there was one problem that existed statewide and clamored for a solution. This was the complex problem of mounting surpluses and falling prices, coupled with the lack of a mechanism to facilitate the efficient marketing of farm products. The problem was aggravated by the ever-deepening depression that, when Ezra began his work in Boise, had been eroding the American economy for months. Falling prices also were accompanied by increasing unemployment that in turn reduced buying power, and that inevitably made the surpluses grow even more. Ezra, borrowing from his heritage and his experiences in Preston, helped fashion a partial solution.

The partial solution Ezra promoted—cooperatives—had its roots deep in Mormon tradition. His people had survived after the 1846 exodus from Missouri because they had worked together as a community. There were no government subsidies or handouts available to help them along; survival depended on their own intelligence and industry and on the cooperation necessary to maximize their efforts. The Mormon settlers later formalized their cooperatives, establishing them on a legal basis and profiting from the synergistic principle upon which they operated. Without attempting to define or to explain it, they knew from experience that the end product of a cooperative exceeded the sum total of its individual contributions.

It was confidence in this concept, born of experience, that had prompted Ezra to organize the cooperatives in Franklin County. Now as the economist and extension specialist for the entire state of Idaho, he took steps to extend it statewide. The keystone of this initiative was the organization in 1933 of the Idaho Cooperative Council (ICC), which Ezra Benson spearheaded. He became the executive secretary of the ICC, whose purpose was to promote the activities of the many small, specialized cooperatives that would function under its coordinating umbrella. Ezra also played an active role in the formation and the functioning of the small, subsidiary cooperatives, including the Idaho Potato Growers' Association and cooperatives for dairymen and for turkey, poultry, cattle, and hog producers, among others. The members of these cooperatives profited not only from the pooling and the controlled sale of their products, but also from the economies realized in the bulk purchases of equipment and supplies needed in their operations.

A major contribution of Ezra and the ICC to the success of the subsidiary cooperatives was in the field of marketing. A key element in the success of a marketer is to create a sense of need or desire in the mind of the consumer. Most often, this is accomplished through skillful advertising. Ezra seemed to have a native talent for advertising, and that talent was used in helping to train the cooperatives in how to make their products attractive through effective advertising.

One of the most notable successes of Ezra and his associates in the realm of marketing and advertising was in making the Idaho potato a household word throughout the United States and elsewhere. So effective has this campaign been that often the mere mention of the word *potato* conjures up the word *Idaho* to go with it. The ultimate coup in marketing and advertising occurred when the ICC and the Idaho Potato Growers' Association persuaded the state of Idaho to add the words "Famous Potatoes" to its automobile license plates. Wherever they go, cars from Idaho act as traveling billboards for the distinguished Idaho potato. As we shall see, Ezra Taft Benson took these marketing skills with him when he entered President Eisenhower's cabinet, where he became the chief agent in marketing United States surplus commodities around the world.

The organization of the ICC coincided with the enactment of the Agricultural Adjustment Act in May 1933, which was the agriculture showcase of President Franklin D. Roosevelt's New Deal. The purpose of the act was to raise agricultural prices and then to maintain them on a parity with industrial prices (taking 1909 to 1914 as a base period) through a system of government control of production of staple crops. The act was administered by the Agricultural Adjustment Administration (AAA), which was created by the act. Through the AAA, agreements between the U.S. secretary of agriculture and producers of major crops were made under which farmers agreed to reduce their acreage and the size of their crops in return for benefit payments derived from taxes levied on all processors of agricultural commodities. It was expected that reduced production would cause the hoped-for increase in prices. Moreover, it was hoped that this arrangement would promote conservation of natural resources through the AAA by removing marginal land from cultivation and by encouraging crop rotation and the planting of soil-building legumes.

As Idaho's agricultural economist and extension specialist, Ezra carried the responsibility to cooperate with the

AAA in implementing the act within the state. This placed him in an awkward position because he disagreed with the basic philosophy of the act, which he felt compromised the independence of farmers. Nevertheless, he suppressed any overt criticism and fulfilled his obligation to explain the provisions of the act to Idaho farmers and even to assist them in negotiating crop-reduction contracts with the secretary of agriculture, although he never encouraged them to do so. However, when the secretary of agriculture, who was pressed to reduce surpluses further, decreed the slaughter of baby pigs, Ezra could remain silent no longer. He denounced the action openly. In doing so, he incurred the antagonism of some farmers and stirred up strong political opposition within the state that surfaced in complaints to university officials in Moscow. So strong were the protests about Ezra's conduct that the dean of agriculture called him in for a consultation. After a long discussion in which Ezra aired his views, the dean said he agreed with them but faulted Ezra for the openness and the forcefulness of his criticisms. Afterward, Ezra seems to have toned down, the only alternative available to him without creating an open rupture with the federal government and, perhaps, jeopardizing his status with the university. His views did not change, however, and he continued to voice them privately. Years later when he became the secretary of agriculture, he was under no such restriction and so he expressed his views about AAA policies without restraint. However, as we shall see, he was gently reined in once by President Eisenhower, not because of his views but because of the strategic wisdom of whether or when to speak out in contentious Washington.

Meanwhile, Ezra found more than enough contention for his liking in rural Idaho. Many farmers did not share his philosophy of government. Some resented his statement that the government did not owe farmers a living, interpreting it as a criticism of their accepting government subsidies. And if studies he published even hinted of opposition to the

New Deal, he would be attacked openly by local Democratic leaders.

Ezra did not allow these attacks to interfere with his chief duty to improve the skills of Idaho farmers. Holding training classes and farm management conferences throughout the state regularly, he taught principles of successful farm management. He gave instructions about proper crop rotation; scientific breeding; insect, rodent, and weed control; proper care of equipment; fertilizers; and economies gained through careful budgeting and bulk purchases. Additional instructions included bookkeeping, negotiating bank loans, and, as already noted, signing up under the Agricultural Adjustment Act. He supplemented this face-to-face instruction with periodic bulletins that discussed market trends and forecasts, marketing strategies, price quotations, and news items of general interest to the agricultural community.

While Ezra was preoccupied with establishing the ICC and learning the intricacies of the Agricultural Adjustment Act, sorrow entered his life. His mother died on June 1, 1933. She was only fifty-five, but bearing and nurturing eleven children had taken its physical toll. Her condition had begun to worsen the first of the year, so by the time her son George left for the mission field in the spring, death seemed imminent. She made him promise he would not return for the funeral should she die while he was in the field. His duty there, she emphasized, came first. Such dedication to missionary work accounts, in significant part, for the impetus that caused all eleven of Sarah Benson's children to fill missions.

All the children except George gathered in Whitney with their father for Sarah's funeral. Elder David O. McKay, who would be called into the First Presidency the following year, traveled to Whitney to offer his condolences in person. So elevating were his words of comfort that the family attended the funeral services with an attitude of thanksgiving instead of sorrow.

That Elder McKay would travel to Whitney unasked to comfort Ezra and his family suggests the affection the Apostle had for him. There seemed to be more to the gesture than the fact that they had been associated in the mission field. Elder McKay undoubtedly saw in his young associate a significant potential for future Church leadership, and he wanted to stay close to him to support him in times of need and to monitor his development. The Apostle assuredly was pleased with what he found. Still only thirty-three years old, his protégé was happily married to a beautiful woman of culture and character, the father of two sons, active in the Church, well educated, and on a promising career path.

Fourteen months later, in August 1934, death visited the Benson family again when Ezra's father, George T. Benson, died unexpectedly. His deep mourning over the passing of his wife seems to have contributed to his sudden death. The family gathered again without George to lay a revered parent to rest. Elder Melvin J. Ballard of the Twelve spoke at the funeral, reputed to be one of the largest ever held in Franklin County. This outpouring of sentiment and support demonstrated the esteem in which George T. Benson Jr. and his family were held by those who knew them best.

As the oldest child, Ezra now assumed chief responsibility to lead his parents' family. His first concern was for George, who was still in the Southern States Mission. He corresponded with the mission president, LeGrand Richards, who made a special trip to Milton, Florida, to tell George about his father's death. George then accompanied President Richards to mission headquarters in Atlanta, where he spent two weeks associating with the Richards family and the missionaries who worked in the mission office. It was a time of healing for George, who was buoyed up by the infectious enthusiasm of LeGrand Richards, who later shared the apostleship with Ezra for more than thirty years. During the last nine years of that association, from January 1974 to January 1983, when Elder Richards died, Ezra, as President of the Twelve, served as LeGrand

Richards's file leader, a period that witnessed a revolution in the missionary work that both of them loved.

The sting of his father's death was eased somewhat for Ezra by the arrival of his first daughter, Barbara, who was born on June 20, 1934. The birth of Barbara began a string of four Benson daughters, all of whom were given names beginning with the letter *B*: Barbara, Beverly, Bonnie, and Beth. The symmetry and euphony of the names were made complete by adding the name Benson to each one. These four daughters, all of whom grew into women of poise, dignity, and culture, added an ineffable quality to the lives of Ezra and Flora Benson with their sweetness, their friendliness, and their music. Despite the aura of prominence in which they grew to maturity, they always maintained a wholesome, unaffected quality in their demeanor, which was as much a tribute to their upbringing as to their native attributes. This quality is aptly illustrated by Barbara's reluctance to ride in the chauffeured black limousine provided for her father while he served as U.S. secretary of agriculture; she felt it just didn't reflect the Benson character.

A few months after Barbara's birth, Ezra took the first major step in his rise to prominent leadership in the Mormon Church. On January 13, 1935, he was sustained as first counselor to Scott S. Brown in the presidency of the Boise Stake. In setting him apart as a counselor, the visiting authority also ordained Ezra a high priest.

This commenced a service of forty-six months (interrupted by nine months of schooling at the University of California at Berkeley), during which time Ezra received a thorough training in Church administration. The only comparable Church position he had had before was his service as the Newcastle Conference president when he supervised several small branches. Now, however, he would share in the responsibility to oversee the work of several large, well-established wards located within a radius of a hundred miles from Boise. His work included training Melchizedek Priesthood leaders throughout the stake, supervising youth leaders, speaking at stake and ward gatherings, and conducting worthiness interviews for those seeking temple recommend renewals or receiving new priesthood offices.

Before going to Berkeley, Ezra also received a few months of training in the first phases of the Church Security Program, later to be named the Church Welfare Program. In the spring of 1936, for instance, he attended a regional conference in Burley, Idaho, where Elder Melvin J. Ballard of the Twelve, chairman of the Church Security Committee, and Harold B. Lee, the managing director, gave instructions about the new program and made production assignments. Ezra and the others in attendance were also briefed about the depressed economic conditions among Church members before the implementation of the Church Security Program. A survey conducted the previous year had revealed that more than 17 percent of all Latter-day Saint families were receiving government assistance of some kind.

A key purpose of the new program was to encourage Church members to provide for themselves, through personal initiative and cooperative efforts independent of government programs. Because of his commitment to the Church, his experiences with the Agricultural Adjustment Act and the AAA, and his strong views about the need for farmers to be independent and to use personal initiative, Ezra enthusiastically endorsed the purpose and the aims of the Church Security Program. After returning from Burley and reporting to the stake president, he was assigned to lead out in fulfilling the commodity production assignments made at the regional meeting. Because of Ezra's move to California in August, he was not present in Boise when the Church Security Program was officially launched Churchwide at the October 1936 general conference. However, when he returned from California, he resumed an active role in the administration of the program in Boise.

Ordinarily the stake president hosts General Authorities during their visits for stake conferences. However, since the Boise Stake president lived eighty miles from Boise, this responsibility fell chiefly on the Bensons. It was a role Flora seemed destined to fill. Her rearing in the gracious Amussen home in Logan had accustomed her to the amenities of urban society, so she received the General Authority visitors with poise and dignity, yet with open friendliness. Because stake conferences were held on a quarterly basis at that time, the Bensons entertained many General Authorities during the years Ezra served in the stake presidency, either as a counselor or as the president. So they would feel no sense of deprivation, Flora insisted the children take their meals with the visitors, rather than be shunted off to the kitchen to eat alone. This practice also provided the children with exposure to adult etiquette and conversation at an early age, training that would be important when the family was thrust upon the stage of national prominence in Washington, D.C.

Of the many General Authorities the Bensons entertained in Boise, none created more excitement and interest than did President Heber J. Grant. The tall, bearded prophet, then nearing eighty, erect and trim, surprised Flora when he graciously asked to be excused from eating at the family table. Instead, he asked to eat alone in the kitchen with only a bowl of milk and some toast as his fare. More than fifty years of traveling around the Church, visiting in the homes of the Saints, had taught him the diet best suited to his health. So he avoided heavy meals at night, a discipline that fostered his robust health yet deprived him of sampling the richest and the best menus his hosts had to offer.

As the prophet prepared to retire, a large delegation of prominent Boise leaders appeared at the home unannounced. Their purpose was to urge that a temple planned for Idaho be built in the Boise Valley. To that end, they offered to donate the land needed for a temple site. Bantering with the delegation, which included some who were not members of the Church, President Grant suggested that they all join the Church and turn their efforts to converting others, and that when the Mormon population was sufficiently large, a temple would be built in Boise. Then in a serious vein, he predicted a temple would be built there ultimately.

President Grant's prophecy saw fulfillment the last week of May 1984, when Ezra Taft Benson, President of the Twelve, and other General Authorities participated in the dedication of the Boise Temple. Regrettably, not all elements of the community shared the joy of the Latter-day Saints for the event. Dissidents distributed defamatory literature at the temple site and held a public prayer vigil, imploring God to enlighten the Mormons. Later the tactics of these dissidents turned ugly. Some of them painted graffiti on the temple walls, which could be removed only by sandblasting. Others detonated an explosive against the walls, thereby shattering several windows. All this was done in the name of Christian concern over the alleged delusion of the members of the Church. Despite this unpleasantness, the dedication was a benchmark in the life of the Bensons, representing the fulfillment of the prophetic promise made by President Grant in their home almost a half century before.

The parade of General Authorities through his home provided the presiding officers of the Mormon Church with insight into the ability and the character of Ezra Taft Benson and the quality of his family life. Ezra would learn when elevated to the Quorum of the Twelve that the General Authorities who stayed at his home in connection with stake conferences had been evaluating him, both for his current service and for his potential future service. It is conceivable that Elder David O. McKay had passed the word among the Brethren to pay special attention to Ezra Benson as a young leader for the future. Since the corporate Church has a continuing existence through time and depends on lay leadership at the local level, its General Authorities are constantly on the alert for the emergence of promising leaders. Who knows but that President Grant's unexpected visit to the Benson home in Boise, coming as it did on his return trip from Alaska to Salt Lake City, was arranged solely to let him gain personal insight into Ezra Taft Benson and his family? Less than a decade after that visit, President Grant called him to the Twelve.

Shortly after the Church announced its security plan at the April conference in 1936, Ezra felt the need to further his formal education. The feeling was impelled by the dual desires to increase his job efficiency and to equip him to provide better for what he expected would be a large family. Learning about fellowship awards offered by the Giannini Foundation for Agricultural Economics, Ezra applied for one of them and was accepted. Supportive as always and uncomplaining about still another move, Flora supervised preparations and, with the three children ranging in age from two to eight, was ready to leave for the University of California at Berkeley on August 1, 1936, as planned.

Their experience at Ames had conditioned Ezra and Flora to economy living. The Giannini stipend, while adequate, was not extravagant. So for the nine months they remained in Berkeley, they lived frugally, shopping for bargains, taking advantage of recreations that required little if any money, and enjoying the social and spiritual life the local ward and stake afforded.

Knowing Ezra planned to return to Boise soon, the stake president did not release him as a counselor when he went to California. This was not an uncommon practice in the Church at the time. It did not preclude him from filling temporary assignments in California. When the stake president there called Ezra to the high council, he accepted willingly. In this role, he filled delegated assignments, working with auxiliary and priesthood leaders, and speaking in wards throughout the stake. Meanwhile, Flora worked in the ward Primary organization.

The work at the university was demanding. As a graduate student, Ezra was allowed some latitude in selecting his field of primary emphasis but then worked under the direction of a faculty adviser or a team who monitored his work. He devoted much of his time to studying the many cooperatives organized in California and the marketing of beef. This entailed many trips that took him throughout California. His observations and findings were summarized in reports submitted to his advisers. These reports, along with oral and written examinations based on lecture courses on campus, provided the criteria by which his scholastic performance was judged. His maturity and discipline, coupled with his work at BYU, Ames, and the extension division in Idaho, gave him high rank as a student at Berkeley. But scholastic distinction came with a price. He arose early in the morning to study diligently through each weekday, and Saturday mornings usually found him at the library or in his cramped study carrel on campus. It was almost a monastic kind of life as he strove to prepare himself for the future.

Ezra's preoccupation with his studies during the days and with his Church responsibilities in the evenings and on Sundays placed a strain on Flora, especially when he was away on field trips. Under the best of circumstances, it was not easy to care for three children, the youngest a toddler of two, in a cramped apartment. It was especially difficult and lonely because in Berkeley the ward members did not live in close proximity, and neighbors generally did not share Flora's lifestyle. Consequently, Flora longed for adult companionship and conversation and for the time when the family could settle down into a more normal routine.

Some of Flora's letters written during this period reveal an untypical sense of discouragement. Apparently sensing this, Ezra made an effort to use Saturday afternoons for family fun and outings. While he couldn't afford the fare for the annual big football game between California and Stanford, he could afford the price of gasoline or the cost of a ferry trip across the bay. The Transbay Bridge, completed in 1936, enabled the Bensons to drive into San Francisco, perhaps the most cosmopolitan of all major cities in the United States. Along the waterfront were merchant ships from around the world and luxury cruise ships that navigated between San

Francisco and exotic ports in the Pacific. Fishermen's Wharf, Chinatown, the Presidio, Golden Gate Park, the Seal Rocks off the coast, the quaint cable cars that crawled up and down the city's steep hills, and mysterious Alcatraz out in the Bay, often shrouded with fog, lent an air of excitement unlike anything these natives of landlocked Cache Valley had experienced since their marriage. Yet in the years ahead, Ezra and Flora Benson would become intimately acquainted with cities, countries, and peoples throughout the world in a way they could scarcely then imagine.

As the summer approached in 1937, Ezra lacked only a few months to complete the work for a doctoral degree. Apparently funding was available from the Giannini foundation to enable him to finish, but his application for an extension of the leave of absence from the University of Idaho was denied. So the Bensons returned to Boise in June 1937.

Flora's joy in returning to their home was heightened because she was carrying her fourth child at the time, Beverly, who was born September 20, 1937. With this addition to the family, Ezra had even greater incentive to apply himself to his work with the extension division. He did so with more than customary enthusiasm, applying the new skills in marketing and cooperatives he had learned at Berkeley. Now thirty-eight years old, he was poised to make major, unforeseen advancements in his ecclesiastical and professional careers, both of which happened within the space of two months.

The first change occurred on November 27, 1938, when he was called as president of the Boise Stake, with Z. Reed Millar and Mathias J. Benson selected as his counselors. At the same time, two additional stakes were spun off from the Boise Stake: the Nampa Idaho Stake, with Peter E. Johnson as president, and the Weiser Idaho Stake, with Scott S. Brown as president. Elder Melvin J. Ballard of the Twelve presided at the meeting where these changes were made. Often when key events occurred in Ezra's life, Elder Ballard was there: he ordained Ezra a seventy, spoke at his father's funeral, presided at the regional welfare meeting in Burley, and set him apart as stake president after the members had sustained him. This ended the string, for Elder Ballard passed away the following July. Years later, Ezra shared the apostleship with Elder Ballard's grandson and namesake, Melvin Russell Ballard.

Almost four years' service as a counselor had trained Ezra well to serve as stake president. He knew the people, understood the program, and was dedicated to the cause. He moved easily into his new duties. As a counselor, his main focus had been on the youth and welfare. He continued that focus as president. After returning from Berkeley, he spearheaded a massive welfare effort that involved every Melchizedek Priesthood quorum in the stake. It yielded vast quantities of fruits and vegetables that were shipped to welfare storehouses for use in the program. Shortly before his call as stake president, Ezra was pleased to report these results at a regional welfare meeting directed by his boyhood friend Harold B. Lee. In less than a decade, this pair of Cache Valley friends, elevated to apostolic status, would team up to conduct a massive welfare operation in Europe, with Elder Lee directing the assembling and shipping of welfare commodities at home, and with Elder Benson directing their distribution in Europe.

As the harvest season was over when Ezra was installed as stake president, his work in welfare was limited to laying the groundwork for future production efforts and administering to the welfare needs of stake members.

Meanwhile, Ezra's reputation was growing rapidly among farm cooperative professionals. His graduate work at Berkeley had elevated him to a new level of expertise and had attracted the attention of leaders in the field. Two of these were John D. (Judge) Miller, president of the National Council of Farmer Cooperatives (NCFC), and Raymond W. Miller, president of the American Institute of Cooperation (AIC). As the executive secretary of the Idaho Cooperative

Council (ICC), Ezra was obligated to attend the annual meetings of these two national groups held in Washington, D.C.

The annual meetings held in January 1938 provided Ezra a conspicuous platform to showcase his skills. He had been invited by Ralph Taylor, executive secretary of the California cooperatives, to deliver the report of the state councils at the NCFC meeting. The report was so carefully crafted and so impressively delivered that Ezra attracted the favorable attention of most delegates, including the two Millers and Charles C. Teague, vice president of the NCFC and president of the California Fruit Growers' Exchange. Because the NCFC was searching for a new executive secretary, Judge Miller and Charles Teague believed Ezra Taft Benson was their man. He was young, articulate, industrious, well educated, and experienced in directing cooperatives at both the county and state levels. Moreover, he had been raised on a farm, had successfully operated a farm, and possessed qualities of integrity and sobriety that would inspire the confidence of the diverse organizations and personalities with whom he would have to deal. In retrospect, it would almost seem that Ezra had deliberately set about to acquire the unusual blend of credentials that qualified him for this unique position.

Several months after his presentation in January 1938, both Judge Miller and Mr. Teague conferred with Ezra about the executive position with NCFC. Once satisfied he would not have to compromise his Mormon standards nor curry influence by wining and dining legislators or others, Ezra expressed an interest in the position. The discussions advanced to the point of an agreement on salary and duties. However, when opposition against him developed on the nominating committee, the negotiations faltered and Ezra withdrew his name from consideration. The opposition rested solely on his lack of experience in Washington, D.C., not on any want of technical, practical, or personal qualification. When a prominent agriculture newsletter published in early August emphatically stated that Ezra would not get the job, he dismissed the idea and concentrated on his duties in Idaho.

Meanwhile, his call as stake president seemed to remove any lingering thought about the NCFC job. He decided his professional future lay in Idaho. Indicative of that mind-set, he had his house repainted, purchased another lot, and otherwise showed by word and deed he was in Boise to stay.

This was Ezra's attitude when he went to Washington, D.C., in January 1939 for the annual meetings. He was surprised, therefore, when he received word that the nominating committee wished to see him. He was even more surprised when the committee members not only offered him the job but also increased the salary 25 percent over the previous discussions and agreed to pick up the tab for his moving expenses.

While personally he was prepared to accept the offer at once, he delayed responding until he had conferred with those who would be vitally affected by his decision. His first call was to Flora. It did not surprise Ezra to learn that his wife had received a spiritual prompting that the family would be moving to Washington, D.C. Indeed, she had begun to make preliminary plans for the move. Since their marriage, he often had witnessed this perceptive quality in his wife on matters affecting him and the children. He also contacted the Brethren in Salt Lake City and university officials in Moscow, Idaho, about the offer. Receiving positive responses from both places, Ezra accepted the offer from the nominating committee, with the understanding that his role as executive secretary of the National Council of Farmer Cooperatives would not obligate him to engage in social activities repugnant to Church standards or to his own sense of integrity. He learned that Judge Miller and Mr. Teague were well aware of his strict adherence to Church standards, for they had been appraising his qualifications for many months. In fact, his teetotaler habits seemed to be a strong reason supporting his candidacy.

107

Chapter 8

To Washington

Despite the trauma of uprooting the family still another time, preparations for the move to Washington worked out smoothly. Ready buyers were found for the home and other real property. More difficult was the severance of ties with church and professional associates. Boise had been home to the Bensons for more than eight years, and during that time they had put down deep roots. Ezra's recent call as stake president had strengthened those roots and had clouded the decision to leave. However, Church leaders had assured him that his leaving after only a few months in office would carry no stigma. In fact, the Brethren seemed pleased at the appointment, for it would enhance the Church's reputation and influence to have a dedicated member like him occupy a position of national prominence. Moreover, the university officials, while regretting the loss of one so capable and well qualified, seemed genuinely proud that one of their own had received such high recognition.

Ezra was released as stake president at a conference held

in Boise on March 26, 1939. It was a deeply emotional experience for him, and so he spoke with great difficulty. The appreciation he felt for his friends was hard to articulate. He and his family owed so much to them. Later a jam-packed testimonial was held in the Boise Tabernacle. The lavish praise heaped upon him was worthy of a eulogy, and gifts given to him provided a lasting memory of the end of one era and the beginning of another.

Before Ezra left Boise, patriarch Mathias J. Benson gave him a blessing. It expressed a principle, reminiscent of Ezra's father's advice, that helped light his way through many dark passages ahead: "Though you will have many perplexing problems," the patriarch told him in the blessing, "and though there will come before you many things that will tax your judgment and ability to decide, but yet, if you place your trust and confidence in the Lord, if you take your problems before Him, the solution will come unto you." Ezra would test this principle often and would be led along by it all his days.

Because Flora would remain in Boise with the children until school recessed for summer, Ezra traveled to Washington alone via Salt Lake City, where he visited personally with the Brethren. Buoyed by their counsel and support, he went on to his great adventure in the nation's capital.

Having visited the city many times, Ezra knew Washington well. He was acquainted with its monuments, its historic sites, and the aura of intrigue and power that pervaded it. He also was acquainted, though in a cursory way, with the role the NCFC played in the complicated patchwork of elected officials, career bureaucrats, and special interest groups like the farm bloc. Ezra speedily learned the details of the NCFC's role and how it meshed with the broad coalition of other groups interested in farmers and farming.

The NCFC was organized in 1929, a few months after Ezra became the agricultural agent for Franklin County. He

had seen it grow in ten years from an infant to a giant organization that represented four thousand local farm cooperatives throughout the country. Through the NCFC's officers
and staff, more than a million and a half farmers, members
of these local cooperatives, had a voice in the halls of
Congress and in the sprawling U.S. Department of
Agriculture (USDA) entirely apart from the voice they had
through their elected congressional representatives.

A function of the NCFC was to keep abreast of and to
advise its constituent members of legislation or executive
policies that impacted on agriculture. In order to serve the
best interests of America's farmers, the council exerted influence on members of Congress and on the USDA bureaucracy to adopt or to discontinue legislation or policies. This
influence usually consisted of briefings to explain the impact
of policies on agriculture and to voice the feelings of the
farm community about them. Included in this process was
testimony given at congressional committee hearings on
proposed legislation. Because of the large number of influential citizens whom the council represented, the views of
its spokesmen were usually given a respectful hearing.
Through its national magazine, *Cooperative Digest*, the council also provided its members with tips on marketing strategies and on economies to be gained by cooperative bulk
purchases of equipment and materials.

The key person responsible to direct the far-ranging
work of the NCFC was its executive secretary. It is a safe
assumption that when Ezra learned the full scope of his new
duties, he was intimidated, not only because of their magnitude but also because they involved skills and aptitudes he
had not yet developed. At the beginning, for instance, he
was a novice in the arts of lobbying and political maneuver-
ing, essential parts of his job description. It was this lack that
had caused some members of the search committee to
oppose him initially. Perhaps their opposition was increased
because of Ezra's announced refusal to exert influence by
wining and dining those whom the council wished to win

to its views. They need not have worried. Ezra Taft Benson was always a quick study and always competitive, as the basketball opponents of the Oneida Academy could attest. Once he had learned the ground rules, analyzed the problems, and become acquainted with the tools and resources available to do the job, he dived in with vigor.

Ezra wasted no time beginning his work. He arrived in Washington, D.C., on a Friday, and the next morning he went to the offices of the NCFC at 1730 I Street to begin his orientation. During the next few weeks, he received in-depth briefings, became acquainted with members of his staff, and was given a taste of his lobbying duties. As he delved into the details of his work, he found it divided into six convenient categories: legislative matters affecting all cooperatives, legislative matters affecting isolated co-ops, public relations, field work, an information service, and the *Cooperative Digest.*

Because his success would depend largely on the skill and the dedication of his staff, Ezra conducted personal interviews with each one to share his goals and administrative philosophy, to learn about their background, and to gauge the depth of their capacity and commitment. It was in this area that Ezra's leadership training in the Church was most valuable. Thoroughly schooled in the principles of unity, delegation, accountability, and goal setting, he utilized these to good advantage in working with the NCFC staff, as he did later in working with his staff in the Department of Agriculture.

Soon after he came aboard, Ezra was taken on the rounds to meet key people in the USDA and in various agriculture associations with whom he would have frequent contact. He also received an early, unexpected introduction to his lobbying duties when the office geared up to lobby against a bill to transfer a division of the Farm Credit Association to the USDA. Ezra and the staff concluded there was no sound reason for the transfer, which he believed was only the dreamy idea of a "crack-brained" staff lawyer. That

Ezra would use such blunt, colorful language to describe the author of the proposed change reveals an important aspect of his character. While he was charitable and kindhearted, Ezra Taft Benson also was a tough, disciplined executive who knew his business, who knew that he knew his business, and who had little patience for incompetence or fuzzy-mindedness. This farmer from remote Idaho would not be cowed or overwhelmed by the intimidating aura of Washington, D.C.

Ezra soon learned, however, that while the capital had many incompetents, it also had many intelligent, resourceful people with ideals and with perceptions of government opposite from his own. Many of this latter kind were found in Congress; their natural inclination to excel was fueled by ambition for higher office and for the publicity thought necessary to make that ambition a reality. So whenever he appeared before a congressional committee, Ezra made sure he was ready, that he had the necessary facts to support his testimony and that he knew the members of the committee and their pet projects and peeves. Thus armed, he was in the best possible position to avoid answering in a way that would leave an opening for anyone on the committee to embarrass him or the council or to jeopardize the interests of the cooperatives that the council represented. Often these exchanges partook of combat, with the questioners and the witness exchanging and parrying verbal thrusts and strokes. There is ample evidence that Ezra rather enjoyed this jousting, provided it was fair and not mean-spirited.

It is obvious that Ezra needed much help in preparing for congressional hearings, especially as the number and the variety of them increased. In addition to his staff, he had the assistance of standing committees of the council whose members were expert in such subjects as legal and tax problems, land-grant colleges, unfair trade practices, farm parity, production credit, commodity exchange, and membership. These sources provided him with extensive notes and briefings necessary to prepare him for appearances before congressional committees. His role was not unlike that of an English barrister who argues cases before the bar based upon briefs prepared by solicitors. Ezra was well qualified to perform this function. His years of academic training had taught him to digest speedily and to organize immense bodies of facts and concepts; his street-meeting experiences in England had trained him in extemporaneous speaking and in adroitly handling objections and criticisms; and his work in the stakes had given him poise and self-confidence in training and convincing others, whether from the pulpit or in counseling sessions. In a sense, therefore, he was the mouthpiece for the NCFC in Washington, a role that gave him broad exposure and an enhanced reputation.

Behind him, of course, were the officers and the directors of the council who established policies and who charted its general course. Most of them were distinguished executives of other organizations who lacked the time to give continuing direction to the council and who met only sporadically for board meetings. Ezra's contact with them was limited. However, he had frequent contact with John D. (Judge) Miller, the president of NCFC, and with his successors, H. E. Babcock and Charles C. Teague. Judge Miller, a lawyer and Pennsylvania dairyman, was one of the pioneers of the cooperative movement. He became Ezra's friend and mentor, was a guest in the Benson home, and retained a close relationship with Ezra even after leaving the council.

During his first six weeks in Washington, Ezra lived a lonely bachelor's life. His challenging work during the day kept him occupied, but off duty he was at loose ends without Flora and the children. Although they kept in frequent contact by letter and telephone, this was hardly a satisfactory substitute for being together. As school wound down in May, Ezra was able to rent a home in the Westgate section of Washington. He traveled to Boise on May 11, 1939, and a week later arrived back in Washington with Flora and the four children. It was a comfort to Ezra to have the family with him again, not only for the personal association but for the counsel Flora was able to provide. Her judgment was always sound, and he relied upon her as much as upon any member of his staff. She added a spiritual dimension to her counsel that no one else could provide. It seemed she prayed her way through the days, seeking insight how she could best serve her husband and the children. Flora's selfless devotion to her family was indeed exemplary.

Within weeks after they arrived in Washington, the Bensons began planning to build a new home. It was a family project in which the children, regardless of how small, also had their say. Soon a choice lot was purchased in the Edgemoor section of Bethesda, Maryland, and architectural drawings were obtained. Construction work begun in June was finished in a hundred days. On September 29 the family moved into their new home, which was made appealing and comfortable by Flora's decorating as well as by the routines of family prayer, family home evening, assignment of responsibilities, and family fun. A visitor to this home not only saw exactly what transpired there every day but also could appreciate the quality of family life that had graced the homes of Ezra's and Flora's parents and earlier ancestors. It was a typical, ideal Latter-day Saint home. Judge Miller never forgot how impressed he was during his visit, especially with the sweet prayer offered by six-year-old Barbara, who prayed their visitor would enjoy himself and would be protected while returning to his hotel.

As they did at Berkeley, Ezra and Flora sought to expose their children to the things of interest near their home. So as Ezra's busy schedule permitted, they were taken on tours of Washington, D.C., and surrounding areas to see and learn about places of historic interest, places like the White House, the Capitol, the Smithsonian Institution, and the Washington, Lincoln, and Jefferson Memorials. Given Ezra's burning patriotic sense, it is doubtless true that his remarks about these and other special historic places imbued the Benson children with a genuine love of country.

Ezra and Flora found strong support for their family in

the Church organizations in the area. They belonged to the Chevy Chase Branch of the Washington District, part of the Eastern States Mission. At the time, there were no organized stakes in the northeastern United States. Soon after Ezra arrived in Washington, Abe Cannon, the district president, called him to the district council, and Flora was called as a counselor in the district Relief Society presidency. The Relief Society president, Louise Bennion, a daughter of President J. Reuben Clark, was married to Captain Mervyn Bennion, a U.S. naval officer then assigned to a desk job in Washington. Later, the "Mormon Colony" in the nation's capital was shocked when Captain Bennion, commander of the SS *West Virginia*, flagship of the Pacific Fleet, was killed at Pearl Harbor.

This "Mormon Colony" was an extraordinary group of Latter-day Saints, mostly from the West, who had come to the nation's capital for education, for government employment or business opportunities, or, as in Ezra's case, for work as executives of private organizations. Among these were Edgar B. Brossard of the U.S. Tariff Commission and his wife, Laura, a sister of Matthew Cowley (who later would be called to the Twelve); J. Willard Marriott, who was then laying the foundation of his food and hotel empire, and his wife, Alice; Ernest L. Wilkinson, prominent Washington attorney and a future president of Brigham Young University, and his wife, Alice; David M. Kennedy, a future bank president and member of the cabinet of Richard M. Nixon, and his wife, Leonora; and the Bennions. These Mormon friends and many others, as well as Ezra's close associates who were not members of the Church, provided the Bensons with an interesting mix of social relations. The nearby universities, libraries, and museums added an important intellectual touch to their lives.

The social life of the "Mormon Colony" in Washington was centered in the chapel located on the corner of Sixteenth Street and Columbia Road. The distinctive building, which featured a replica of the angel Moroni statue atop the Salt

Lake Temple, was dedicated in 1933 and soon became a city landmark. The chapel soon became a second home to Ezra when, in late June 1940, he was called as the first president of the Washington Stake, with offices located in the building. Hours before or after work at the council, as well as weekends, often found him there counseling with his associates, conducting interviews, and planning for the future of the stake.

The call came as a distinct shock. Ezra had lived in the area for less than fifteen months, and he was not well acquainted with members in the area. In addition, there were many able men who did not have these drawbacks. So when President Rudger Clawson and Elder Albert E. Bowen of the Council of the Twelve said the Lord wanted him to serve as stake president, Ezra protested, citing the reasons mentioned earlier. The Brethren were unmoved, as Ezra surely knew they would be. He had been through this process in Boise and knew how it worked. He knew these men made such decisions by spiritual means after exhausting their investigative and analytical abilities. There likely had been discussions in Salt Lake City about the leadership of the new stake. This was hinted at in a letter from President J. Reuben Clark, who said he had the impression, when Ezra called on the Brethren before going east, that Ezra would be a good president for a stake in Washington, D.C. And, of course, Ezra's former mission president and mentor, David O. McKay, was at that time a member of the First Presidency. Moreover, President Heber J. Grant knew firsthand that the Benson family was a fine model for all Latter-day Saints; and because Ezra had served as a stake president before, he was a good candidate for the position. After conducting the usual interviews with local leaders and praying for guidance, the visiting Apostles received spiritual confirmation that the Lord approved of calling Ezra Taft Benson as stake president.

Ezra selected Sam Carpenter, secretary of the Federal Reserve Board, as his first counselor and Ernest L. Wilkinson as his second counselor. Ernest's legendary frankness surfaced early in their relationship when he told Ezra he had recommended someone else as stake president. Instead of being offended or put off by the remark, Ezra welcomed it as indicating he would receive his counselor's honest opinions about stake issues, an essential quality for a good counselor.

The new stake embodied four wards and two branches in an area extending from southern Pennsylvania to Richmond, Virginia. Knowing he and his associates had limited time because of heavy responsibilities in their daily work and with their families, Ezra sought to streamline and simplify their Church duties by preparing a pocket calendar for their use, an innovation in that day. He also sought to make the time spent in Church meetings more productive, exemplified by a pulpit light that indicated when a speaker's time had elapsed.

As stake president, Ezra's main areas of focus were missionary work, training local leaders, and tithing. He saw proselyting as a three-pronged instrument of redemption for the convert, growth for the Church, and fulfillment for the members; training as the means of strengthening the Church for the present and the future; and tithing as the tool to build faith and temporal security.

In focusing on missionary work, he broadened the use of the Washington chapel to include organ recitals and tours of the building for visitors, gave special attention to stake missionary work, and, on a personal basis, always carried with him a Book of Mormon, to read or share with others as he traveled about. As for leadership training, he met regularly with stake priesthood and auxiliary leaders, instructing them in their duties and in the way they should relate to those whose work they supervised. His influence upon individual members was best exerted through training bishops and branch presidents during regular personal interviews with them. By this means he was able to instruct them in their duties, ascertain areas of needed improvement, suggest

117

remedies, and follow up in later interviews, in all this emphasizing the lines of priesthood authority and account- ability between him and those with direct responsibility to shepherd the local congregations. As for tithing, he never missed an appropriate opportunity to talk about it in coun- seling sessions or in public meetings at the stake or local lev- els. Converted to the principle from his youth through the teaching and example of his father, Ezra knew that once the members could be persuaded to test the pertinent scriptural promises, they too would become converted to tithing, thereby increasing their faith, their commitment to the Church, and their enjoyment of the spiritual and temporal blessings that flow from its observance.

As Ezra geared up to stress the importance of the tithe, it was his conviction that if the principle were observed by all, there would be no necessity to call on members for other financial contributions, for all fiscal needs of the Church could be met through tithing funds. He shared this convic- tion with the presiding authorities at the time, but nothing came of it until years later when, as President of the Church, he initiated the policy now in effect under which all local operating expenses and welfare costs are satisfied out of the tithing and fast-offering funds, thus obviating the need to generate local budgets for those purposes, as Ezra was obligated to do as president of the Washington Stake.

That he emphasized these few things is not to suggest that Ezra concentrated on them to the exclusion of every- thing else. He regularly addressed and gave training on many other subjects as circumstances required.

Adding these Church duties to an already overburdened schedule at the NCFC heavily taxed Ezra's energies. It seemed to the family that he was almost constantly on the move during this period. This shifted more of the family responsibilities to Flora, who on March 30, 1940, three months before her husband's call as stake president, had given birth to their fifth child, Bonnie. Inevitably, her added load had another domino effect within the family—more responsibility for twelve-year-old Reed and brother Mark, age eleven, and, to a lesser degree, for the two little girls, Barbara and Beverly, who were six and three years old.

The children had their own challenges, chiefly of adjustment to an entirely new culture, which added to the stresses within the Benson family. This is best illustrated by Reed's foray into fisticuffs. When subjected to unprovoked harassment by another student, Reed slapped him in retaliation. After friends pulled the boys apart, the teacher, hoping to avoid a brawl, ordered they settle their dispute later in the ring with boxing gloves. With typical efficiency and foresight, Flora decided that if her son was to have an equal chance, he needed some training. So she obtained a book on boxing and proceeded to train him in the fundamentals. More important, she fasted on the day of the fight, and while he was in the ring she prayed for him. It is inferred that the burden of her prayer was not that Reed would "win" the fight, but that he would not be injured, would fight with skill, and would emerge from the bout with his dignity and self-confidence intact. So it was that in all their trials and travails, the Benson children knew their mother was there to train and to encourage them and to elevate them spiritually through her prayers and fasting.

Ezra had always received this same kind of practical and spiritual support from Flora and always would. By his own admission, he never could have achieved what he did had it not been for her constant support and encouragement. As the burdens upon him increased, he was comforted to know she was there on the home front, meeting without complaint the added pressures and problems that his outside responsibilities created.

Soon after his call as stake president, these responsibilities were taken up a notch. In September 1940 he was appointed secretary of the newly created National Committee for Farm Production Supplies, whose purpose was to lobby for adequate farm supplies to meet increased demands on agriculture created by the war in Europe.

Because the elaborate system of government agencies and controls created by the New Deal had clogged the channels of a free market, the new committee had to convince government bureaucrats of the need to make essential supplies available to the farm community. Given the inherent inertia of a bureaucracy and the density of some bureaucrats, it was tedious and discouraging work.

An episode that glaringly revealed the system's weakness, and the incompetence of some of its administrators, occurred when a bureaucrat denied the request for more canvas needed for lambing sheds with the direction to postpone the lambing! Undoubtedly, such experiences helped solidify Ezra's implacable opposition to government interference and control and his constant advocacy of free-market principles. Notwithstanding, he stubbornly stayed at his task, contending almost daily with the bureaucracy, to facilitate the production and the smooth flow of agricultural commodities in furtherance of the committee's slogan, "Food to Win the War." It was Ezra's skillful work on this committee, as he steered its way through the brambles and thickets of Washington politics, that established his reputation among farming interests and earned him the praise of professionals in the field.

More outside pressures were added later in 1940 when he was elected as a member of the National Farm Credit Committee. The purpose of this committee was to counsel government agents about management of farm surpluses under government policies. The assignment was difficult for Ezra because he disagreed with most of these policies. But because changing them was beyond his control, he worked within the system as best he could in the interests of the country and the farm community.

Ezra's most prestigious government appointment came later when he represented the NCFC in meetings of the National Agricultural Advisory Committee, which President Franklin D. Roosevelt organized to give him insight into agriculture's problems and potential. The advisory

committee, which consisted of representatives of the four
national farm organizations—the NCFC, the Farm Bureau,
the National Grange, and the Farmers' Union—met
monthly with the president. President Roosevelt always listened respectfully to Ezra's opinions about farm matters
because of Ezra's academic and practical knowledge of the
subject. Following one of the early meetings of this group,
in which Ezra had said very little, President Roosevelt said
of him, "Who was that fine-looking young man? If they will
make him their spokesman, I will talk with him anytime"
(*Improvement Era*, Jan. 1953, p. 27).

The complexion of Ezra's duties as an agricultural executive in Washington changed radically with the bombing of
Pearl Harbor by the Japanese on December 7, 1941. Before
then the management of farm surpluses was a continuing
problem. Later the hungry demands of the U.S. military and
its allies for farm products created shortages. This change
effectively ended the agricultural depression that had lin-
gered since the end of World War I. With this change, Ezra's
focus shifted to encouraging greater production and to
efforts to prevent price ceilings.

When in October 1942 Congress gave the U.S. president
authority to place ceilings on wages, rents, and prices, Ezra
spoke against it on national radio. His philosophy, as
always, was to let the market decide these matters. When
his views were not accepted, he began to press for an
increase in price ceilings for agricultural products. As a
result, he encountered strong opposition from labor interests
who contended this would wreck family budgets and
require wage increases. In advisory committee meetings
with President Roosevelt, Ezra and other farm leaders found
him reluctant even to discuss the issue. They believed he
feared reactions from the powerful labor lobby. In the spring
of 1943, however, declining farm production, caused in large
part by the drain of agricultural workers to high-paying
defense plant jobs, caused the president to listen and to
approve a remedial five-point program put forward by

agricultural interests through Ezra Taft Benson. While this brought some relief to farmers, Ezra considered it to be inadequate and continued to argue for a free market, but without effect.

Meanwhile, the war impacted heavily on Church work in the Washington Stake. Soon after Pearl Harbor, President Benson began to counsel the members to conserve on travel, to store food for emergencies, and to support the war effort. Since many servicemen flocked to the city, the cultural hall of the Washington chapel was converted into a dormitory to accommodate them. In addition, there was a redoubling of effort in stake missionary work, which was aimed chiefly at members' friends and relatives who had not yet joined the Church.

Sadness came into the Benson family again during 1942 when word came that Flora's mother, Barbara Amussen, had passed away. The news was especially painful because she had planned to visit the family in Washington but inexplicably had changed her plans. The events surrounding her death underscored the depth of her spirituality. In September she told a daughter, Mabel, that her deceased husband, Carl Amussen, had appeared in vision to say she would die the following Thursday. Despite Mabel's efforts to disabuse her of the idea, she deliberately set about to prepare for the event: she withdrew her savings from the bank, paid all her bills, closed up her house, and moved in with her daughter. She bore such a powerful testimony on Sunday that the bishop closed the meeting after she sat down. On Wednesday evening she told Mabel that she wished to retire early and that she did not want to be disturbed. The next morning they found her dead, as she had predicted. She apparently passed away peacefully in her sleep early Thursday morning.

The incident was typical of Barbara Amussen. Throughout her life she had shown an unusual spiritual affinity. Like her daughter Flora, she was habituated to prayer, constantly seeking spiritual direction as she prayed her way through the days. It is undoubtedly true that Flora Benson's similar aptitude was learned in large part from her saintly mother. Another illustration of Barbara Amussen's spiritual sensitivity was her impression, which she shared in a letter to the Benson family in Washington some time before her death, that her son-in-law Ezra would be called to a high position of leadership in the Church.

Chapter 9

Called to the Twelve

As summer approached in 1943, Ezra decided to take a lengthy trip to the West Coast. He wanted to visit personally with Charles C. Teague, recently installed as the president of the NCFC, who was a prominent California citrus grower. Also he wanted to visit some of the migrant-worker camps and key agricultural operations and leaders in the Golden State. And before returning home, he wanted to visit some of his old professors and colleagues at Berkeley, to counsel with Church leaders in Salt Lake City, and to make a nostalgic side trip to Idaho. As a reward for Reed's exemplary conduct at home and his distinction as the first Eagle Scout in the Washington Stake, he decided to take Reed with him.

Father and son boarded the train at Silver Springs, Maryland, on June 21, 1943. In one of those curious quirks of history, Rudger Clawson, President of the Twelve, died in Salt Lake City on the same day. Before he returned to Washington, Ezra would be called to fill the vacancy in the Twelve created by the passing of President Clawson.

President Clawson's death actually created a second vacancy in the Twelve, because Elder Sylvester Q. Cannon had passed away on May 29, 1943, at age 65. There appears to be no indication in Ezra's diary or conversation that, when he headed west on this trip, he had any inkling he would be called to the apostleship. Yet there were too many hints for an observer not to believe that at least subconsciously he recognized he might be a prime candidate for such a call. There were the predictions of his mother, his uncle Serge Benson, and, more recently, Mother Amussen. And there were other considerations: the long mentor-protégé relationship with President McKay; congratulatory letters Ezra had received in Washington from President Clark, including the last one inquiring about his next trip west and encouraging him to visit in Salt Lake City; and many positive experiences with President Heber J. Grant and other General Authorities, who had enthusiastically recommended that he take the Washington job. There also were his leadership experiences abroad and at home, especially his service as a conference president in England and as president of two stakes in the United States; his expertise in agriculture, both academically and in practice, a subject of basic importance to the welfare program and to Latter-day Saints in general; and (although his modesty would not have allowed him even to think it) his sterling character, his positive and enthusiastic outlook, his good reputation both inside and outside the Church, and his penchant for hard work. Underlying all this, of course, were his solid testimony, his faith, his love for people, and the unqualified support of an accomplished wife and an exemplary family.

If, in fact, these imposing credentials made no impression on Ezra Taft Benson, nor hinted to him that he might be in the cross hairs of the Brethren as they aimed toward filling the vacancies in the Twelve, they certainly had an impact on the Church leaders. In June there were discussions at Church headquarters when a member of the First Presidency revealed that both Spencer W. Kimball and Ezra

Taft Benson were being considered by President Grant as potential members of the Twelve. Some high leaders of the Church had similar feelings; so did others outside the hierarchy, as shown by Barbara Amussen's letter.

Ezra and Reed's first intermediate stop was in Chicago. From there they angled southwest into Texas and then across New Mexico and Arizona into California. The long hours together on the train enabled father and son to address in-depth topics that Ezra's hectic schedule had excluded from family discussions. The experience helped fuse their natural affinities and foster the understanding that marked their future relationships.

They spent more than two weeks in California, visiting Mr. Teague, scouting the agricultural scene, and retracing some of Ezra's steps taken while he studied California's cooperatives and marketing strategies in the 1930s. Mr. Teague, aware of lucrative offers made to Ezra by other farm groups, urged him to remain with the NCFC. As an inducement to stay, he told Ezra to name his own salary. At San Francisco Ezra addressed a gathering of agricultural leaders that included some of his Berkeley professors. Their presence was unsettling at first. In the end, his superior grasp of farm issues gained in the arena seemed to bolster his self-confidence. Indeed, the student had passed his tutors in the night.

The travelers arrived in Salt Lake City on Thursday, July 15, 1943, unaware of the drama played out the week before when the Brethren approved Spencer W. Kimball as a member of the Twelve and President J. Reuben Clark extended the call to him in Safford, Arizona, by telephone. Ezra visited his mentor, President David O. McKay, on July 16. It is apparent that Ezra's name had figured prominently in discussions of the Brethren on both July 8 and July 15; but President Grant had not yet received spiritual confirmation about calling Ezra to the apostleship. President McKay said nothing about this, of course, but being aware of the developments, he was interested to know about Ezra's itinerary.

He was told that Ezra and Reed planned to spend a few days in Idaho and then would return to Salt Lake before going east. That proved to be enough time to bring the question of his status to a head.

The visit to Whitney and Preston was a journey into the past for Ezra and a time of awakening for his son. Reed was only a toddler when the family had moved to Boise, so most of what he saw seemed new and strange. But for the father it was a return to the familiar place he would always call home, the place where he had been born and nurtured and taught and from where he had gone into the world to make his mark. It was a warming experience to visit the family farm, the Whitney chapel, and the academy in Preston and other landmarks, as well as to greet many old friends and relatives who still lived in the area. Already the reputation of the name Ezra Taft Benson in Cache Valley was due as much to his own achievements as to those of his ancestor and namesake. Ezra's conspicuous role on a national stage had gained much more notoriety than had the deeds of his great-grandfather, although Ezra would have been the first to admit they were of less significance. Yet during this Idaho visit, events were maturing in Salt Lake City that would elevate Ezra to the same apostolic status his ancestor had reached, an essential step to his becoming the President of The Church of Jesus Christ of Latter-day Saints. Indeed, on Thursday, July 22, 1943, the Council of the First Presidency and the Twelve affirmed President Grant's decision that Ezra Taft Benson be called as a member of the Quorum of the Twelve Apostles.

Unaware of this decision, Ezra and Reed returned to Salt Lake City on Monday, July 26, for a last round of visiting before heading east. Learning of his whereabouts after he arrived in the city, Joseph Anderson, the secretary to the First Presidency, contacted Ezra and advised him that President Heber J. Grant wanted to visit him at his cabin in a canyon east of the city. Thinking the cabin might be some distance away, he wondered whether he could go there and still catch his train. Learning it was only a few miles from the center of the city, Ezra welcomed the opportunity to shake the prophet's hand once more.

George J. Cannon, one of President Grant's sons-in-law, picked up the Bensons in his car and drove them up Emigration Canyon to the prophet's secluded hideaway, where he had gone to relax over the long July 24 weekend. Still mentally alert and active, President Grant had a slight physical disability caused by a stroke he had suffered several years before. Since then he had carefully husbanded his strength and often went to this rustic cabin for rest and renewal.

After entering a spacious, comfortably furnished living room whose walls were adorned with pictures of the large and gregarious Grant family, Ezra was shown into an adjoining room that served as the prophet's bedroom and study. Fully dressed and reclining on his bed, President Grant welcomed his guest, asked him to close the door, and motioned him to a chair near the bed. Sitting up, the prophet took Ezra's right hand in both of his and, without any preliminaries and with tears in his eyes, told him he had been called as the youngest member of the Quorum of the Twelve Apostles. With that, President Grant congratulated him, invoked God's blessings upon him, and told him of the enthusiastic response of all the Brethren when his qualifications were discussed in the upper room of the Salt Lake Temple.

Ezra was shocked. At first he was almost speechless. Later he only remembered repeating several times the words, "Oh, President Grant, that can't be," as tears filled his eyes. As his young friend struggled to compose himself, the prophet spoke words of comfort and encouragement, giving assurance that the Lord would magnify him in this new calling. Once he was able to speak more coherently, Ezra expressed his love and his dedication to the work. There followed an hour of quiet conversation during which, among other things, they discussed the timing of Ezra's severance from the NCFC, the announcement of his call to the Twelve, and his ordination. At a later date, George J. Cannon, who had known nothing about the reason for the visit to his father-in-law, commented that Elder Benson had been talkative and friendly on the way up the canyon but had sat still and silent on the way back. Indeed, the new Apostle had much to think about and little to say as he began to sort out what this call would mean to him and his family.

As previously arranged, George J. Cannon delivered the Bensons to the home of David O. McKay. Upon seeing his protégé, President McKay embraced Ezra, congratulated him, and assured him of his love and support. We do not doubt that President McKay had feelings akin to those of a pleased parent as he considered how in only two decades the young Elder Benson he had known in England had grown into an able, accomplished man with a national reputation who now had been called to join him in the apostleship. When Reed was told what had happened, he too embraced and congratulated his father, the man whom he admired and sought to emulate above all others.

A tight schedule prevented Ezra from calling Flora before he left Salt Lake City. But after a sleepless night on the train, absorbed in thoughts about the future, he called her from Grand Junction, Colorado. There then occurred a repetition of what had happened when he was appointed to the NCFC. Flora, seeming not surprised by her husband's announcement, told him she had had a premonition something significant would occur during his trip. And later she confided that she had known early in their relationship that he was destined to fill a high office in the Church. From that early time she had turned her efforts toward helping him to become qualified.

Before leaving Grand Junction, Elder Benson also called C. C. Teague to tell him what had happened. His friend, though loath to lose him from the farm cooperative movement, was understanding and offered congratulations and best wishes for success in his new assignment. Severance of his professional relationship with men like Mr. Teague was one of the few regrets Ezra had in accepting his call to the Twelve.

The First Presidency announced Elder Benson's call in the *Deseret News* on Tuesday, July 27, 1943. Once published in the press, the story spread rapidly, so by the time he reached Washington, D.C., everyone seemed to know. This touched off an avalanche of congratulatory calls and letters. The volume was bewildering. They came from members and nonmembers alike. Many reported they had known all along that he was destined for the apostleship.

Once the initial excitement of the call and the flood of felicitations had subsided, Ezra began to focus on the complex task of gearing up for the move to Salt Lake City. He had been told by President Grant to take as much time as necessary to terminate his connection with the NCFC. This would take several months as the council went through the laborious process of finding a suitable replacement and as the transition to a new administration was effected. Meanwhile, he was to continue serving as stake president until he heard otherwise from Salt Lake City.

Into this challenging mix were added Flora's announcement that she was expecting their sixth child and uncertainty about Ezra's financial future with the Church. Not once had the question of money come into his discussions with President Grant and President McKay. He learned later that he would receive a modest living allowance as a General Authority and that he would be expected to bear the cost of his move west, to find his own accommodations in Salt Lake, and to care for the support and education of his large family. While Ezra had received a substantial salary with the NCFC and by this time owned his home free of indebtedness, he was only forty-four years old and had been unable to build up any substantial surpluses. In effect the call put him under financial stress, for he would be required to uproot his family and to start again in a new locality with only a minimal assured income and with little prospect of being able to provide his family with the kind of temporal security his continued employment with the NCFC would have guaranteed.

Those who viewed Elder Benson's call from the outside were oblivious to these real and upsetting problems. They saw only the distinction the call carried: the close association with the living prophets; the opportunity to travel around the Church, meeting and counseling with the leaders and members; and the prestige attached to sitting in those upholstered seats at general conferences. Yet, Ezra and Flora Benson had faced challenges before and so were prepared to take their new challenges in stride. They accepted Ezra's call with gratitude and enthusiasm, and with the faith that any attending problems would be resolved in time.

Aside from the continuing flow of congratulatory messages, the months of August and September passed as if nothing had happened. His stake duties, work at the NCFC, and family responsibilities absorbed Ezra's time as before. A quarterly stake conference held in September was a highlight in Ezra's service as Washington Stake president. He was deeply touched by the outpouring of love and admiration from the leaders and members of the stake, who seemed to feel his call in some way was also a recognition of them. During the same month, he and other farm leaders were heavily involved with President Roosevelt, discussing plans to deal with the major economic dislocations that would occur in agriculture at the end of the war.

Flora was invited by the Brethren to accompany her husband to the October general conference in Salt Lake City, where Ezra would be presented for sustaining vote as a member of the Twelve. Flora and Ezra were provided with accommodations in the Hotel Utah, sandwiched between Temple Square and the Church Administration Building. During several days before the conference, they visited with members of the First Presidency and other General Authorities and were briefed on matters pertaining to their

131

pending move to Salt Lake City and on the procedures to be
followed at the conference. They also mingled with many
friends from Cache Valley, Boise, California, and
Washington, D.C., who had come to Salt Lake for the conference and were staying at the Hotel Utah. In this environment the excitement was electric as everyone looked
forward eagerly to the conference where two new members
of the Twelve would be sustained.

The earlier announcements of the calls of Elders Spencer
W. Kimball and Ezra Taft Benson seem not to have diminished the fascinated interest of members at the conference.
They were eager to get a good look at the new Apostles and
to hear them speak so they might come to know them better and gauge the depth of their spirituality and knowledge.

The General Authorities were presented for sustaining
vote at the first general session on Friday morning. When
the names of the two new Apostles were read, anticipation
seemed to wash through the Tabernacle audience. After the
Brethren had been unanimously sustained, Elders Kimball
and Benson were invited to take their places on the stand,
Elder Kimball to the left of Elder Harold B. Lee and Elder
Benson to the left of Elder Kimball, at the end of the row of
Apostles. As he arose and made his way forward, Ezra was
conscious of all eyes in the Tabernacle being fixed on him
and Elder Kimball, watching their every move. And as he
sat there on the stand, waiting his turn to speak, Elder
Benson felt conspicuous, ill at ease, and incredibly appre-
hensive about what he would say and how he would say it
when called on. Indeed, it seems that, under the circumstances, his seat on the stand was not nearly as comfortable
as it appeared to those in the audience.

Elder Ezra Taft Benson's maiden speech in the Salt Lake
Tabernacle was short and well spoken, carrying a deep
undertone of spirituality and conviction. Elder Kimball,
who had preceded him in addressing the conference, later
expressed, in his typically self-deprecatory way, the wish
that he had done as well. In his remarks, Elder Benson

Elders Spencer W. Kimball and Ezra Taft Benson in October 1943, when both were sustained to the Quorum of the Twelve Apostles

expressed his gratitude, his testimony, his commitment to the work. There would be ample time through the years ahead for him to elaborate on these themes and to develop many others as circumstances would require, themes rooted not only in the scriptures but also in his deeply held sense of patriotism. Yet, as we shall see, Elder Benson felt this patriotic sense was a branch growing out of the same root as the scriptures.

The final act that officially ushered Ezra Taft Benson into the circle of the Twelve Apostles occurred on October 7, 1943. On that day the First Presidency and the Twelve assembled in the First Presidency's council room, located in the north end of the main floor of the Church Administration Building. President Grant had used this large, impressive room intermittently as his private office. The special meeting was held there rather than in the upper room of the Salt Lake Temple, where it ordinarily would have been held, in order to accommodate President Grant's physical disability.

Speaking slowly, but with clarity and emphasis, the

aged prophet gave the two new members the apostolic charge, which obligated them to put their new calling above everything else; enjoined upon them the principles of unity and confidentiality; and encouraged them, collegially, to express their honest views on all issues coming before the council. After both had accepted the charge, President Grant, who was unable to stand unaided for long periods, invited Elder Kimball to kneel before him. The President and the other members of the apostolic council who had gathered around placed their hands on his head and, with President Grant acting as voice, ordained him an Apostle and set him apart as a member of the Quorum of the Twelve Apostles. The same procedure was followed with Elder Benson. The effect of these actions was to confer on Elders Kimball and Benson all the authority necessary to lead the Church as its prophet, to be held in an inchoate or suspended form until the happening of two events, at which time the authority would become fully vested and operative. Those two events were to survive to be the senior living Apostle and to have the other living Apostles ordain him as the President and the prophet of the Church. Never before, as in the case of Elders Kimball and Benson, had two men been ordained to the apostleship on the same day, each of whom later survived to become President of the Church. It may never happen again.

When Elder Benson returned to Washington, D.C., he wore two ecclesiastical hats—stake president and member of the Twelve. He would fill that dual role for five more months, although his apostolic duties were minimal. A week after his return from Salt Lake City, he traveled to Annapolis, Maryland, where he organized a new branch composed of naval personnel and their families. He urged the midshipmen who were training at the academy to use their contacts with nonmembers as opportunities to create goodwill for the Church and perhaps to open the way for them to desire membership in the Church. President Grant had given Ezra a similar charge when he called him to the

Twelve, and from that time forward Ezra was always alert to missionary opportunities.

His first stake conference assignment took him to New York City. Although he had attended many such meetings over the years, none had produced in him so much apprehension. He found that presiding over a stake conference as a visiting General Authority was much different than merely attending one. He had missed the opportunity as a new Apostle to attend stake conferences in company with other General Authorities to learn their philosophy and objectives. Thus he was left to his own instincts and to spiritual promptings. He fretted before the conference and wondered afterward how effective he had been. The comments of those present were not a reliable gauge. The only true test was how his conduct or remarks had made an impact for good on his listeners. He returned to Washington not knowing whether he had met the test. Ezra learned later that it was a rare thing to receive convincing evidence of success at a stake conference. His own feelings had to suffice.

In January he attended his last annual meeting of the NCFC, held in Chicago. Afterward he received many letters of appreciation for his services. A recurring theme in them dwelled on Ezra's energy and his positive approach to problems, qualities that typified everything he did and that followed him into his apostolic service. Later at a formal farewell given by the board, emotions ran high as he was lauded for his work and rewarded with a gold watch as a memento of his service. Everyone present, including the guest of honor, undoubtedly assumed his professional career in agriculture was at an end and that this was his swan song.

Yet Ezra's severance from agriculture was not complete. He continued to serve as an NCFC director and attended meetings of the Agricultural Postwar Planning Committee as a consultant. He retained these connections not only because of his interest but also because both President Heber J. Grant and George Albert Smith, President of the

Twelve, had urged him to do so. It was felt he could render an important service to the country while enhancing the status and the influence of the Church. Moreover, a contact he made during his final weeks as NCFC executive secretary foreshadowed a continuing influence in agricultural matters with high political leaders. In late February 1944 he attended a series of agricultural meetings, including one in Albany, New York, the state capital. While there, he met with Governor Thomas E. Dewey, who was known to have presidential aspirations. Later in the year he acceded to the governor's request to sketch out a national agricultural program, and four years later when the governor was a presidential candidate, Ezra accepted the invitation to serve on his agricultural advisory committee. As the 1948 election approached, Ezra learned from a reliable source that he was being considered as a member of Dewey's cabinet.

Elder Benson was released as president of the Washington Stake on March 5, 1944. Elder Spencer W. Kimball, who had previously attended meetings in Chicago and New York, was assigned to conduct the reorganization. It is ironic that the first stake reorganization Elder Benson participated in as a member of the Twelve was the one in which he was released as stake president. Also significant was that Elder Kimball, though ordained the same day as Ezra, presided at the conference, for he had been called and ordained first. This seniority in the apostleship accounted for Spencer W. Kimball's preceding Ezra Taft Benson as President of the Church.

The two Apostles were inspired to call Edgar B. Brossard as the new stake president replacing Elder Benson. In the evening after the conference, Elder Kimball and his wife, Camilla, who was traveling with him, visited in the Benson home, where they played games and had refreshments. The next day, Elder Benson took Elder Kimball to his office at NCFC headquarters and conducted a tour of the facilities and introduced him to some of his coworkers.

Because Flora was within a few months of delivering her

sixth child, she did not accompany her husband to the April general conference in 1944, although she had been invited to do so by the Brethren. So in late March Ezra traveled alone to Salt Lake City, where he attended all the conference sessions as well as his first quarterly meeting of the Twelve. At these meetings, which convene every three months, the Twelve Apostles counsel together, report their activities, and bear testimony. Held in the council room of the Twelve on the fourth floor of the Salt Lake Temple, this meeting gave Elder Benson his first real insight into the collegial traditions that bind the Twelve together in a brotherhood that is unique in the world.

Unlike the First Presidency, which is dissolved at the death of each succeeding President of the Church, the Quorum of the Twelve Apostles has had a continuous existence since first organized in 1835. The instructions given to the original members of the Twelve defined their global responsibilities, admonished them to diligence in their life-long callings (referred to as the "Imperious Mandate"), and instructed them to come together periodically to report, to renew their fraternal ties, and to share their testimonies. Elder Benson learned that the procedures used by the Twelve in their council room had been handed down through the generations of Apostles who had preceded him. As he sat in this room, where hang portraits of the members of the Twelve, Elder Ezra Taft Benson represented the sixty-third Apostle called to the Twelve and ordained in modern times. His great-grandfather and namesake, Ezra T. Benson, was number twenty.

Ezra was uplifted and challenged by associating with the members of his quorum. The bonds of loyalty and friendship forged among them were akin to those in the family. Although they were men of diverse backgrounds and skills—educators (John A. Widtsoe, Joseph F. Merrill, Harold B. Lee), attorneys (Stephen L Richards, Charles A. Callis, Albert E. Bowen), businessmen (George Albert Smith, Spencer W. Kimball), a farmer (George F. Richards),

Elder and Sister Benson with their children in 1943: Bonnie (on her father's lap), Mark, Barbara, Beverly, and Reed (standing)

a historian (Joseph Fielding Smith), a newspaperman (Mark E. Petersen, called a year later)—they shared convictions of the divine origins of the Church and were dedicated to its worldwide mission. Their knowledge and expertise gained in their earlier careers bolstered the soundness of their deliberations.

Before leaving for the East, Ezra rented a temporary home on Military Drive, on the east bench of Salt Lake City. Back in Washington, D.C., he divided his time between making the final transition to his successor at the NCFC, working with Flora to sort and pack their belongings for the move west, and negotiating for the sale of their home and the liquidation of other assets.

The Washington Stake honored the Benson family at an emotional farewell in late April. It was difficult to leave their many friends, their beautiful home, and the exciting lifestyle they had enjoyed in the nation's capital. Ezra especially would miss the associations with stake leaders and members and with his coworkers in the farm cooperative movement. He would always look upon his five years in

Washington as one of the most productive periods of his life, a period during which his reputation as an agricultural and an ecclesiastical leader was firmly established and when the members of his family had grown in unity and personal achievement.

Once the family was comfortably settled in their new Salt Lake home, Elder Benson finally was able to devote himself full-time to his calling in the Twelve. His first headquarters assignments included service as Executive Secretary of the Melchizedek Priesthood Committee, adviser to the YMMIA and YWMIA, and member of the committees responsible to make stake conference assignments and to review manuscripts written for publication. In addition, of course, were the weekly report and planning meetings with his quorum and the weekly meetings of the Council of the First Presidency and the Quorum of the Twelve held in the upper room of the temple. Sandwiched between these meetings were numerous personal interviews with local Church leaders who came for counsel and with individuals who sought direction or solace from the Apostle or who came merely to renew acquaintance or to reminisce. In time Elder Benson became a favorite of young people to perform their temple marriages. He also participated regularly in instructing missionaries preparing to enter the mission field and in setting them apart. Added to these varied activities was a voluminous correspondence Elder Benson carried on with Church leaders whom he had met in the field, with individual members who wrote seeking counsel, and with his associates in the NCFC, for which he continued to serve as a member of the board of directors. He also had continuing duties with the Agricultural Postwar Planning Committee, which entailed meetings and correspondence.

Elder Benson's work in Washington, where the three branches of government seemed to be at odds constantly, increased his appreciation for the operation of the Church at the highest level. While many lauded the separation of powers in the federal government as providing a needed system of checks and balances so one branch could not dominate the others, members lauded the Church system in which the ultimate executive, legislative, and judicial authority is vested in one man, the prophet, aided by his counselors. Ezra, who was familiar with Alma's warning against kingly leadership (see Mosiah 23:7–8), nevertheless approved of the Church system because of its greater efficiency and the unquestioned integrity of the prophet. Moreover, he found in the leading councils of the Church a disposition to hear the views of all and a reluctance to move forward unless there was a unanimity of feeling, despite the authority of the prophet to act unilaterally.

Elder Benson's field duties consisted mainly of conducting stake conferences and mission tours. During the first weeks of his full-time service, he usually attended stake conferences in company with a senior member of the Twelve to receive training in procedure and to gain insight into personalities, problems, and the apostolic agenda by confidential visits with his companions. So on June 18, 1944, Elder Benson attended the conference of the Salt Lake Cottonwood Stake in company with the president of his quorum, George Albert Smith. With this spare, bearded, gracious man, Ezra soon developed a close rapport that was solidified by their common interest in Scouting. President Smith had served on national boards of the Boy Scouts of America (BSA) for many years; and shortly after his call to the Twelve, Elder Benson was appointed to the national board of the BSA for rural Scouting. At the time, they were the only two General Authorities of the Church serving on national Scouting boards. Soon after Elder Benson's move to Salt Lake City, his relationship with President Smith was further strengthened when he purchased a home on Harvard Avenue, which was in the Yale Ward of the Bonneville Stake and where President Smith also lived.

When the last of the six children, Flora Beth, was born on August 12, 1944, it became important for the Bensons to find a larger and permanent residence in Salt Lake City. The

*The Benson family
during the 1944
Christmas season*

home they decided on was distinctive looking, on a quiet,
tree-lined avenue, and the backyard bordered a heavily
wooded ravine through which ran a clear mountain stream.
It was located near the Uintah grammar school and only a
few blocks from Roosevelt Junior High, East High School,
and the University of Utah. A shopping center and the bus
route were nearby. The Yale Ward chapel was within easy
walking distance. Unlike Boise and Washington, D.C., their
neighbors were predominantly members of the Church. The
Bensons were welcomed with warmth and enthusiasm and
immediately made to feel part of the ward family, a close-
knit community whose families lived within the radius of a
few blocks from the ward chapel. As Ezra began his lengthy
and frequent travels for the Church, it was consoling for him
to know that his family was established in such a comfortable and secure place.

Elder Benson's first mission tour took him to the East Central States Mission, which included North Carolina, Tennessee, Kentucky, Virginia, and West Virginia. At the time there were no stakes within this vast area and very few chapels. Two years earlier Elder George Albert Smith had toured the mission in company with the mission president, James P. Jensen, and his wife, Belle, when a highlight of the tour was the dedication of a new chapel at Huntington, West Virginia, and a renovated chapel at Louisville, Kentucky, which the Church had purchased from a protestant group.

Elder Benson toured the mission by automobile in company with the mission president and his wife and an elder from the mission office who drove the car. Automobile travel at the time was an adventure because of gas and tire rationing caused by the war. Meetings were held with missionaries and members in twenty-eight cities over a period of twenty-six days. Ezra's orientation to missionary work and his practical experience in the field enabled him to give effective training to the missionaries and to motivate them to increase their efficiency and productivity. Testimony bearing, which was always part of the meetings with the missionaries, invariably touched Elder Benson and doubtless reminded him of similar experiences in England with his mission presidents, Orson F. Whitney and David O. McKay.

Because the districts in the mission were incipient stakes, Elder Benson gave training to the local district leaders in the principles of Church administration applicable to both stakes and mission districts. (The first stake within the mission area, at Richmond, Virginia, was not created until 1957, thirteen years after Elder Benson's tour.) In his public addresses, Elder Benson sought to inspire and to lift his audiences and to correct them when he saw the need. It was an exhausting but rewarding tour.

While in the East, Ezra also traveled to Washington, D.C., where he attended meetings of the American Institute of Cooperation. To his surprise he was elected as a vice president and a member of the executive committee. Obviously the institute was anxious to retain its relationship with this man, not only because of his expertise in cooperatives but also because of the reflected prestige it gained by Ezra's service in the high echelons of a growing international church. It was a case of reciprocity as Elder Benson sought to promote the interests of the Church by his service to the institute.

Speaking at general conference was a major trial for Elder Benson. The intimidation of a crowded tabernacle and a large unseen radio audience created extreme tension and required more care in preparation than for talks given at stake conferences or during mission tours. The anxiety was increased by not knowing in what session or in what order he would be called on to speak. To be called on during the last session of a conference, as occurred occasionally, meant he was kept on edge throughout three days. Yet these tensions paled in comparison with those he experienced in preparing and delivering the nationally broadcast "Church of the Air" talk during the 1944 October general conference. The theme of this talk, the first major talk delivered by Elder Benson after his call to the Twelve, "America, a Choice Land," sounded a message that would be repeated over and over, with variations, throughout his apostolic career. In it he declared that the Constitution of the United States was written by inspired men, that the freedoms and the productivity enjoyed in the land derive from a divine source, and that conduct offensive to the divine will should be abandoned on pain of losing these rich bounties. It was a direct appeal for national repentance, something quite unheard of in that day. And it was a clear reflection of the speaker's character and of what to expect of him in the future. Here was an honest, forthright, intelligent man who did not mince words and who spoke his mind regardless of the consequences.

Elder Benson's concern about the moral climate in the United States hinted at by this talk doubtless arose in large part from the traumas and the dislocations caused by the war. At the time he moved to Salt Lake City in May 1944, the war in Europe was building to a crescendo. For weeks the Allies had been pounding German cities with thousands of bombing sorties, creating the devastation Elder Benson would witness personally much sooner than he then could have imagined. And on June 6, 1944, two weeks before he joined President George Albert Smith at the Cottonwood Stake conference, the Allied forces under the command of General Dwight D. Eisenhower swarmed over the beaches at Normandy. Thereafter until the end of the war, newspapers regularly listed the names of American servicemen killed, wounded, or missing in action. There were few who were not touched personally by these tragedies, whether through family ties or friendships.

The end of the war came with unexpected suddenness. Germany surrendered on May 7, 1945, and the Japanese followed suit on August 14, 1945, after atomic bombs were dropped on Hiroshima and Nagasaki. Between these two events, a major happening occurred within the Church when, on May 14, 1945, President Heber J. Grant passed away. A week later, on May 21, 1945, the First Presidency was reorganized. At a special meeting in the upper room of the temple on that day, George Albert Smith was sustained and ordained as the eighth President of the Church. He selected J. Reuben Clark and David O. McKay as his counselors, and they were set apart on the same day. The new First Presidency was sustained by the members of the Church at the October 1945 general conference. At the same time, Elder Matthew Cowley was sustained as a member of the Twelve, filling the vacancy created by George Albert Smith's ordination as the President of the Church.

Chapter 10

Shepherding the Saints in Europe

President George Albert Smith's first major initiative was to alleviate the suffering of the destitute Latter-day Saints in war-torn Europe by shipping food, clothing, bedding, and other welfare commodities to them. More important, he sought to reestablish the lines of priesthood authority and responsibility among them and to provide them with spiritual direction and motivation.

Following the 1945 October general conference, President Smith appointed Elder John A. Widtsoe of the Twelve, a native of Norway and a former president of the European Mission, to direct this work. Elder Thomas E. McKay, an Assistant to the Twelve who had recently served as a mission president in Europe, was appointed to assist Elder Widtsoe. President Smith accompanied these two brethren and others to Washington, D.C., in late October to confer with government officials about obtaining passports and visas for them and about clearances to ship the commodities. Because of political complications at the end of the war and the disruptions caused by Allied bombings, they were told there would be an indefinite delay in obtaining the needed approvals.

In late December, Elder Widtsoe suffered a recurrence of serious physical problems and advised President Smith that he felt incapable of performing the arduous work in Europe. The need to act speedily prompted President Smith to convene a special meeting of the Brethren three days before Christmas where a replacement for Elder Widtsoe would be appointed. The designation of Elder Benson to direct the relief effort in Europe came as a surprise. Although it was felt that his large, young family would preclude his selection, the wisdom of his appointment soon became apparent. Shortly after Christmas he flew to Washington, D.C., where in a few days he obtained passports and visas and arranged transportation to Europe for himself and his traveling companion, Frederick W. Babbel, a task thought impossible by some in such a short time. His experience with the NCFC had taught Ezra how to navigate the murky waters of Washington's bureaucracy; he knew whom to see, what to say, and how to say it. His administrative skills, added to a prophetic blessing and Ezra's zealous faith, would open many doors during the coming weeks in Europe.

The blessing was conferred on Elder Benson by President George Albert Smith on January 28, 1946, when the prophet set him apart as president of the European Mission. He was promised "every power and gift" needed to accomplish the work of "putting the missions of Europe in order" and doing "that which is so important to be done at this time," namely, the alleviation of physical want. Ezra was admonished "to appeal to the Lord" in the performance of this work, for the Lord would give him strength "to accomplish everything that is necessary to be done." He also was promised the ability to break down prejudices, to exert influence with men of prominence, to avoid obstacles thrown up by the adversary, and to soothe the feelings of those embittered by the war. Finally, he was told to go in peace, to not worry about his family, and "to keep close to the field until every organization is in satisfactory condition and you will be able to report all is well" (Ezra Taft Benson, *A Labor of Love* [Salt Lake City: Deseret Book Co., 1989], Appendix A).

Elder Benson called his family together, gave counsel about their conduct in his absence, expressed his love, and in imitation of the ancient patriarchs pronounced a father's blessing on each member. The following evening, January 29, 1946, Ezra and Flora were driven to the airport by their friends, Harold B. Lee and his wife, Fern. Waiting there were other associates from the Twelve: Spencer W. Kimball, Mark E. Petersen, and Matthew Cowley. It was snowing heavily, a harbinger of the harsh weather Elder Benson would find in Europe, reported to be the most severe winter there in eighty years. After a tender moment aside with Flora, Ezra embraced his brethren and disappeared into the waiting airliner with his traveling companion.

The trans-Atlantic flight was an adventure. Following several days of storm en route to New York and on the East Coast, their plane left La Guardia Airport in New York and, after skirting the coasts of Massachusetts, Maine, and Newfoundland, landed at Gander, Newfoundland. There mechanics tried to correct the malfunction of two of the motors by replacing spark plugs. Tension escalated that night while crossing the Atlantic as passengers watched the engineer repeatedly shining his flashlight on the two offending motors. In Ireland the next morning, while the passengers ate breakfast and admired the Irish countryside near the River Shannon, mechanics again tinkered with the two cranky motors, this time removing water from the magneto.

Elder Benson was greeted in London by Hugh B. Brown, president of the British Mission, and his wife, Zina. Illustrating the shifting tides of hierarchical leadership in the Church, Elder Brown, who was not a General Authority at the time and was subordinate to Elder Benson, would later become his superior as a member of the First Presidency. Then, upon the death of President David O. McKay, he would become once again a member of the Quorum of the Twelve, over which Ezra would preside during the final years of Elder Brown's life.

Elder Brown briefed Ezra about the condition of the Saints in Great Britain, showed him the devastation caused by German bombing, and then demonstrated that culture was not dead in London when he and Zina hosted him at a Tchaikovsky concert by the London Philharmonic Orchestra in the famed Royal Albert Hall. "Thank the Lord for great music," wrote Elder Benson after the concert. No experience better illustrated the vast difference between the effect of the war on England and on Germany. London and other English cities were badly scarred but retained their basic integrity, while the major German cities were literally demolished. The consequences of this difference were tragically shown in the condition of the people. While there were shortages, inconveniences, and traumas among the English, there was vast destruction, social and political chaos, and abject poverty in the once magnificent cities of the Third Reich.

Not wanting to intrude on the British Mission's already cramped quarters, Elder Benson sought separate housing nearer to the centers of government, business, and transportation. Undeterred by reports that lodging was not available in crowded London, Ezra, after fervent prayer, was able to rent a ground-floor flat only a block from Grosvenor Square, where the U.S. Embassy and other U.S. offices were located. Consisting of two bedrooms, a bath, and a sitting room, it would serve both as living quarters for him and his secretary and as the headquarters of the European Mission. According to counsel received from President Smith, Frederick Babbel would be Elder Benson's constant companion throughout his tenure as European Mission president.

On February 11, 1946, Elder Benson began his first tour of the Continent. The two-week trip took him to France, Holland, Denmark, Sweden, and Norway. Flying to Paris on a stripped-down army transport whose only amenity was a parachute, he made arrangements to purchase seven Dodge half-ton pickup trucks for the use of local Church units. Plans to drive one of them to Holland were abandoned when a check revealed the front bearings were dangerously worn, so they went by train instead.

At the Hague, as he did at other mission headquarters, Elder Benson counseled with the local leaders to ascertain their needs, the status of their people, and to impart necessary advice. Everywhere he found the Church organizations functioning as well as could be expected under the circumstances. The members had received many small relief packages sent directly from the United States, and during this tour Elder Benson learned that four carloads of commodities he had requested were on their way from Welfare Square in Salt Lake City. The most critical shortages were linens, which also were hard to find in the United States, and fuel.

While in Copenhagen, Elder Benson made a side trip to nearby Koge, where Flora's father was born. There he obtained leads on new genealogical data and made arrangements for local researchers to pursue them further. The visit aroused sweet memories of his companion on whom he relied so heavily for solace and motivation. The correspondence between them during this anxious period reveals the depth and the tenderness of their loving relationship.

In Stockholm, Sweden, Elder Benson held three press conferences, report and training meetings with leaders and missionaries, and a large public gathering attended by many nonmembers. Reports of the visit of a modern Apostle kindled much interest among people starved for spiritual nourishment after years of wartime deprivations.

On the flight to Oslo, Norway, the temperature fell to twenty degrees below zero. This and heavy snows blanketing northern Europe aggravated the fuel shortages that Elder Benson found everywhere. There was little he could do to alleviate this problem.

After a week back in London to prepare reports, catch up on correspondence, and refurbish his wardrobe, Elder Benson was off again to the Continent. Flying to Paris, he was driven through peaceful Switzerland, untouched by the war, into Germany. "My heart was made heavy as we drove through towns and cities leveled to the ground as a result of war," he confided to his diary. "Occupation troops were everywhere. . . . Freiburg presents a vast amount of devastation, and this scene was multiplied many times along the way" (ibid., pp. 39–40).

Karlsruhe looked like an immense rubble heap. No building seemed to have escaped the devastation. Yet, off the main boulevard, beyond the facade of destruction, was a severely damaged building that was still usable. Here Elder Benson found 260 people assembled in a conference that had been in progress for an hour and a half when he arrived. All arose in respect and silently watched as he mounted the stand. On their faces was evidence of the fears and privations the war had spawned. Their clothing was threadbare, accentuating the chill in the poorly heated room. Yet a warm glow shone from their eyes. Elder Benson was the first General Authority to visit Karlsruhe in seven years; they listened intently to everything he said.

Stifling his own deep emotions, Elder Benson, speaking through an interpreter, expressed his love, extended greetings from the prophet and other Church leaders, assured them of temporal assistance to come, admonished them to live righteously, bore testimony, and invoked God's blessings on them. Later, as he shook hands with each person in the audience, "it was gratifying to see the look of faith and devotion that lighted their faces" (ibid., p. 41).

In Karlsruhe Elder Benson was briefed about the war's impact upon Church members in Germany. Many had been killed by the bombings. In Hamburg, for instance, twenty-seven members were killed during one night's raid. In succeeding nights, many more were killed or wounded, and countless others were left homeless. Those who survived

150

lacked adequate shelter, clothing, and food. Some lived in unheated quarters without water or cooking facilities. There were serious sanitation problems. Most of the meeting-houses had been destroyed. These problems were worsened by the many refugees who fled to West Berlin from the Soviet zone and Poland.

At first it was a case of Berliners sharing their poverty. Then Elder Benson, as a stopgap, purchased supplies in Switzerland and arranged for the Red Cross to deliver them to Church members in Berlin. He was anxious, however, to obtain permission for the Church to transport and to deliver its own supplies to its members. To that end, he traveled to Frankfurt, Germany, on March 16, 1946. Calling at the head-quarters of General Joseph T. McNarney in the I. G. Farben Building, a colonel at the desk told Elder Benson he could not see the general for three days. Undeterred, he and Frederick went to their car to pray for guidance and for doors to be opened to them. They returned for another try to find a new officer at the desk. Within fifteen minutes they were in the presence of General McNarney.

At first the general was adamant; their supplies could be distributed only by the military. Convinced this system would prevent most of the supplies from reaching the Saints, Elder Benson persisted in an adroit yet determined way. "When he saw we were somewhat determined, he said, 'Well, you go ahead and collect your supplies, and probably by the time you get them collected the policy will be changed.'" The general was incredulous when told the supplies were already gathered in warehouses in Salt Lake City and that carloads of food, bedding, clothing, and medical supplies would be moving toward Germany within twenty-four hours from the time Elder Benson wired the First Presidency. "I never heard of people with such vision," the general responded. "And before we left him," wrote Elder Benson, "we had written authorization to make our own distribution to our own people through our own channels, and from that moment we had wonderful cooperation" (ibid., p. 49).

Though badly damaged, the mission home in Frankfurt was still in livable condition. Here Elder Benson received further briefings about the impact of the war on the area's Church members: eighty-two were killed while serving in the armed forces, seventy-one civilians were killed by bombings and shell fire, fifteen hundred were unaccounted for; between 80 and 85 percent of the mission membership were bombed out of their homes and were living in makeshift quarters outside the city.

Helpful Mormon GIs escorted Elder Benson out of Frankfurt when he left for Hanover. He found these men everywhere in Europe. Many were returned missionaries who were continuing their conversion efforts while in uniform. They were a great strength to the local Saints and their leaders. All enmities generated by the war were swallowed up in the unity of the gospel and the Church.

"This, I believe, is the worst we have seen," Elder Benson wrote of his visit to Hanover. "It appears that not one building in the city proper is undamaged, and most buildings are leveled to the ground. To look up some of the streets with every building laid waste fills one's heart with a weird and sad feeling. People walking about in the ruins seem almost as though they were from another world." Still, with only two hours' notice, 175 Hanover Saints assembled in a heatless, partially bombed-out schoolhouse to hear the Apostle. "The spirit of the meeting was marvelous to feel and behold. How I longed for power to lift these good people from their heartrending state. We did all in our power to help them and offered such assistance as we could and promised we'd see them again soon" (ibid., pp. 54–55).

The trip from Hanover to Berlin was tedious. Bombed-out bridges caused many wearisome detours. Armed troops with fixed bayonets were positioned at intervals all along the route. "We were permitted to pass safely through unmolested in spite of the many warnings and stories of danger passed on to us by the various military units," wrote Elder Benson of the trip. "The sight of Berlin is indescribable. Not a building has escaped damage, and miles of the city are laid in utter waste. It is a scene of shocking desolation" (ibid., p. 57).

All Latter-day Saint church buildings in Berlin were destroyed by the bombing, including the mission headquarters. "The office force and missionaries went over to the rented home of Brother Langheinrich the night before the bombing on his recommendation, otherwise they would all have been killed as the building was completely ruined." But this destruction hardly compared with the human wreckage. "As I rode through the streets and walked through some impassable by auto," Elder Benson wrote, "I smelled the odor of decaying human bodies, saw half-starved women paying exorbitant prices anxiously for potato peelings. I saw old men and women with small hatchets eagerly digging at tree stumps and roots in an effort to get scraps of fuel and then pulling those home for miles on anything that would roll." Most touching of all was a conference meeting with 480 cold, half-starved Latter-day Saints, held in a half-wrecked third-floor auditorium. "It was an inspiration to see the light of faith and hear their harrowing experiences, including murder, rape, and starvation of their loved ones. Yet there was no bitterness or anger but a sweet reciprocation and expression of faith in the gospel. We were together in a partly bombed building for three and a half hours" (ibid., p. 65).

The faith and confidence shown by the Latter-day Saints was not shared by other segments of Berlin's population. It was reported there were "well over one hundred suicides daily due to the mental attitude of the people who have no hope in view of the ravages of the war" (ibid.). The spirit of confident survival in the face of overwhelming physical devastation shown by the German Saints was a marvel to Elder Benson. It reflected no personal superiority over those who wilted under the enormous pressures and took their own lives. Instead, it was a demonstration of the profound influence of gospel principles in the lives of the people.

Obviously, this was the remedy most needed by those who had been so tragically touched by the war. It was a spiritual balm whose healing influences surpassed by far any physical remedies Elder Benson was able to provide. So when he had established the framework for the efficient delivery of Church welfare commodities, and when he saw that wave after wave of shipments were on their way from the Church larders in Salt Lake City, he focused his main attention on the training of local leaders and on the calling and motivation of missionaries.

Anxious to ensure that the delivery channels he had arranged would remain open and that there would be a suitable environment in which the nurturing and proselyting work of the Church would thrive, Elder Benson counseled with General Lucius D. Clay, U.S. Deputy Governor for Germany. "Our group was assured of his full cooperation," he reported, "and we received his appreciation that the church was on the job in the occupied areas ready to help in the mammoth work of rehabilitation" (ibid., p. 61). The general also approved the resumption of the pre-war Church program, including MIA activities, missionary work, and the organization of Boy Scout work.

With these assurances, Elder Benson continued with his tour, visiting Nuremberg, Munich, and Stuttgart, Germany; Prague and Pilsen, Czechoslovakia; Vienna, Austria; Paris, France; Liège and Antwerp, Belgium; and Amsterdam, Utrecht, and The Hague, Netherlands, before returning to London. Later he visited Warsaw, Poland, and Helsinki, Finland, and toured extensively in Great Britain. The last included a nostalgic visit to Newcastle, where in memory he relived the days of his youthful ministry.

During these tours, Elder Benson laid the groundwork for his service as president of the European Mission. Afterward, he made numerous other trips to follow up with his training, to make necessary organizational changes, and to ensure that the temporal and spiritual needs of Church members were being met.

During the months of this difficult service, Elder Benson was under constant pressure—traveling under adverse conditions, changing beds almost every night, eating erratically, juggling his personal needs of wardrobe and hygiene, and wrestling all the while with the seemingly endless problems of organization and nurturing that faced him on a daily basis. Sometimes the burden seemed too heavy to bear.

However, three things sustained him throughout. Paramount was spiritual direction. He prayed incessantly for guidance. In answer came promptings of where to go, whom to see, and what to say. He proceeded like his hero, Nephi, confident that God would show him, step by step, how to do the work he had been instructed to perform.

Akin to this godly direction was Flora's loving support. Her letters, dog-eared from countless readings, buoyed him constantly. Sentences like the following could not have failed to imbue him with renewed strength and determination: "My apron and handkerchief are wet with tears of appreciation for you as I write this letter." And, "You know we are always thinking and praying for you, dearest, and hundreds of your dear friends and loved ones are doing the same." Then followed words demonstrating, as nothing else could do, that her expressions of love and support were genuine: "Wouldn't you like me to send you some tuna fish, sugar, etc.? I am sending you some candy and nuts, and I'll try and make you some better cookies than the ones I have already sent you and pack them better. Tell me what you would like sent." And the conclusion conveyed the comforting knowledge that all was well at home: "The Lord is constantly blessing our efforts. If we do our part, the Lord never fails us. I feel His constant care over me continually. May you have peace of mind always, T, and know that things are going well with us—and don't worry about us. We miss you greatly, but it shall bring its blessings" (ibid., p. 43). Later, when little Beth became ill, it was comforting to know that the prophet was near to bless her and to give comfort to Flora: "President George Albert Smith, with his son-in-law, administered and blessed the baby. . . . I know the Lord blessed her because we were almost forced to take her to the hospital. But I know it was the administration that made her keep a lower temperature. . . . Please don't worry about Beth, dear. I know the Lord will bless her to be well and strong again" (ibid., p. 56).

Finally, Elder Benson was buoyed by his native enthusiasm and positive outlook. He also used music to encourage the Saints and to lift his own spirits. While in Stuttgart, for instance, he joined with Fred Babbel, Max Zimmer, and Chaplain Badger to form what was jokingly called "The K-Ration Quartet," which provided lighthearted entertainment for themselves and their audience.

By November 1946 Elder Benson felt that the organizations in Europe were "in satisfactory condition" and that he could report to the prophet that "all is well," as his setting-apart blessing had required. On November 16, 1946, he met his replacement, Elder Alma Sonne, Assistant to the Twelve, who arrived at Southampton, England, with his wife on the SS *Washington*. Also on board were mission president Walter Stover, who was on his way to Berlin, and missionaries destined for Switzerland and France. After giving them instructions, Elder Benson accompanied Elder and Sister Sonne to London. During the following three weeks, Elder Benson took Elder Sonne on a lengthy tour throughout the European Mission, briefing him on the work and introducing him to local Church leaders and key military commanders and government personnel.

On Wednesday, December 11, 1946, Elder Benson dictated final letters and, after transferring all inventories, finances, and other mission affairs to Elder Sonne, boarded a Pan American flight at Heathrow Airport. Reports of foul weather over the Atlantic prompted a delay in leaving Shannon, Ireland. It was decided to fly to New York via Goose Bay and Labrador, Newfoundland, instead of via the

Azores. Unlike the balky plane ten and a half months earlier, this one was mechanically sound. Still, the prospect of a wintry crossing of the Atlantic was unsettling. A safe touchdown at Goose Bay relieved the tension. Here Ezra was astonished by the huge mounds of snow that lined the runway. Giant snowplows stood ready to build them higher as the snow fell. The temperature stood at fourteen degrees below zero, which discouraged a leg-stretching walk.

Elder Benson welcomed the warmth and the spaciousness of New York's enclosed air terminal. Even the tedious delay in clearing customs could not dim his genuine joy at being back on American soil. And the absence of rubble and grotesque, bombed-out buildings was a reminder of America's favored status. Elder Benson's experience in Europe seems to have magnified his intense loyalty to the United States and his determination to combat any influence threatening its freedoms. Through the years ahead, his voice would be raised repeatedly, extolling his country's virtues and warning against the intrusion of alien doctrines.

Ezra called Flora from New York to tell her he had landed and was scheduled to arrive in Salt Lake City at 4:30 A.M. on Friday, December 13, a day he said was "anything but unlucky." He enjoyed a warm bath, put on clean clothing, and, after an unforeseen delay, boarded the plane. Heavy turbulence between New York and Chicago caused more delay, but the remainder of the flight was smooth. It is unlikely that the flight conditions made much difference to Ezra, caught up as he was in the excitement of seeing Flora after such a long separation. They had never been apart this long before. The delays postponed his arrival in Salt Lake City until 6:00 A.M. Flora was waiting. It was an emotional reunion as they embraced, hardly able to speak. But words were not needed to convey their joy at being reunited.

The family had acquired a new automobile during Ezra's absence. The cozy warmth and the new-car smell of the Pontiac Six provided a sharp contrast with the old jalopies Ezra had used in Europe. The joyous reception of the four girls, warm and safe in their gracious home, well clothed and well fed, accentuated the wide gulf that separated America and the ravaged civilization he had seen abroad.

Reed and Mark, who were attending BYU, came up from Provo in the afternoon, completing the family circle. Anticipating her husband's arrival, Flora had restocked the refrigerator and had prepared some of the family's favorite dishes and delicacies. These, and the endless conversation throughout the remainder of the day and into the night as the Bensons endeavored to fill in the gaps caused by their separation, created one of their most memorable days.

The next day, Ezra and Flora met with President George Albert Smith and President J. Reuben Clark, to whom Elder Benson made a preliminary report of his mission abroad.

Chapter 11

Apostolic Initiatives

Because of Ezra's exhausting schedule during the past months and because Flora faced major surgery, they were urged to take a vacation and to enjoy the Christmas holidays with their family. Leaving Reed and Mark to supervise the younger children, they spent four days in Cache Valley. No resort seemed as alluring as this special place; and with their new car and surfaced roads, it was only a two-hour drive. After passing through Ogden and Brigham City and emerging from Sardine Canyon, they entered the wide valley, now blanketed with snow, whose early history was so intimately interwoven with the name Ezra Taft Benson.

This was home. Here their ancestral roots ran deep. In Logan was the imposing temple where Ezra had been endowed and his parents had been sealed; here, too, were the places where they had first met and become better acquainted, the college campus and the gracious Amussen home. Driving northward through Smithfield, Richmond, and Cove, they entered Idaho at Franklin. From there it was only a few minutes' drive to Whitney and then on to Preston. Places all along this route aroused memories of the past, good memories of family, friends, schooling, youthful aspirations, courtship, and early married life.

At Whitney was the old family home where Ezra was born, then occupied by Orval and his family. This loyal brother, his partner and friend, had remained on the family farm and, in the tradition of his ancestors, had become a pillar in the community, tilling the soil while serving for many years as bishop of the Whitney Ward. Despite the distinction Ezra had attained, one wonders whether he harbored a benign envy of his brother, who was living the kind of life Ezra had always aspired to. Regardless of the worldwide travels that lay ahead and the even greater distinctions the future held, Ezra Taft Benson's heart always remained in this remote place that was sacred to him. He would end his mortal journey here, buried beside Flora in the small Whitney cemetery, near his parents and other kin.

Four days after a joyous Christmas with all the family gathered around, Flora entered the hospital to undergo three hours of corrective abdominal surgery. She was hospitalized for ten days afterward. During her convalescence, Ezra divided his time between the home and his office. At the office he settled into his headquarters assignments. A key responsibility was as Executive Secretary of the Melchizedek Priesthood Committee. This committee, of which he also was a member, filtered out matters affecting the priesthood worldwide, bringing to the Twelve, and later to the First Presidency, the crucial items the committee had studied and the recommendations it proposed. Under Elder Benson's direction, the committee prepared a new *Melchizedek Priesthood Handbook.* Later he also resumed duties as an adviser to the YMMIA and YWMIA and as chairman of the committee to analyze all reports and statistics and to make recommendations. In his role as a member of the Twelve, he also served as a member of the Church Missionary Committee.

During January, Elder Benson was honored by appointment as a trustee of the American Institute of Cooperation. This connection enabled him to exert a continuing influence on American agriculture and its leaders and kept him in the public eye. It also provided an important national platform from which he could expound his economic and political views that always were intertwined with moral themes.

Before Elder Benson started again on the merry-go-round of stake conference assignments, it became apparent to the Brethren that he was spent. Nearly a year of living on the emotional edge had taken its toll. He had lost weight, tired easily, and did not seem as focused as before. Because of this and the fact that Flora still had not regained full strength, the First Presidency urged the couple to take a longer vacation. The family doctor recommended three weeks. Ezra agreed to one. They drove the Pontiac to the Salt River Valley, which Phoenix boosters had named the Valley of the Sun. No publicity was given to their trip, else Elder Benson would have been inundated with requests to speak. They quietly holed up and while absorbing the warmth of the desert sun, read, wrote in their diaries, drove about the valley, ruminated about the past, and planned for the future. They returned to Salt Lake City, rested, relaxed, and ready to go to work.

In late February, Elder Benson resumed stake conference assignments with a vengeance. Over a period of several weeks, he held training and general meetings in the Chicago, New York, Florida, and Washington, D.C., stakes. Because his work in Europe had been well publicized in the Church press, he had acquired something of a celebrity status. This attracted large crowds to the public meetings where his eloquence and fervent testimony lifted and motivated the people. His most effective work, however, was performed behind the scenes while he trained the local leaders, bringing to bear the weight of his rich administrative experience gained at home and abroad.

The conference in Jacksonville, Florida, was especially

161

significant. Except for a stake created in Cache Valley on February 2, 1947, this was the newest stake in the Church. It had been created on January 19, 1947, by Elders Charles A. Callis and Harold B. Lee. Two days later, Elder Callis died in Jacksonville. Elder Lee conducted his funeral there and returned home with the body. Because of the unity in the Twelve, Elder Callis's death was like losing a member of the family. So Elder Benson's feelings were subdued as he met with the Jacksonville Saints, who, because of Elder Callis's long service in the South as mission president, looked upon him as a father. The vacancy in the Twelve created by Elder Callis's death was filled at the general conference in April 1947, when Elder Henry D. Moyle was called.

Flora joined her husband for the stake conference in Washington, D.C. It was like a homecoming, as their many friends showered them with love and attention. Afterward, on assignment from the Brethren, Ezra inspected and reported on farming properties owned by the Church near Palmyra, New York. While there, at the cradle of the Church, he and Flora visited places of historic interest: the homes of Joseph Smith Sr., Martin Harris, and Peter Whitmer Sr. Most significant, however, were visits to Hill Cumorah, where the Book of Mormon plates were delivered to the Prophet Joseph Smith by the angel Moroni, and the Sacred Grove, where the Restoration began. Seeing these places, and reflecting on the extraordinary events that took place there, imbued the Bensons with a deeper sense of awe about the divine origins of the Church.

Elder Benson's celebrity status prompted more speaking requests than were received by most General Authorities. Although it was not possible for him to accept all of these invitations, he did accept what seemed to be an inordinately large number. These included talks given at ward sacrament meetings, firesides, civic groups, and agricultural associations. He also continued with the many council and report meetings at headquarters, personal interviews, and a burgeoning correspondence. This latter activity grew following his mission to Europe because he kept in touch with many he had met there. His prominence and youth and his pleasing personality also attracted an increasing number of young people who asked him to perform their temple sealings. All this was interspersed with regular stake conference assignments.

The summer of 1947 brought a welcome pause in Ezra's crowded schedule. It began with a farewell for Reed on June 22, prior to his departure for a mission in Great Britain. Ordinarily his call would have come nearer his nineteenth birthday, January 2. However, the complications and commitments attending his father's return from Europe dictated a delay that enabled Reed to complete another semester at BYU before leaving. The meeting was held in the Yale Ward chapel, the building where President George Albert Smith also worshipped. It was filled to capacity. The prophet was present and made brief concluding remarks. In them he wished the missionary godspeed and characterized the Bensons as one of the most exemplary families in the Church. It was an accolade Ezra treasured. His diary typically gave the chief credit to Flora, who reciprocated that same feeling toward her husband. Family rearing was a team effort with Ezra and Flora Benson. Whatever success they attained in rearing their six children they attributed to the blessings of heaven and to the love, cooperation, and diligence they brought to the task.

In early July following Reed's departure, the rest of the family enjoyed a week's vacation at Yellowstone National Park and Jackson Hole, Wyoming. It was the kind of outing that mirrored the Benson character, featuring hiking, horseback riding, and enjoyment of the scenic beauty of the park. Later in the month they enjoyed the festivities connected with the centennial celebration of the arrival of the Mormon Pioneers in the Salt Lake Valley. The family attended the July 24 unveiling of the impressive monument at the mouth of Emigration Canyon in commemoration of the event. At the unveiling, hundreds of sea gulls flocked around the

monument, drawn there by the foresight of centennial committee members who all summer had had feed strewn
around the monument in mid-morning each day.
Accustomed to receiving breakfast there, the birds appeared
at the usual hour on the twenty-fourth, adding a symbolic
significance to the occasion. For the family, the unveiling
had a deeper and far more personal meaning. While paying
public homage to the pioneers as a group, they privately
honored their ancestor, the first Ezra Taft Benson, who was a
member of the pioneer company led by Brigham Young. The
family also enjoyed other happenings connected with the
centennial—the mammoth parade, sporting events, and the
play titled *Promised Valley*, staged outdoors at the University
of Utah Stadium and featuring an original score and prominent performers.

In August, Elder Benson traveled to Colorado with
Mark to attend the annual meeting of the American Institute
of Cooperation (AIC). He was the concluding speaker.
Influenced undoubtedly by the devastation he had seen in
Europe and by the initial clashes between the Soviet Union
and the West, precursors of the cold war, Elder Benson
developed themes that would be sounded over and over
during the following decades. He underscored America's
status as a land choice above all others, warned that peace
was fragile and that dangers lurked ahead, deplored the tendency toward indifference, and admonished all Americans
to be more faithful, prayerful, and loyal. Though composed
mostly of people who were not members of the Church, the
institute received the talk with appreciation, even enthusiasm, as did many others throughout the land. It was rare for
a public figure to treat such topics with the frankness and
fervency shown by Ezra Taft Benson. He never failed to
exhibit these qualities in his speaking, regardless of the time
or the place.

There was a similar reaction to a talk he gave before the
AIC in Omaha, Nebraska, in March 1948. On this occasion,
however, he shared the spotlight with seven-year-old

Bonnie, who had accompanied her dad to Omaha. The press was so intrigued by the poise of the little girl, and by the anomalous example of a father bringing such a young child on such a long trip to attend such a distinguished function, that a picture of Bonnie was featured on the front page the next morning. But to Elder Benson the incident was not an anomaly. He frequently took the children with him on out-of-town trips, both as a means of cementing good relations and of educating them.

The themes developed in these two talks before the AIC were condensed afterward in an article Ezra prepared for the *Improvement Era,* titled "Survival of the American Way of Life." Some in the Church thought it strange that Elder Benson would speak out so strongly on such a subject so soon after America and its Allies had thoroughly defeated their enemies in World War II and while the United States was in the midst of shifting from a wartime economy. A main reason for his anxiety clearly is traceable to his experiences in Europe. He had seen how civilization could be shattered as the result of ideological extremism. And while Naziism had been crushed, he saw a greater danger in monolithic communism, whose clearly stated aim was to export its atheistic beliefs and rigid political and economic dogma throughout the world. He seemed driven to awaken America to the dangers he foresaw, and no amount of criticism could deter him from speaking out. He later was bolstered in this attitude by eight years of experience at the heart of American government and by encouragements from President David O. McKay, who shared his concerns about the aims and the dangers of international communism.

Meanwhile, there was more excitement within the Benson family. In the spring of 1948, Mark received a call to serve in the Eastern States Mission, with headquarters in New York City. His farewell testimonial was held in the Yale Ward chapel on May 2, his nineteenth birthday. An overflow audience attended. A reception was held in the Benson home afterward. Mark's departure nine days later created mixed feelings in the family—happiness he was worthy to serve, and sadness at losing his companionship for two years. His departure also created a nagging concern in the parents about which the children were unaware. Supporting two sons in the mission field at the same time created a serious financial drain that ate into the Bensons' small savings. However, like so many other Latter-day Saint couples faced with the same problem, they swallowed hard and went back to work.

The work for Ezra was one continual round of travel, meetings, interviews, study, writing, counseling, and speaking. His talk at the April 1948 general conference, the first general conference to be televised, was especially challenging. He used the occasion to expound what had now become his favorite themes—the choice status of America and the dangers to it posed by alien doctrines. He traced the evolution of the Jaredite and Nephite civilizations in America and, citing 2 Nephi 1:7, said it would be a "land of liberty" to those who possessed it if they would serve Jesus Christ "according to the commandments which he hath given." He identified the chief danger facing America as "the spread of coercive man-made systems." Then becoming specific, he warned against communism, whose militant doctrines, he said, posed "one of the greatest conflicts ever known to man." To him the conflict went far beyond the bounds of earthly politics and statesmanship and involved "eternal principles of right and wrong." While acknowledging that the message of the Church to the world was one of peace, love, and the restored gospel, he added, "At the same time we stand firmly in support of the principles enunciated in the Constitution and the Declaration of Independence, and every Latter-day Saint would defend to the last those eternal principles" (in Conference Report, Apr. 1948, pp. 82–87).

Much was heard about the issue of communism during 1948, a presidential election year. Thomas E. Dewey, a conservative Republican, was opposed to the incumbent Democrat, Harry E. Truman. Because of Ezra's expertise in agriculture, his conservative views, and his high profile position in a church known for its conservatism, the Dewey campaign targeted him for support, for counsel on key issues, and for possible service in the administration should Dewey be elected. The candidate visited Elder Benson in Salt Lake City during the campaign, and later at Dewey's request the two visited in Chicago. Out of these contacts came feelers about Ezra's joining the Dewey cabinet, but Ezra put off any serious discussions about that possibility until after the election. They never took place because of Truman's upset victory, a victory Ezra attributed in large part to the overconfident attitude of Dewey and his team. Still, Elder Benson's involvement in behind-the-scenes activities of this 1948 campaign, his sound counsel, his professional credentials in agriculture, his personal appeal, and his proven ability as a Washington operative doubtless impressed the political professionals in the Republican party who had him in mind for the future.

A few months after the election, Elder Benson had an opportunity to visit President Truman in the White House. This occurred while the Apostle was in the East to be inducted as a member of the executive board of the Boy Scouts of America. Flora was with him. He extended to President Truman the best wishes of President George Albert Smith and discussed with the chief executive the Church's predominant emphasis on the family, while assuring him of the support and the prayers of the membership of the Church.

On the way home, Ezra and Flora paid another visit to the Sacred Grove, near Palmyra, New York. Swept up in a spiritual reverie as they stood together alone in that special place, they received a powerful confirmation of the truth of the Prophet Joseph Smith's account of what took place there when he kneeled to pray as a young boy.

During this period Elder Benson developed problems

with his digestive system. It was a disorder shared by not a few of his brethren. The main causes were an erratic diet induced by constant travel, overwork, tension from personal or ecclesiastical concerns, and lack of adequate exercise. Recognizing the problem, which was aggravated by the rapid growth of the Church, the Brethren took a major step in 1949 to reduce their work load when it was decided that General Authorities would attend stake conferences semi-annually instead of quarterly. This provided for more week-ends at home. As he did not participate in recreational sports, Elder Benson began to get more exercise by working more often in his big yard. He also began to spend more time relaxing with Flora and the girls in family outings. All this had a positive effect on his health and outlook.

Two significant family events drew Ezra and Flora to New York in December 1949. The first was a performance of the Utah Centennial Chorus at a meeting of the National Association of Manufacturers in the Waldorf-Astoria Hotel. The chorus, of which Mark was the president, was composed of missionaries in the Eastern States Mission. The missionary achievements of this son revealed a talent for leadership and administration that later would find expression in many positions of responsibility, including service as a mission president and as a stake president.

A few days after the performance of the Centennial Chorus, Ezra and Flora met Reed in New York City as he debarked from the *Queen Mary*. He had completed two and a half years of successful missionary work in Great Britain. It was a source of gratitude to his parents that Reed had served as president of the Newcastle District, which included the same area in northern England over which Elder Benson had served as conference president almost thirty years before. This son, too, developed good leadership and speaking skills in the mission field. These were evident later when he served as a mission president and as a regional coordinator of the John Birch Society, a patriotic organization whose object was to thwart the spread of international communism.

At the direction of President George Albert Smith, Reed was called on a short-term mission in the eastern states. The mission president appointed him to serve with his brother in Washington, D.C., where Mark was the district president. Here many doors were opened to the brothers through the influence and wide reputation of their father and through their own initiatives and hard work. Six months later when Reed and Mark were released, Elder Benson took Barbara and Beverly with him to meet their brothers in the East and to come home together. Flora did not accompany them because she had not fully recovered from additional surgery she underwent in April. As he always did for the sake of economy, Elder Benson joined this pleasant outing with his children with a responsibility he had to attend special meetings of the Boy Scouts of America.

Once the duties were behind and the sons had been released, Elder Benson and the four children started westward by automobile on a leisurely journey to visit Church historical sites. From New York, where the early events took place, they traveled to Kirtland, Ohio. The stately temple, and streets bearing names like Joseph and Cowdery, reminded them that this was the site of the first permanent Latter-day Saint community. This made Kirtland famous, as did the spiritual phenomena that occurred when the temple was dedicated.

The area around Nauvoo, Illinois, held special interest for the Bensons. To the south was Quincy, where the first Ezra Taft Benson was converted and baptized. And southeast was Carthage, where the Prophet Joseph Smith and his brother Hyrum were martyred. While they were unable to locate the site of their ancestral home in Nauvoo, the home of Bishop Vinson Knight, where Ezra T. Benson and his family first stayed in Nauvoo, still stood, adjacent to the home of Brigham Young and a short distance north of the Prophet's Mansion House.

The long drive across Iowa—past Garden Grove, where Grandfather George T. Benson was born in a wagon box; past Council Bluffs, where Great-grandfather Ezra T. was ordained to the apostleship—and across Nebraska and Wyoming was enlivened by reading excerpts from Church history and by reflecting on the vast changes in transportation and accommodations and in the status of the Church that had occurred in a hundred years.

Following their arrival in Salt Lake City, Reed and Mark reported their missions in the Yale Ward chapel. While they were traveling home, their neighbor and friend, President George Albert Smith, had been in the East to attend the unveiling of monuments in Whitingham, Vermont, and in the rotunda of the Capitol in Washington, D.C., honoring President Brigham Young. Later in the summer, the prophet traveled to Hawaii to participate in the centennial of the beginning of proselyting in Hawaii. On August 8, 1950, during President Smith's absence, Elder George F. Richards, President of the Twelve, passed away. This set in motion a chain of events that had far-reaching impact on the Church and on Elder Benson and his brethren of the Twelve. At the following general conference in October, President David O. McKay was sustained as President of the Quorum of the Twelve, while retaining his position as Second Counselor in the First Presidency. At the same time, Elder Joseph Fielding Smith was sustained as the Acting President of the Twelve, and Elder Delbert L. Stapley was sustained as the newest member of the Twelve, filling the vacancy created by the death of President George F. Richards. And President Smith hinted at still more changes to come when, during his remarks concluding the conference, he said, "But in six months, we do not know what may occur" (*Improvement Era*, Dec. 1950, p. 1023).

This was the last time President Smith addressed a general conference of the Church. During the ensuing six months, his health, which always had been fragile, began to deteriorate. By the first of April 1951, it was apparent the end was near. The aged prophet passed away quietly on Wednesday, April 4, his eighty-first birthday. Because of the timing of President Smith's death, it was necessary to rearrange some of the general conference sessions. The funeral was held in the Salt Lake Tabernacle on Saturday morning, April 7. In the passing of President Smith, Elder Benson lost not only a respected leader but also a good friend. Despite the difference in their ages, there was a close, congenial rapport between them. Both were the descendants of distinguished Church leaders whose names they bore. It was at the suggestion of President Smith that Elder Benson began to use his full name to distinguish him from his great-grandfather Ezra T. Benson. President Smith had done the same, using his full name to distinguish himself from his ancestor George A. Smith, an Apostle and former member of the First Presidency.

Because the worldwide demands of the rapidly growing Church required it, there was no delay in reorganizing the First Presidency. The Twelve assembled in the upper room of the temple on Monday morning, April 9, for this purpose. After discussion, and on motion duly seconded, David O. McKay was approved as the ninth President of the Church and ordained and set apart by the other Apostles. He then dropped an unexpected bombshell by nominating Stephen L Richards as First Counselor and J. Reuben Clark as Second Counselor. Everyone was stunned. All had assumed President Clark, who had served as the First Counselor to both President Heber J. Grant and President George Albert Smith, would be renamed to that position. Realizing that President McKay was entitled to designate whom he wished to work beside him and in what order, Elder Benson joined with the other Apostles in sustaining this action. Yet he and the other members of the Twelve were concerned that President Clark would be distraught. While he struggled over what was interpreted by some as a demotion, President Clark was resilient and stoically accepted the change. At the solemn assembly where he was sustained as second counselor, President Clark taught Elder Benson, and indeed the whole Church, a great lesson when he emphasized that the criterion for success is not where one serves but how. Influenced by President Clark's example, Elder Benson later formulated two catchphrases he used repeatedly in guiding and motivating his brethren: "It's the Spirit that counts," he would often tell them, and "What's best for the Church?"— the criterion he would apply in arriving at difficult decisions.

The ascension of President McKay to the prophetic office had little effect on Elder Benson's work as a member of the Twelve. He continued to fill the same quorum assignments as before and to travel throughout the Church as before, holding stake conferences and touring missions. He continued to speak out on public issues, using the platform of the AIC to reach a national audience. And as the presidential campaign began to heat up in 1952, he became more concerned about the political and social issues facing the nation.

He spoke out forcefully about these issues, as he did about any issue that troubled him, regardless of the forum. So at the April 1952 general conference, he gave "frank and forthright consideration of some of the problems" faced "not only as a Church but also as a great Christian nation." Continuing, he told the Tabernacle audience, "We seem to live in a world of conflict, insecurity, uncertainty, and almost bewilderment." He then characterized the United States as "the richest nation in all the world," noting this had been accomplished "on about 6% of the land area of the world by a relatively small group of people, only 7% of the world's population." He attributed this to divine causes. "The prophets of God foreshadowed these achievements," he said, "when they predicted that this would be a land choice above all other lands and that it would be preserved for a righteous people."

He ascribed the nation's economic plenty to heavenly influences and its political strength to a benign constitution established "by the hands of wise men . . . raised up unto this very purpose." Despite this picture of peace, plenty, and prosperity, he sounded a dire warning: "I feel in my own heart that during the hour of our success is our greatest danger. I feel firmly that even during the hour of great prosperity, a nation may sow the seeds of its own destruction." He cited several conditions tending toward that: sexual excesses and the limitation of families, the waste of natural resources, the failure to teach high moral principles, the rising cost of government, depreciation of the currency, confiscatory taxation, and an expanding bureaucracy. He then prescribed tests to be applied in deciding future policies and strongly admonished his listeners: "I think, my brethren and sisters, as Latter-day Saints and as American citizens, we need to rouse ourselves to the problems that confront us as a great Christian nation. . . . We need a nationwide repentance to rid this land of corruption. We must return to the fundamental virtues that have made this nation great." Finally, he offered a prayer toward that end: "God help us that we may not drift farther from the principles of faith and honor established by those noble founding fathers and the pioneers who settled these valleys" (in Conference Report, Apr. 1952, pp. 57–61).

This talk, with its strong political overtones, would not have gone unnoticed by the leaders of the Republican party, who had had their eye on Ezra Taft Benson for several years. And at the time it was given, these political leaders were engaged in a major effort to persuade General Dwight D. Eisenhower to run for president on the Republican ticket. General Eisenhower was then the supreme commander of the Allied powers in Europe, the military force of the North Atlantic Treaty Organization (NATO). The general resigned his NATO command in late May 1952; and in early June he delivered an important address in Abilene, Kansas, at the dedication of the Eisenhower home as a memorial to his parents. The talk focused on four key points that he said were threats to the American way of life: the substitution of punitive laws for the cooperative spirit among the people, inflation that debased the value of money, excessive taxation that destroyed incentives, and bureaucracy that usurped functions of the local community and the individual.

The similarity of the views and the style of these two men is apparent. Both came from a rural background and looked for a revival of American values they felt had been lost. Both were forthright men who minced no words and who had no secret agenda. They had a crusading spirit and were vigorous and positive in their outlook. Both had a deep-seated faith, and both loved their country and the American way of life and sought to perpetuate them for future generations. The mutual confidence that grew between them when finally they were brought together is easy to understand.

Chapter 12

Into the Maelstrom

Elder Benson watched the 1952 presidential campaign with great interest. Although his position in the Church made it impossible to be involved actively, he had strong views about it and expressed them privately. His choice among the Republican hopefuls was Senator Robert Taft, not because they were distantly related, but because the senator's conservative views accorded with his own. Those views were rooted in the basic concepts of maximum freedom for the individual and a limited role for government in domestic affairs. He did not know General Eisenhower personally, although he shared the positive view of him held by most Americans, that of a genial, likable man who had done an excellent job as the commander of Allied forces in Europe during World War II, and later as the commander of the military forces in NATO. Nor did he know anything about the general's political views, other than what he might have learned from reports of his Abilene speech.

Unlike 1948, when he was aggressively courted by the

Dewey people, Elder Benson had received no overtures from the Eisenhower campaign after the general had been nominated at the Republican convention. For that reason it came as a surprise when, on Thursday, November 20, 1952, he received a telephone call from a friend, Utah Senator Arthur V. Watkins, who said major support for Ezra's appointment as U.S. secretary of agriculture was being generated. The senator asked whether Elder Benson would be interested in the position and available to accept. Senator Watkins, a former stake president, understood perfectly when Ezra told him that decision rested with President David O. McKay.

The next morning, President McKay advised Ezra that he had been contacted about his availability for a cabinet appointment. The prophet said his mind was "clear in the matter" and that Ezra should accept if the invitation came "in the proper spirit" (Ezra Taft Benson, *Cross Fire: The Eight Years with Eisenhower* [Garden City, N.Y.: Doubleday & Co., 1962], p. 5). Ezra doubted the invitation would come. He had never even seen General Eisenhower in person, much less met him or spoken to him. Had it been Thomas E. Dewey four years earlier, Ezra's reaction would have been otherwise.

The following weekend, Elder Benson and Mark E. Petersen were assigned to divide the Sharon Stake in Utah Valley, creating the two hundredth stake in the Church. Ironically, Arthur V. Watkins had been installed as the first president of the Sharon Stake in 1929. On Saturday afternoon between meetings, Flora reached her husband in Clark's Men's Store in downtown Provo, where he had gone to purchase a new suit. She said General Eisenhower's headquarters in New York City were trying to reach him. He went immediately to the nearby campus of Brigham Young University. Finding a secluded office, he first sought direction through meditation and prayer. He next called President McKay to advise him of the contact from Eisenhower's headquarters. The prophet repeated his previous counsel. Ezra then called Republican headquarters in New York and, in the absence of the general, talked with his brother, Milton S. Eisenhower, who was helping organize the new administration. Apparently Elder Benson ranked high on the list of potential cabinet members, largely because of the recommendations of his friend Milton Eisenhower, who had served as director of information and as land-use coordinator for the Department of Agriculture during much of the time Ezra served as the NCFC executive secretary. Because Milton also had served as editor of the *Yearbook of Agriculture*, he knew personally of Ezra's work and reputation not only as a professional but also as a devoted and patriotic American. Milton's recommendation of Ezra Taft Benson as secretary of agriculture would have carried great weight with General Eisenhower.

After completing the organizational work for the new stake with Elder Petersen, Ezra drove to Salt Lake City that Saturday evening. Shortly after midnight, he boarded a red-eye flight for New York City. Flora, with customary efficiency, had packed his bags. Most important, she had expressed confidence in the purpose and outcome of his trip and to that end had joined him and other members of the family in a special fast and in prayer. It was a typical Benson approach to a new and unstructured situation.

Arriving in New York at noon on Sunday, Ezra went right to bed. A nagging cold and medication he had taken, combined with the night flight, had exhausted him. He arose refreshed on Monday morning. After engaging in fervent prayer for direction, he joined Milton Eisenhower for lunch. There his friend briefed him about the two o'clock appointment with the general. Ezra was surprised to learn that he was the only one being interviewed for the appointment as secretary of agriculture. Milton's recommendation, and endorsements by Republican leaders, including Senator Robert Taft, had convinced General Eisenhower that Ezra Taft Benson was his man, subject to a personal interview.

"He looked younger than his pictures indicated," Ezra

wrote of his first introduction to Dwight D. Eisenhower. "As vigor was his dominant quality, the lively, blue, direct eyes were his most striking feature. You knew in an instant they mirrored the inner man, that they would reveal all his quick changing moods; interest, welcoming warmth, delight, icy rebuke or cold anger" (ibid., p. 11).

Obviously satisfied with what he saw in his visitor, Mr. Eisenhower came directly to the point, inviting Ezra to join his cabinet as secretary of agriculture. Responding, Ezra raised several questions concerning, for instance, the fact that he did not support Eisenhower before the convention, the prudence of appointing a clergyman to the cabinet, and his reservations about the wisdom of a military man serving in the White House. The answers were disarming, being in essence that politics necessarily entails diversity, that Eisenhower's aim of improving America's moral fiber would be enhanced by the presence of a clergyman in his cabinet, and that concern about the general's military background underscored the need for civilians to surround him. Once assured he would never be asked to promote any measure with which he disagreed because of conscience or philosophy, and after Mr. Eisenhower pointedly said Ezra could not refuse to serve his country, Ezra accepted.

The news of Ezra Taft Benson's appointment evoked widespread and conflicting responses. The farm professionals were almost unanimous in their approval, confident his policies would be dictated by principle, not political expediency. Even the leaders of the American Farm Bureau Federation and the National Farmers' Union, consistently at odds on key issues, were together on this one. Conservative Republicans could not have been happier. And there was a sense of euphoria among members of the Church, many of whom felt the appointment, in some way, was a vindication of the Church.

Not everyone shared these complimentary views. Most Democrats in Congress, who had either crafted or had consistently endorsed the existing farm policies, were wary of the appointee. His conservative views were well known to most of them. There was justified concern he would endeavor to scale back, if not eliminate, the bloated system of farm subsidies that had grown up over the years. And there were many farmers, regardless of political affiliation, who enjoyed the benefits of generous farm subsidies and who, therefore, were not enthusiastic about the appointment. Other opposition came from an expected source: from those who believed the appointment of a clergyman violated the principle of separation of church and state, and from those who disparaged the views of Elder Benson's church. Among the most outspoken of these was the general secretary of the American Council of Churches, who complained that pagan religions were no more hostile to the Christian faith than was Mormonism. He never made clear the relevance of that criticism to Ezra Benson's ability to direct the affairs of the Department of Agriculture.

The vast majority of Americans greeted the appointment with typical indifference. The novelty of a clergyman in the cabinet, the first since Edward Everett was appointed secretary of state in 1852, soon subsided. The general public seemed willing to let Mr. Benson go about his work, whatever that was, while reserving the right to weigh in with criticisms at will.

Meanwhile, the impact of the appointment on Elder Benson was bewildering. He was inundated with hundreds of letters, telegrams, telephone calls, and personal contacts congratulating him or seeking some favor or endorsement. While trying to cope with these, responding personally to as many as possible, he faced the daunting task of laying the groundwork for his administration, attending confirmation hearings, temporarily laying aside his Church duties, and making necessary arrangements for the family, all in a period of less than two months.

He left Salt Lake City on December 2, 1952, on a twenty-day tour of the United States. His purpose was to gain a broad perspective of his new duties by interviewing farmers, farm professionals, educators, business and government leaders, and any others directly affected by agriculture policies. In the process he also was looking for qualified people to serve on his staff and on an agriculture advisory committee. It was a pressure-filled trip, entailing long hours in meetings and crowded travel schedules complicated by increased passenger loads as the holidays neared. Ezra was encouraged by the positive reception he received and by the caliber of those who pledged their support, including former president Herbert Hoover and General Douglas MacArthur. He was heartened by President Hoover's volunteered public endorsement of his plans to reorganize the sprawling agriculture department. Ezra interrupted the tour long enough to return home to perform the temple sealing for his son Mark to Lela Wing of Alberta, Canada, the first marriage among his six children.

The confirmation hearing was a combative prelude to what lay ahead in Ezra's frequent jousts with Congress. He sparred with Senator Milton R. Young of North Dakota, who tried unsuccessfully to elicit a statement from the nominee about his stand on price supports. Senator Allen J. Ellender of Louisiana attacked him for failing to prescribe specific remedies for defects he saw in the current policies. Ezra's previous experience with congressional committees had prepared him well for these encounters. He sailed through the confirmation process without serious difficulty.

What he found more difficult was severing regular contact with his brethren of the General Authorities. He genuinely loved them, and he loved his responsibilities in the Twelve. To give up the rewarding associations with these men, and with leaders and members throughout the Church, if only temporarily, was not easy. Had the decision been his alone, he would not have accepted the cabinet appointment. But when General Eisenhower had placed the appointment on the ground of patriotic duty and when President McKay had encouraged him to accept it, he had no viable alternative.

A blessing given him by President McKay put the matter in proper perspective and filled him with vigorous resolve. In it the prophet endowed him with sound judgment and clear vision, urged him to function in the spirit of his apostolic calling, promised his decisions would be inspired as he prayed and lived as he ought, and admonished him to defend the rights and privileges of the individual guaranteed by the Constitution and to be fearless in condemning any subversive influences that threatened them. This last element of the blessing would assume an ever-increasing importance to Elder Benson, extending into the years following his service in the cabinet.

Ezra attended a pre-inaugural meeting of the new cabinet on January 12, 1953. Flora joined him later in Washington, D.C., for the inaugural ceremonies, as did Reed who was then serving as a chaplain in the air force stationed at San Antonio, Texas. The girls stayed in Salt Lake City, where they and their mother would live until school ended for the year. Mark was in Palo Alto, California, with his new bride and occupied with graduate studies at Stanford.

The inauguration ceremonies at the Capitol on January 20 launched what was later called the "Eisenhower Crusade." After being sworn in by Supreme Court Chief Justice Fred M. Vinson, the new president led the mammoth inaugural parade down Pennsylvania Avenue to the White House. Seated in a convertible with Flora, Ezra was in awe of the cheering, waving crowd, estimated at 750,000, gathered to usher in a new administration of the world's most powerful nation. The pageantry of the event, the flags, the floats, the bands, the martial airs, and the disciplined, razor-sharp drill teams seemed to immerse him in a sense of unreality. It was a long and tortuous track that had led him from the remote and sheltered anonymity of Whitney to this place upon which the eyes of the world were focused.

Chief Justice Vinson administered the oath of office to Ezra the next day in the Gold Room, located in the east wing of the White House. Looking on were President Eisenhower

With President Dwight D. Eisenhower looking on, Elder Benson is sworn in as U.S. secretary of agriculture in January 1953 by Fred M. Vinson, chief justice of the Supreme Court

and other dignitaries. Most interested of all were Flora and Reed, who shared the notable event with their husband and father. Later they were driven to the USDA headquarters in a black Cadillac limousine, one of the many perquisites of Ezra's new position. Elder Benson had been in this building many times during his years of service with the NCFC, when he was only one of the nameless thousands who entered it to transact business or to seek information and direction. Now it was different. Everyone recognized him immediately, greeted him warmly, and deferred to his every wish.

The spacious private office of Secretary Benson had an intimidating aspect about it. From this command post, he would direct the work of 78,000 USDA employees. About eight thousand of these were housed in the USDA Administration and South Buildings in Washington, D.C. The remainder worked out of ten thousand branch offices located throughout the United States and in fifty countries. The budget needed to operate this vast bureaucracy in its multiple activities was $2.1 billion for 1953, the second largest of the civilian departments. The task of streamlining, harnessing, and motivating this huge army of workers to reach his goals was the first major challenge of the new secretary. As he inspected the office with Flora and Reed, the place where he would spend most of his waking hours during the next eight years, Ezra Taft Benson doubtless felt the weight of that challenge. And doubtless, too, he approached it in the same attitude with which he had approached countless other challenges through the years, an attitude of prayerful self-confidence devoid of arrogance.

Ezra had rented a small apartment in Washington where he planned to get along on his own until his wife and the girls would join him in five months. Before returning to Salt Lake after the inauguration, Flora had arranged her husband's clothes, stocked the refrigerator, placed family pictures about, and left him a note filled with expressions of love and instructions about where to find things and to buy things. It was typical of the way she had cared for him from the beginning, freeing him up to provide for the family and to do the work she had always felt he was destined to do. And aside from these mundane things and her emotional love, she had filled the role of adviser and counselor to her husband, providing perceptive observations about policies, politics, and personalities. Her departure created a great void in Ezra's life. The magnitude of that void was brought home when he returned to his little apartment the first night after she left. Seeing all around the evidences of her love and concern, he broke down and cried aloud. It was to be a lonely and stressful five months.

Aside from the immense task of taming, instructing, and moving the bureaucracy of his department, Ezra's main responsibilities were centered around his work with President Eisenhower and the cabinet and his dealings with Congress. From the moment of their first meeting in New

York, there had been an immediate bonding between Ezra and the president. They seemed to recognize in each other qualities in their own background and character. Both had been raised in a rural setting where they learned as youths to work hard, came from families who were prayerful and God-fearing, had excelled scholastically and in their professions, were deeply religious and patriotic, were vigorous and positive in their actions, and were anxious to elevate the spiritual tone of the nation. This last aspect of their relationship had emboldened Ezra to suggest to the president that the pre-inaugural cabinet meeting on January 12 be opened with prayer. Although the president was noncommittal when the subject was broached, he later called on Ezra unexpectedly to open the meeting with prayer.

The response had been so favorable that Ezra hoped that opening cabinet meetings with prayer would become a regular practice. However, at the first regular cabinet meeting after the inauguration, the president failed to call on someone to pray. Ezra was disappointed. After mulling over the matter for several days, he sent the president a memo, asking about commencing all cabinet meetings with prayer. Eisenhower said he would take the matter under advisement; he wanted to be sure other cabinet members would feel comfortable about it. Later, without explanation, the president announced that all cabinet meetings would be commenced with prayer. The practice continued throughout Eisenhower's tenure. Ezra was highly gratified. He was convinced that the American nation owed its existence to divine favor, and he believed its future prosperity depended on God's approval, to be acquired by right conduct and earnest pleading. This conception is rooted deep in Mormon theology, which teaches that America is a land choice above all other lands and that the nation that possesses it must serve God or be swept off (see Ether 1:42; 2:9). So prayer in cabinet meetings was not an idle gesture to Ezra Taft Benson. It was fraught with deep significance and to him tapped the wellsprings of America's freedom and prosperity. Accordingly,

Ezra also followed the practice of commencing USDA staff meetings with prayer.

Ezra took the same approach in selecting his staff. "I [chose] my team prayerfully and carefully, asking God to give me a spirit of discernment" (*Cross Fire*, p. 31). That process prompted him to select Dr. Don Paarlberg of Purdue University as economic adviser, True D. Morse as under secretary, J. Earl Coke as assistant secretary, Clarence M. Ferguson as administrator of the extension service, and John H. Davis as president of the Commodity Credit Corporation. The only one of these Ezra had known previously was John H. Davis, whom he had selected as his successor as executive secretary of the NCFC. He learned about the qualifications of the others through his networking contacts among the agriculture experts and the academic community. He selected them for their professional competence without regard to religious affiliations. However, he wanted to know whether they were active in their own church, were happily married, and enjoyed their work. On the other hand, all his personal assistants were Latter-day Saints, who sometimes were called "the Mormon Mafia." They included D. Arthur Haycock (former personal secretary of President George Albert Smith), Milan Smith, Lorenzo Hoopes, and Daken Broadhead.

With his staff and assistants in place, Ezra lost no time in getting down to work. On his first day in office, he announced a regrouping of the twenty agencies and bureaus in the department into four main categories, each headed by a staff officer. This major change had been worked out before he took office with the aid of an advisory committee and using some ideas proposed by former president Herbert Hoover. "Instead of the heads of all these agencies and bureaus reporting directly to the Secretary as in the past," Ezra explained, "only four persons would now have to do so. We expected this to increase the effectiveness of internal operations and improve service to farmers" (ibid., p. 48).

These regroupings stirred up emphatic protest from

185

some Democratic quarters. The main source of complaint was the transfer of the Agricultural Conservation Programs (ACP) from the Production and Marketing Administration and the new requirement that the chairmanship of county ACP committees be rotated.

This controversy at the threshold of his administration robbed Secretary Benson of the usual period of grace accorded to new officeholders in Washington. His opponents lost no time in attacking him in Congress and in the media. He was put on the defensive immediately. His opponents scrutinized his statements intently, looking for hooks on which to hang their criticisms. They found a sharp one in his memo to the field explaining the department's reorganization. He had written that the country was entitled to expect "that everyone of us will give a full day's work for a day's pay." This was interpreted as an accusation that the department was filled with loafers and as a slur against the dedication of department employees. It created an explosion of protest. "I was learning that every word had to be twice weighed," Ezra wrote ruefully (ibid., p. 53).

As a means of calming the turmoil, and of placing his philosophy before the public, Ezra held a press conference on February 5, 1953. He was surprised at the apparent lack of rancor among the hundred or more media representatives present in the USDA auditorium. He affirmed that the department would uphold rigid price supports through 1954, honoring a campaign pledge made by the president. After that it would favor only flexible supports, necessary to protect farmers against disaster or to stabilize the economy but not to guarantee the farmer a living. To support this future policy, Secretary Benson expounded some of his ideas on government. In his view, subsidies to farmers that were not necessary to prevent disaster or stabilize the economy were an unwarranted invasion of the farmers' freedom. To him, freedom was more important than life itself; and to become dependent on unnecessary subsidies bound the farmer with subtle cords of restraint, weakening his will,

stifling his initiative, and blurring his vision. He then suggested that the criterion for judging the propriety of any policy or legislation was whether it improved the character and
the morale of the people.

This was stiff medicine for a generation of farmers who
had become accustomed to overgenerous subsidies; indeed,
some farmers had come to regard them as a matter of right.
Surprisingly, Secretary Benson's views, considered extreme
against the background of twenty years of Democratic rule,
evoked little adverse comment in the media. Perhaps misled into thinking this mild response meant his views had
wide acceptance, Ezra prepared confidently for his first
major address scheduled on February 11, 1953, in St. Paul,
Minnesota.

The forum was a meeting of the Central Livestock
Association. A continuing slide in beef prices made the three
thousand livestock operators present a tough audience for
Ezra's stiff-upper-lip philosophy. But he pulled no punches.
He told them straight out essentially what he had said at the
press conference. Cattlemen like farmers should operate in
a free market, unfettered by government subsidies, except
in cases of dire emergency. He urged the audience to return
to the "fundamental virtues" of freedom and independence
that had made America great. He said the United States
rested on a spiritual foundation and suggested that tamper-
ing with the spiritual verities of freedom and independence
placed the nation at peril.

The warm applause, and the lack of a strong reaction in
the St. Paul press, misled Ezra into the false belief that his
doctrine had carried the day. He learned differently when he
returned to Washington. He found the talk had stirred up a
hornets' nest of dissent. This confused him because his
remarks were almost a replay of the comments he had made
at the press conference. Suddenly he was catapulted into the
public eye like no other member of the new administration.
And standing alone in the glare of national publicity, he
became the favorite target of all who had grievances against

the Eisenhower regime. The media, sensing a good story, ran with it, giving wide coverage to Ezra's controversial ideas and his Mormon background. His picture found its way on to the covers of national magazines, including *Time*. He was caricatured, lampooned, and ridiculed, especially by the Democratic politicians. Senator Eugene McCarthy, for instance, said Secretary Benson reminded him of a man standing on a riverbank calling to a drowning man to take a deep breath of air.

So loud and insistent was the furor that dire predictions began to appear to the effect that because the secretary of agriculture was such a liability to the president, he would soon be dumped. Living alone, working long hours, and striving to get control of his unwieldy department, Ezra was almost overwhelmed by the weight of this constant drumbeat of criticism and abuse. Not having heard the president's reaction to all this, Ezra felt isolated and vulnerable. He was sustained during the ordeal by the unfailing support of Flora and the children and by the sense that the positions he had taken were sound and in the best interests of the country. When at last Ezra was invited to meet with the president, it was pleasing to hear him say he agreed with everything Ezra had said in St. Paul. He only questioned the timing of the speech. Accustomed to planning military campaigns, the president was inclined to map out a strategy long in advance and to approach an objective slowly and deliberately, sometimes using feints and subterfuge to mask his moves. Ezra, on the other hand, always used the direct approach, focusing like a laser on the objective and driving toward it with fixed intensity. This difference in method would appear again in their long relationship. But there was never a difference in their objectives nor in their patriotic commitment to the United States.

During the height of these attacks, Elder Harold B. Lee came to Washington, D.C., to conduct a stake conference. Feeling his friend had a special need to be buoyed up, he invited Elder Benson to sit on the stand and to speak. It was

Secretary Benson inspecting farmland during a period of drought

a welcome change for Ezra to be in the midst of his people and to enjoy the spirit of the meeting. In his remarks, Elder Lee said there would be many who would attempt to belittle Elder Benson and to destroy his reputation and influence and even to destroy him. But he declared that "the glory and majesty attached to the name Ezra Taft Benson" would never die as long as he continued to live the gospel, while those who sought his destruction would be "forgotten in the remains of Mother Earth" and "the odor of their infamy" would ever be with them. Ezra appreciated the strength and encouragement his friend offered and returned to his desk the next morning with renewed enthusiasm.

That was dampened, however, when he received a call

advising that Flora and Barbara had been injured in an automobile accident. Learning the injuries were not critical, he did not travel to Salt Lake City because of the press of his duties, but instead asked Reed to go there to render necessary assistance. He then commenced a special fast while praying for their rapid recovery. Flora and Barbara were soon up and about and suffered no permanent effects from their accident.

Ezra was able to break away to attend April general conference. His appearance in the Tabernacle was the first since his appointment to the cabinet. It created an electric effect among the audience. The members of the Church had watched the drama being played out in Washington and understandably were concerned about the rough treatment Elder Benson had received in the media. So his appearance at the pulpit of the Tabernacle was greeted with more than the customary interest. He told how grateful he was to be present and how he missed regular contacts with the Brethren. The solicitous concern of members of the Washington Stake, he said, especially President J. Willard Marriott, had in part compensated for his inability to fulfill regular Church assignments. He also expressed gratitude for the honor of serving in the cabinet, repeated the test he applied in determining the wisdom of government policies—whether they improved "the morale, the character, and the well-being of our people"—and urged Church members to pray for President Eisenhower. He then had this to say about America:

"Brethren and sisters, I love this great nation in which we live. To me it is not just another nation. It is my firm belief that the God of heaven raised up the founding fathers and inspired them to establish the Constitution of this land, and I believe that is Mormon doctrine. This is a part of my religious faith as it is of yours. This is a great and glorious nation, with a God-given, divine mission to perform for liberty-loving people everywhere. This mission cannot be performed unless America is kept strong and virile, unless this people adheres to those eternal principles embodied in the gospel and in the Constitution of our land" (in Conference Report, Apr. 1953, p. 40).

In his admonition to keep America "strong and virile" is seen the basic reasoning that underlay Elder Benson's strict policies governing agriculture in the United States. The talk also reveals his conception that the "divine mission" of the Church imposed by the Constitution carried with it responsibilities for "liberty-loving people everywhere."

Ezra sincerely believed his views would be widely accepted by the farmers of America, and others, if they but understood the issues and the principles involved. Because he felt they had been misled by the policies of past administrations, he decided to try to change their thinking through education and persuasion. He did this by means of articles and instructions published by the USDA (sometimes jocularly called the "epistles of the Apostle") and by speaking to farmers' groups throughout the country. The second means was more effective. Ezra was a gifted, persuasive speaker. Endowed with a natural eloquence developed by experience speaking at street meetings, at countless Church gatherings, and in public forums over the years, Ezra often could win people to his views if he could once get their ears. Utilizing that talent, he regularly sought opportunities to speak to groups interested in agriculture.

Secretary Benson also aggressively sought to speak to gatherings of those who were openly opposed to his views. So when Senator James Eastland of Mississippi on the Senate floor called him an enemy of the farmer, Ezra instructed his staff to accept the first invitation he received to speak in Mississippi. The opportunity came in April 1953, shortly after the general conference of the Church in Salt Lake City. The forum was a gathering of the Delta Cotton Council. The senator, a wealthy plantation owner in southern Mississippi, invited Secretary Benson to stay at his gracious manor. The night before the meeting, Ezra invited the senator to read his speech. In introducing the speaker the next day, Mr. Eastland told the twenty thousand listeners present they would not like what they were going to hear but that it would be good for them because it was the truth. Ezra was incredulous. It amazed him that the senator's thinking had been reversed merely by reading the speech. He also was astonished by the enthusiastic applause that followed and by the warm congratulations of many who were present. Afterward, Senator Eastland became a staunch supporter of Secretary Benson. The same could hardly be said of other Democratic legislators who were plotting to bring about the downfall of Ezra Benson and his upsetting philosophy.

Chapter 13

The Battle over Subsidies

The controversy between Secretary Benson and the legislators who chided him for his talks in St. Paul and Mississippi revolved around the question of subsidies. As it applied to agriculture, the word *subsidy* acquired a provocative meaning from policies developed in the 1930s as part of the New Deal. The means adopted by the Roosevelt administration to heal an agriculture crippled by the Depression was the Agricultural Adjustment Act. Its main purpose was to raise agricultural prices and to maintain them on a parity with industrial prices, using 1909 to 1914 as the base period. The device used to increase farm prices was to control production by paying farmers a subsidy to restrict their crops. The theory was that the reduction of crops, creating artificial scarcity, would translate into higher farm prices. The amount of the government subsidy was the difference between market price and parity.

When Secretary Benson took office, the prices of major crops were pegged at 90 percent of parity. As noted, he was committed to maintain these through 1954 because of President Eisenhower's campaign promise. But Ezra had made it clear he opposed rigid price supports beyond that date. Ideally, he preferred there be no supports at all. Realistically, he recognized the need for flexible supports to protect the farmer from unfair economic conditions. But he did not want to cripple the farmer by guaranteeing him an assured, fixed income, removing him from the economic tensions others faced.

With that, the battle lines were drawn. The proponents of rigid price supports decided that the best way to win was to get rid of the chief advocate of flexible supports, Ezra Taft Benson. To that end he was attacked relentlessly by members of Congress opposed to his views. The liberal press joined in with derogatory editorials and with telling cartoons that satirized his views. In addition, the professional Democrats combed Ezra's talks and writings, searching for ammunition with which to attack him.

The criticism of Secretary Benson escalated when price supports for other commodities were sought. In the autumn of 1953, several hundred cattlemen caravanned to Washington, D.C., to demand subsidies for beef. Secretary Benson refused firmly but not arbitrarily. He explained his thesis that beef prices were down temporarily because of a cyclical swing in the market, that they would rebound soon, and that it was important that cattlemen not be fettered by subsidies. The large number of supportive letters he received convinced Ezra that most cattlemen endorsed his views. Moreover, he suspected that many of the caravanners were "suitcase cowboys," speculators who had gone into the cattle business to take advantage of high beef prices and who had panicked when prices fell.

Ezra also denied requests that eggs be subsidized. This caused friction within the administration when Sherman Adams, Eisenhower's chief of staff, urged that the requests be granted. When Ezra refused, Adams, in an angry pique, accused him of unreasoning stubbornness and told him to get off his "puritanical white horse." Ezra continued to refuse, ignoring the exasperation of his colleague. It was a typical reaction. Ezra Taft Benson always held his temper in check. His refusal to retaliate in kind took the edge off many controversies and won many admirers. Sherman Adams later characterized him as being "rugged and right." President Eisenhower shared that appraisal, although he said Ezra did not always express his views with "the maximum of tact" (in Dwight D. Eisenhower, *The White House Years* [Garden City, N.Y.: Doubleday & Co., 1963], p. 354).

As the Eisenhower administration neared the end of its first year, there were many calls for Ezra Benson's dismissal. They came from both Democratic and Republican sources—from those who worried about his stand on subsidies and from those Republicans who feared his presence in the administration would hurt the party in the 1954 elections. Democrats in the House dramatized the rift by adopting two resolutions demanding Secretary Benson put price supports under livestock. These tactics did not shake the president's confidence in his secretary of agriculture, nor did they weaken his support of Ezra's policies. Indeed, in January, 1954, Ezra was elated when, in his address to Congress, President Eisenhower formally approved the policy of flexible supports on major commodities and recommended a modification of the formula for computing parity.

With this victory behind, Ezra's main objective was to drum up support for the president's package when it would come before Congress for debate and vote. To this end he launched a five-week talking tour during which he delivered eleven major speeches, three in the Corn Belt, two in Oklahoma, one in Colorado, two in the Deep South, one in California, one in New York, and one in Washington, D.C. In addition, he delivered many informal talks, participated in several press conferences and radio and television programs, and testified before congressional committees. His message was always the same wherever he spoke. He decried the existing policy of strict production controls. "But

Secretary Benson speaking to a national radio audience

America did not become a great country by restricting production," he told his audiences. "Progress and prosperity do not come from idle land any more than they do from shutdown factories. We need production for progress, efficiency for progress, wisely used abundance for progress" (*Cross Fire*, pp. 174, 175).

Ezra was heartened by the response he received to his message. At a meeting of the National Farmers' Union in Denver, for instance, an organization that consistently opposed his policies on price supports, he received a standing ovation. It was difficult to conceal his emotion as farmers crowded around him afterward. He was heartened, too, by a talk President Eisenhower gave on national television advocating flexible supports. Alluding to counsel he had received to avoid attempting a solution of the farm problem during an election year, the president said, "Though I have not been in this political business very long, I know that what is right for America is politically right" (ibid., p. 195).

Meanwhile, the battle in Congress was fought with intensity. The House Agriculture Committee created a furor by voting to raise price supports on dairy products. This would have taken agriculture in the opposite direction Ezra intended, broadening instead of shrinking subsidies. It obviously was an attempt to position the Democratic party for the election, portraying it as the friend of the dairy farmer. The effect of it was to stir Ezra into even greater activity to promote his ideas, not only personally, but through influential and loyal friends who shared his views. Typical of these was a group of close friends called the "He-Coons," who styled themselves as "agricultural minutemen." Ezra wrote of them: "Whenever agricultural storm clouds appeared particularly dark, they told me, they intended to gather in Washington on a moment's notice" (ibid., p. 69). Ezra was not reluctant to call on friends when he needed them. Relying on these and other dependable supporters, and backed solidly by the president, Secretary Benson launched an aggressive counter-offensive to persuade Congress to pass the Agricultural Act of 1954, which included the concept of flexible price supports. In the process it became necessary to make some concessions, something he was willing to do as long as it did not require a compromise of principle or of his main objective of obtaining flexibility in fixing subsidies.

Ezra brought a spiritual influence to bear on the outcome of this legislation when Flora and the children joined him in a special fast. He also used a psychological device to buoy up his resolve and self-confidence. This consisted of statements of Abraham Lincoln and Thomas Jefferson copied on a piece of paper that he carried in his wallet. "I do the very best I know how," read the Lincoln statement, "the very best way I can; and I mean to keep doing so till the end. If the end brings me out all right, what is said against me will soon be forgotten." The Jefferson statement included this: "To hesitate for fear of criticism is cowardly. If our cause is right be not afraid of criticism, advocate it, expound it, and, if need be, fight for it" (ibid., p. 71). President Benson apparently used this psychological device through the remainder of his life. Shortly before he was sustained as President of the Church, he showed the author a slip of paper removed from his wallet on which was typed 3 Nephi 22:17: "No weapon that is formed against thee shall prosper; and every tongue that shall revile against thee in judgment thou shalt condemn. This is the heritage of the servants of the Lord, and their righteousness is of me, saith the Lord."

The showdown came on August 9, 1954, when the Senate voted on the farm bill. The tension in the chamber spilled out to engulf the White House and the offices of the Department of Agriculture. Both the president and Ezra Benson were on trial. Despite strong counsel to the contrary, they had placed their reputations on the line by seeking major changes in agriculture legislation during an election year. Most pundits had predicted a major defeat. Instead the bill passed the Senate 49 to 44. In addition, Congress passed the Agricultural Trade Development and Assistance Act, known as Public Law 480. This provided for moving a billion dollars' worth of commodities into special trade and relief channels over a three-year period. "These two measures" wrote Ezra, "gave us the ability to launch a limited one-two punch against the complex farm problem" (ibid., p. 211).

The congressional action created a great sense of relief within the administration—and a sense of disbelief outside it. How had it happened? How had the administration won such a smashing victory against what appeared at first to be such insuperable odds? Most commentators ascribed it to Ezra Benson. "The principle of flexibility is established to replace rigidity," read the *Kiplinger Letter* for August 14, 1954. "To ram this through Congress took guts . . . in both Benson and Eisenhower. Benson was David against Goliath. . . . Eisenhower was his firm backer, contrary to much political advice. It was principle vs. politics, and much of the betting was on politics. Yet principle won." *Colliers Magazine* of September 17, 1954, referred to it as the biggest legislative victory of the Eisenhower administration and called Ezra Benson its hero.

Overnight the secretary of agriculture was transformed from the ugly duckling of the administration to its superstar. His endorsement or his active help on the political stump was sought by many legislators who were up for reelection, legislators who earlier in the year would have shunned him like the plague. Now, however, they sought to bask in the reflected renown of his achievement. Ezra accommodated as many of them as he could. He spent all of September on the road up through November 2, speaking every day except Sundays, in behalf of Republican congressional candidates. While overall the Republicans lost ground, a typical result for a mid-presidential term election, the candidates in farm states, whether Democrats or Republicans, who had endorsed Ezra Benson's views fared well.

When he accepted President Eisenhower's invitation to join the cabinet, Ezra agreed he would serve at least two years. As the second year wound down in December 1954, he wondered whether the time had come for him to leave. He reasoned that the notable successes in Congress and the recent election would enable him to depart "if not in a blaze of glory, at least with a few scattered bonfires." The opportunity to broach the subject arose four days before Christmas when Ezra took President Eisenhower to visit the beef cattle research station at Front Royal, Virginia. During the hour-and-a-half drive, he reminded the president of his commitment and told him, "I want to do what you wish in the matter, but for my part I would be more than happy and content to go back to my life's work in Utah." Flashing a quick look at him, the president shot back, "If you quit, I quit." With a smile, the president then offered to go to Salt Lake City to urge that he continue. Learning there was no pressure from his leaders to return, the president affirmed he was anxious that Ezra stay on in Washington. Ezra agreed willingly. (See ibid., p. 221.)

By this time, the Bensons were comfortably settled in their new home in the nation's capital. With the enthusiastic agreement of Flora and the children, Ezra had purchased a new home near Rock Creek Park, only a fifteen-minute drive from his office. There was something about it that reminded them of their home in Salt Lake City, although it was architecturally different. "There was plenty of room for the whole family," wrote Ezra. "The basement recreation area, I knew, would appeal to the children. A shuffleboard court could be built into the floor and there was space for our ping-pong table and for the group dancing we always liked as part of our family home nights" (ibid., p. 138). In their new home the Bensons perpetuated the simple, wholesome lifestyle they had always followed, despite the aura of fame and distinction surrounding Ezra's service in the president's cabinet. Their routines were marked by regular prayer and family home evenings; the children attended public schools; Flora, with the assistance of the girls and, indeed, of the whole family, managed the household without a maid; and they avoided the glitzy social life and entertainment so many Washington luminaries doted on. As already noted, the children at first were embarrassed to ride in the chauffeur-driven limousine; and when they were driven to school, they insisted on being let out several blocks away from it. Flora created a sensation when, in hosting a luncheon for the cabinet members' wives, she managed the whole affair with only the assistance of her daughters.

Such anomalous conduct for Washington society attracted widespread attention. Sensing a good story, Edward R. Murrow, host of the popular television show *Person to Person*, sought permission to televise the Benson family at home for one of his episodes. At first, Flora was adamantly opposed, not wanting the privacy of the home invaded in such a public way. She relented, however, when

Reed suggested it would be a good missionary opportunity to portray the lifestyle of a devoted Latter-day Saint family. The show simulated a Mormon family home evening with the girls singing and dancing, the boys talking about missionary work, and the parents discussing family values. Murrow reported it generated more positive public response than any show he staged.

The Bensons' social life was centered largely in the Church. They had many close Latter-day Saint friends with whom they socialized. The ties of Church and common goals shared with these friends provided Ezra and Flora with a relaxed ambience in which to enjoy themselves, away from the glitter and fame of the Washington social whirl.

Chapter 14

The Battle
against Surpluses

The New Deal policy of creating market scarcity with non-production incentives and subsidies had also created enormous surpluses of farm commodities. Government silos and warehouses bulged with ever-increasing quantities of wheat, corn, butter, cheese, nonfat dry milk, soybeans, and cottonseed products, to mention a few. In April 1954, for instance, the dry milk inventory had increased to 566,000,000 pounds; and by July there were 467,000,000 pounds of butter on hand. To keep ahead of these mounting inventories was like bailing water from a leaky boat. "No question about it," Ezra wrote in the summer of 1955, "surpluses had become the number-one problem in U. S. Agriculture. No real hope of improving farm income was in sight until the surpluses could be liquidated" (*Cross Fire*, p. 258).

As Secretary Benson and his staff wrestled with this complex problem, four possible solutions emerged: release the surpluses into the domestic market, destroy them, sell or give them away overseas, or pay farmers for not producing.

The first two were dismissed out of hand. Flooding the domestic market with the surpluses would wreck farm prices, thereby increasing government subsidies and the quantity of new commodities to be warehoused. The repugnance Ezra had for the policy of destruction, tracing back to his experiences in the 1930s, had never changed. Only a little less repugnant to him was the concept of paying farmers for not producing. Yet he was reluctantly coming to the view that he might have to yield on this issue because, under the circumstances, failure to do so could render great harm to agriculture. So he set his staff to work, devising the least objectionable program that would reward farmers for lowering production. This came to fruition in May 1956 when Congress, at the request of Secretary Benson and the administration, created what was called the Soil Bank, which compensated farmers for removing part of their acreage from production. It was the major instance in which Secretary Benson placed pragmatism ahead of his farming philosophy while he served as secretary of agriculture. He was always apologetic in mentioning it.

Meanwhile, he turned to the other alternative to reduce the surpluses—increasing commodity exports. When Ezra took office, exports were at a seven-year low. Government subsidies had kept farm prices artificially high, which crippled U.S. farmers in efforts to compete for global markets. The passage of the Agricultural Trade Development and Assistance Act of 1954 had provided an important tool to increase farm exports. Under the act, farm surpluses could be sold for foreign currencies, bartered, or donated to the poor. Other strategies to promote exports included cooperative arrangements with trade and agriculture groups, participation in international trade fairs, and diplomatic efforts to lower trade barriers against U.S. farm products.

On February 19, 1955, Secretary Benson launched his first international tour to monitor and stimulate these programs. The destination was Latin America. The decision to go there first was dictated chiefly by President Eisenhower's desire to promote hemispheric solidarity. Personally, Ezra was anxious to go because of his intense interest in the architectural remnants of the ancient civilization that thrived in Latin America during Book of Mormon times. The two-and-a-half-week trip, which took him to Cuba, Puerto Rico, the Virgin Islands, Trinidad, Costa Rica, Venezuela, Colombia, Panama, Nicaragua, Guatemala, and Mexico, gave him a panoramic view of those countries, their potential as targets for U.S. farm exports, and their relationship to the Book of Mormon drama, a drama that constantly absorbed Elder Benson's interest.

Flora accompanied her husband for the visits to Cuba, Puerto Rico, and the Virgin Islands and then returned to Washington. In Cuba, Secretary Benson was hosted by Dr. Osvaldo Valdes de la Paz, Cuban minister of agriculture. Together they attended a livestock show in Havana, conferred with officials of the Hershey Company about the sugar industry, and toured several poultry farms and a potato farm. Ezra was pleased to learn that the potato farmer purchased his Red Bliss potato seeds from a producer in North Dakota. During their time together, Ezra and Dr. Valdes developed a close rapport. Ezra gave his new friend a 4–H tie clip as a memento, explaining it symbolized head, heart, hand, and health. Along with the Boy Scouts, this was a youth organization that Ezra Taft Benson promoted aggressively all his adult life. Later, while in Mexico, he was gratified when told that the man from whom a prosperous Mexican dairy farmer had purchased a prize bull was Leness Hall, who was Ezra's cousin by marriage and who had been one of his top 4–H Club leaders in Idaho in 1929.

A recurring question during the tour was raised again at a press conference in Bogotá, Colombia, when Secretary Benson was asked whether U.S. policy contemplated dumping huge commodity surpluses on the international market. "The United States Government," he assured the questioner, "will not drive world prices down by unloading our surpluses into foreign markets. We intend to compete for a reasonable share of world markets, but always fairly" (ibid., p. 240). A sign that the marketing strategy was working appeared in Nicaragua when Ezra's host proudly announced a local dairy cooperative had ordered ten thousand pounds of surplus butter from the United States. In Guatemala, a country thought by some of the Brethren to be the location of ancient Zarahemla, there was much to cause reflection upon the events of long ago recorded in the Book of Mormon, a copy of which was usually found in Elder Benson's briefcase.

After returning from this trip, Ezra attended a stag luncheon in the White House that President Eisenhower hosted in honor of Prime Minister Robert G. Menzies of Australia. Following the luncheon, the president asked Ezra to remain to brief him on the Latin America tour. "He seemed pleased," wrote Ezra of the briefing. "As I was leaving, he said, 'I hope you'll be able to go back there again and elsewhere, too, and do the same kind of job in other countries'" (ibid., p. 242).

It did not take Secretary Benson long to accept the president's invitation. By June the government's investment in price-supported farm commodities had increased to more than $7 billion, which would balloon to nine billion by the end of the year. "I knew how a ship captain must feel as he watches his badly leaking vessel take water," mused Ezra, "watches the sea creep higher and higher in the hold. The surplus disposal programs were our water pumps, and we had them going full speed. But for the time being the leak was bigger than the pumps could handle. Would this sea of surplus crops overwhelm us and sink us before we could plug the leak?" (ibid., p. 257).

Ezra was an activist when faced with a problem. The solution he saw to this one was to "sell our farm products for dollars. To do that, we had to get out and sell" (ibid., p. 260). Designating himself "Salesman at Large," Secretary Benson organized his second international trip. It would take him to Great Britain and Europe for eighteen days of aggressive selling, interspersed with moments of personal privilege and reflection.

The organization of such a trip by a member of the cabinet was of itself a major undertaking. It entailed voluminous correspondence and numerous conversations with the State Department, embassies, the department's attachés, and the ministers of agriculture in the countries to be visited.

Everything was in readiness by August 28, 1955, when Ezra and Flora left Washington, D.C. At Prestwick Airport near Glasgow they were met by the U.S. consul general, Francis Flood, who was their guide and host in Scotland. Ezra's objective here, as elsewhere, was to try to open official doors and to break down barriers for U.S. traders and trade organizations. To this end he conferred with key government officials and business leaders. When time permitted, he also visited local agriculture projects, as he did in Scotland when he inspected an Ayrshire farm operated by the Scottish Cooperative Wholesale. Driving south through "Bobby Burns Country" into England, Ezra enjoyed a nostalgic visit to Carlisle, his first field of labor as a missionary in Great Britain. Visiting Carlisle's old landmarks, he was able to share with Flora the memorable events she had learned about only through correspondence and his retelling of them. Now to see these places in person brought home to her a new reality of the events and caused a further bonding to the unusual man who had risen to positions of such high eminence in the three intervening decades.

In London Ezra attended a series of conferences on British-U.S. trade with the Board of Trade and the Ministry of Agriculture. He also held promising discussions on U.S. cotton imports and on the possibility of the British opening their market to imports of U.S. fruits, especially citrus fruits.

Crossing the Channel, Ezra visited the Netherlands and Denmark, marveling at the similarity between farm life in Europe and the United States. Farmers everywhere, he had found, shared a common bond that transcended nationality, language, and politics. It was rooted in the bedrock principles of faith and work, faith that the good earth would yield its plenty in proportion to the intelligent and diligent work devoted to its cultivation. Yet, forces beyond the farmer's control introduced uncertainty into the orderly processes of planting, nurturing, and harvesting—the forces of weather, blight, pestilence, and vagaries of the marketplace. The object of this tour was to attempt to introduce more reason and certainty into the latter.

Secretary Benson was intrigued by experiments being conducted at a "hog progeny station" in Denmark. There scientists and breeders were developing "meat-type hogs," animals with more meat and less fat. The experiments were of special interest to the secretary because of similar work being carried on at a USDA facility at Beltsville, Maryland. They also stimulated his own scientific interests and forward-looking attitudes.

The visit to Denmark was a personal high point for both Ezra and Flora. There Ezra was privileged to show his wife around Koge, the birthplace of her father, where Ezra had visited during his 1946 European mission. To see the home where her father had lived, beautified by the same kind of cultivated garden about which Carl Amussen had told his family, filled Flora with an ineffable feeling of love for this honored parent. She wept at the sight.

Traveling to Paris, through areas devastated by the recent war, Ezra was amazed by the transformation that had taken place. Few physical evidences of the destruction remained. It attested to the resiliency and the industry of the people.

At Paris Secretary Benson conferred not only with French farm leaders but also with twenty U.S. agricultural attachés whom he had summoned from all over Europe. After receiving reports from these associates, the secretary instructed them in the international trade objectives of their government. In pursuit of those objectives, he told them of the "urgent need for cooperation, goodwill, and under-standing among people" (ibid., p. 263).

In Rome Secretary Benson spoke at the opening session of the annual conference of the International Federation of Agricultural Producers. There he enunciated the basic prin-ciples of the U.S. policy on the export of agricultural prod-ucts—fair but aggressive competition for world markets, determination to compete in quality, and willingness to participate in mutually profitable international trade pacts. The secretary's remarks were translated simultaneously into the several languages of the multinational audience. "The world rapidly gets smaller," Ezra wrote of the experience (ibid.).

The Bensons were hosted in Rome by U.S. ambassador Clare Boothe Luce, who opened many official doors for them and who introduced them to some of the historic trea-sures of the ancient city. St. Peter's had special significance for Ezra. His role as one of the modern Apostles gave him a unique affinity with Peter, the chief ancient Apostle, an affin-ity shared only by Elder Benson and his associates in the Twelve.

From Rome Ezra traveled to Bern, Switzerland. There he joined President David O. McKay and other General Authorities of the Church for the dedication of the temple, located a few miles outside the city. Aside from the excite-ment attending any temple dedication, this one had special significance. It was the first temple built by the Church in Europe. As such, it symbolized the international character of the Church and the intention of its leaders to reach out invitingly to people everywhere.

A solemn quietness permeated the temple as Elder and Sister Benson took their places in the celestial room. Surrounding them were friends from home and Church members from all over Europe. In this setting, differences in nationality and language lost their meaning. Here all were brothers and sisters in the family of the Church. During the period of silence preceding the ceremony, Elder Benson's mind seems to have dwelled on themes of family as evidenced by his talk during the service. "Being privileged to speak," he reported later, "I told something of the history of . . . my progenitors, particularly my great-grandfather, Serge Louis Ballif" (ibid.). This ancestor first heard about the Church in 1852 in Lausanne, Switzerland. At the time he was serving as a clergyman in the Cathedral of Lausanne. As such, he had assisted in publishing "The Gospel of the Holy Ghost," a treatise that disputed Protestant claims to divine authority. With that background, he was immediately attracted to the unique message of two Mormon elders, delivered in halting French, who told him about a church that had been established by divine authority through the ministration of angels. He was converted and baptized soon afterward. Before migrating to the United States, he filled a mission for the Church in Switzerland and assisted in publishing Mormon tracts. "As I spoke," reported Elder Benson, "somehow I had the impression that those ancestors were with us in spirit at the services that morning" (ibid., p. 264).

Periodic illuminations like this induced much of the fervency Elder Benson displayed in his work. His convictions were grounded in personal revelation from God, not in mere intellectual assent. The power of these convictions was conveyed to those who heard him speak, as it doubtless was to those present at the dedication of the Swiss Temple. The ceremonies were capped by the moving rendition of "The Spirit of God Like a Fire Is Burning."

Meetings with Swiss agriculture leaders the next day ended a fruitful trip to promote the export of U.S. farm commodities. By now Ezra Benson had the ball rolling. His personal efforts through these international tours, added to the other programs he had initiated, had begun to swell the government's farm commodity exports. In the year beginning July 1, 1954, they increased by $200 million; and in the following years they ballooned, with a $350 million increase in the year 1955–56 and a $1.33 billion increase in 1956–57. Indeed, during this last year the maritime industry was pressed to find enough tonnage to handle the flood of exports. So grateful was the Italian government for Secretary Benson's efforts in helping to solve its food shortages that it awarded him the High Cross of the Order of Merit of the Italian Republic in recognition.

Ezra had little time to savor the success of his European tour. Only days after he returned, the government was thrown into turmoil when President Eisenhower suffered a heart attack. It occurred on September 24, 1955, while the president was visiting his wife's family in Denver, Colorado. The prognosis about his condition and whether he could carry on was uncertain. Through it all Ezra had a calm assurance that the President would recover and endeavored to buoy up those around him with the same confidence.

Meanwhile, there was work to do. The next morning he flew to Ottawa, Canada, with other government officials to attend a meeting of the Joint United States-Canadian Committee on Trade and Economic Affairs. In the discussions, there was outspoken criticism of the U.S. government's vigorous surplus disposal policy. "We [made] it clear," reported Ezra, "that we did not intend to sit back and let our markets go by default." He told the committee that the United States intended to compete aggressively for its share of the international market but that "we'll compete fair and square" (ibid., p. 270).

These urgent public affairs occurred in the midst of private arrangements for Barbara's marriage to Dr. Robert Walker, a Canadian physician. The ceremony was scheduled for Thursday, September 29, in the Salt Lake Temple. Flora and Barbara, accompanied by Beverly, had flown west earlier to make final arrangements for the wedding and to enroll Beverly at BYU. Ezra and the other two girls joined them on Tuesday, September 27.

The quiet ceremony was performed in the temple following the customary monthly meeting of all General Authorities. Afterward a wedding breakfast was held in the Hotel Utah. At the request of her parents, Barbara sang "I

Love You Truly," the song that had been sung at their wedding breakfast twenty-nine years before. The incident was typical of the Bensons' reliance on tradition to promote family unity.

Three days later, Elder Benson stood at the Tabernacle pulpit to address the general conference of the Church. He alluded to the improved condition of President Eisenhower and to the public prayers offered in his behalf during the conference. He also mentioned the privilege of attending the dedication of the temple in Bern and the spiritual outpourings that had occurred there. "I think I have never felt in all my life the veil quite so thin as it was three weeks ago this morning as we met in the opening session of that dedication service," he told the audience.

After sketching the sharp contrast between the current conditions in Europe and those he found in 1946, and after mentioning the favorable perceptions the general public had of the Church, he did something the members of the Church almost had come to expect of him. He sounded the voice of warning. "But I would like to raise this warning," he said to the audience. "In this period of apparent goodwill—good feeling toward the Church—when it seems as if we have no great obstacles any more as we once had, there should be deep concern. In my judgment, in the hour of our success is our greatest danger. And apparently this is an hour of great success." He then identified the main source of the danger he foresaw. "I realize that the devil is alert. He is the enemy of this work. He is the enemy of all righteousness, and I know that he is clever, that he never takes a holiday. He works overtime. He is ingenious. I am confident he will devise new ways to fight this work. We may not know just what form those schemes will take, but we must be vigilant" (in Conference Report, Oct. 1955, pp. 106–10). He then identified a practice adopted by some young Mormon couples that troubled him, the practice of providing liquor for their guests at home while abstaining themselves. He felt this was too much of a concession to the ways of the world and held

the risk of great mischief. Because of his extensive experience among those not of the faith, he assured his listeners
that if they demonstrated the Mormon lifestyle in their
homes as elsewhere, guests would understand and would
hold them in higher regard because they adhered to their
standards.

Chapter 15

Global Salesman

As Eisenhower's first term drew to a close in 1956, Ezra wondered whether he should leave the cabinet. Many were anxious that he go, both Democrats and Republicans: the Democrats because of his stand on price supports, and some Republicans because they feared his presence in the administration would be detrimental to the party in the fall election. Yet there were many who supported the secretary and who had been won over to his realistic though unpopular policies. His chief supporter was President Eisenhower.

Although the president questioned some of his secretary's strategies and his tendency to take unyielding positions, he endorsed his agricultural philosophy without question; and he personally admired Ezra's integrity and his deep spiritual nature. Consequently, the president dismissed emphatically any suggestions that he dump Secretary Benson. While Ezra was willing to stay if Ike needed him, his preference was to return to his life's work as a member of the Twelve. Regarding this concern, President McKay's

213

counsel to Elder Benson was that he stay on if President Eisenhower needed him. When Ike said he did, that ended it: Secretary Benson turned to his work in the department and to the campaign for the president's reelection.

In receiving Ezra's commitment, Eisenhower was the beneficiary of the Benson family's propensity for unity in all things. Everyone joined in the effort, whether behind the scenes or on the stump. Flora proved to be an effective campaigner. At a rally in Toledo, Ohio, for instance, attended by several cabinet members' wives, Flora, after delivering her prepared speech, cast it aside and talked to the audience as the wife of a farmer. The women present, most of them also wives of farmers, felt a special kinship to her when told Flora had cooked for threshers and did all her own housework without the help of a maid, even when Mamie Eisenhower and other dignitaries came for lunch. She received an enthusiastic ovation. Reed also was openly active in the campaign. At the time, he worked for the National Republican Congressional Committee and filled speaking assignments, even substituting for his father in an emergency. With a natural bent for speaking, honed in the mission field and as a military chaplain, he was a persuasive and entertaining speaker and, once his skills became known, was much in demand at party rallies. This exposure, added to his role as a valued political confidant of his father, doubtless was a factor that induced him to run for Congress after he returned to Utah.

Ezra's knowledge, eloquence, temperament, and stature combined to make him one of Eisenhower's most effective campaign speakers. He was constantly on the move during the critical phases of the campaign. Regardless of the time or place of a rally, he always projected the same image and, with variations, delivered the same message. The image was one of integrity and skill. The message dwelled on the future needs of America. He eloquently explained how agriculture and American taxpayers had become shackled by the bloated system of excessive subsidies and artificial

scarcity. His remedy was to cut those shackles while preserving a necessary safety net for the farmer in times of
emergency and to let farm prices find their own level
according to market demands. The market, in Secretary
Benson's view, was not restricted to the boundaries of the
United States. He thought in terms of worldwide markets.
Ezra apparently believed that through aggressive marketing
abroad, American farm products could receive global acceptance in ways similar to how he and his marketing friends
had made the Idaho potato a household word in the United
States. The whole thrust of his training and experience had
been toward creative marketing of farm products, beginning
with the Benson brothers' catchy motto, "You can whip our
cream, but you can't beat our milk." And, of course, marketing was the main object of his graduate work at Ames
and at Berkeley and of his farm extension work at Preston
and Boise.

Secretary Benson's views were readily accepted by
many in the farm community who sought freedom from the
dead weight of government supervision and control. His
views received an even wider acceptance by American taxpayers wearied by the burden of paying for the liberal farm
subsidies. It is not surprising, however, that his agricultural
philosophy was bitterly rejected by many in the farm community who received government grants. In addition, candidates who advocated the status quo were harshly
outspoken in denouncing these views and their author, Ezra
Taft Benson.

In the heat of the campaign, these enmities aroused bitter reactions. Often Secretary Benson was confronted by
hecklers who taunted him openly or who sought to disrupt
meetings by walking out as a group. He also became the
butt of many jokes, such as when President Eisenhower's
opponent, Adlai Stevenson, wisecracked that the only way
to dismantle the seemingly invincible New York Yankee
organization was to place Ezra Benson in charge of its
farm system. The cartoonists also made sport of him with

215

exaggerated caricatures and insulting captions. At one farm meeting, eggs were thrown at him. This tactic boomeranged, however, when a wave of public indignation turned many former opponents toward him.

When the political rhetoric ended, the voters had their say: Eisenhower was reelected by a landslide. The results in the so-called farm states were mixed. Some Republicans who supported the administration's farm policies were defeated; others were reelected. Overall, Ezra and the candidates who endorsed his farm policies fared well. The political disaster some had predicted never materialized. Personally, Ezra came out of the election with an enhanced reputation. Even his opponents admired his integrity. And the tenacity shown in advocating his views caused many in the press to refer to him as a man of great courage and determination, even a man of "guts."

President Eisenhower's reelection caused no significant changes in Secretary Benson's work. He continued to lobby Congress for support for his farm policies and to promote the interests of farmers generally by a consistent administration of his department. He also continued to push the initiatives intended to reduce farm surpluses. Moving these huge stores of farm products continued to be his major problem.

A few months after Eisenhower's second term began, Ezra commenced to plan a world tour designed to promote the export of America's surplus farm commodities. The complex arrangements were completed by October 1957. He was accompanied by Flora, Beverly, Bonnie, and five staff members who were specialists in various phases of agriculture. Their itinerary would take them to Japan, Hong Kong, India, Pakistan, Jordan, Israel, Turkey, Greece, Italy, Spain, Portugal, France, and England. Ezra referred to the tour as "Around the World in Twenty-Five Days." "The purposes of this trip," he explained, "were to observe the agricultural and economic development of the countries visited; to talk with governmental leaders and officials of trade groups to see if a further expansion of U.S. farm exports for dollars could be arranged, and to look into the effectiveness of the various surplus disposal programs under which our farm products were moving abroad" (*Cross Fire,* p. 364). It was Secretary Benson's conviction that aside from reducing the nation's surpluses, the export of U.S. farm commodities, whether purchased for dollars or local currency or obtained by barter or donation, "was an important thread in the fabric of world progress toward peace and plenty" (ibid., p. 366).

Since Japan had become the United States' best cash market for farm products, the tour logically commenced there. In Tokyo the secretary learned how efforts to promote the use of U.S. farm products were bearing fruit. He was pleased to see a thousand children eating a school lunch consisting mostly of bread and milk produced on American farms. Mobile kitchens were being used to demonstrate to Tokyo housewives how to prepare bargain wheat dishes. Here, as elsewhere on the tour, Ezra visited Japanese farms. He was impressed by the intensiveness of Japanese agriculture. On land area less than 3 percent of the farmland in the United States, the Japanese produced enough food to feed seventy-two million people, representing 80 percent of their population.

In Hong Kong, Pakistan, and India, Secretary Benson became acutely aware of a problem whose magnitude he had not understood before. There he saw thousands of refugees, the world's "unwanted," crowded into squalid camps, people without a country who had little hope of ever enjoying more than the scanty subsistence provided by the charity of their hosts. Ezra was devastated by the sight of these helpless people but heartened to know that some of America's surplus foods were helping to feed them.

In India, Secretary Benson saw personally for the first time how agricultural aid provided under Public Law 480 was being administered. Here U.S. farm imports had increased from $40 million to $205 million in one year alone.

Prime Minister Jawaharlal Nehru of India, assisted by

his daughter, hosted the Bensons in the prime minister's ornately furnished home. While Ezra discussed some matters of agricultural policy with his host during the evening, it was essentially a pleasant social affair.

Mr. Nehru, poised and affable, who spoke impeccable English with a noticeable British accent, presided over a country with more domestic problems than any other country Secretary Benson visited during the tour. Overpopulation, ancient religious conflicts, and a rigid caste system created social stresses that defied resolution. An agriculture that lacked modern equipment and cultivation skills was unable to produce enough to feed the people adequately. Thus the import of farm products was an urgent necessity. This led to discussions about extending the commodity import agreement with India under Public Law 480, which benefited both countries by siphoning off some of America's suffocating surpluses to help alleviate India's chronic scarcities. Such stark contrasts served to enhance Ezra's appreciation for the bounties of the United States, notwithstanding the headaches its mounting surpluses caused him in his role as secretary of agriculture.

The Bensons' night with Mr. Nehru was an exception to their usual routines, for it was a working trip for Ezra and his duties had to take precedence over family matters. However, to make the trip exciting for Flora and the girls, arrangements were made for them to see things of historic and cultural interest while Ezra tended to business. When possible, he joined them, sandwiching personal things between slices of his official obligations. A night like the one spent with India's prime minister was ideal for Ezra, blending just enough business to take the edge off his inordinate sense of responsibility with a pleasant, relaxed interlude with his family and newfound friends.

The highlight of the tour for Secretary Benson was the two days he spent in Israel. He conferred with "hundreds of government officials, farmers, business and trade people, and leaders in the professions" (ibid., p. 369). He was driven by automobile into rural and urban areas and flown in a small plane at low elevations over much of the country. He was impressed at the way desert land had been reclaimed for productive use by intelligent husbandry. His grounding in the sacred scriptures would have recalled the ancient prophecies about how in the last days the desert would be made to blossom as the rose.

Secretary Benson conferred with David Ben-Gurion, Israel's head of government. The meeting was held in the hospital where Ben-Gurion was convalescing from injuries suffered in a recent bombing. This resilient, outspoken man made a profound impression on his visitor. "He was not afraid to oppose his own people, or his Cabinet, or anyone else," Ezra wrote of the Jewish leader. "Like De Gaulle, he spoke his mind. You knew exactly where he and you stood" (ibid., p. 368). To the American, the elderly Ben-Gurion resembled his conception of how an ancient Israelite prophet would have looked, with his quiet, confident demeanor and piercing brown eyes. That perception, and Elder Benson's status as one of the Twelve, led them into a discussion of Old Testament prophecies. And that, in turn, caused Ezra to allude to revelations in the Doctrine and Covenants and to the mission of Orson Hyde and John E. Page to dedicate the land of Palestine for the return of the Jews. Surprisingly, Ben-Gurion was already aware of these things, although he expressed no opinion about them. "I left," Ezra wrote later, "convinced that he is a noble soul with a deep love for his people and a determination to give them faithful and courageous leadership" (ibid., p. 369).

Leaving Israel, Secretary Benson and his party visited Turkey, where he discussed wheat reserves the country needed to back up its army; Greece, where he felt that future economic development would provide increased markets for U.S. commodities; Italy, where he saw good prospects for future sales as government leaders reshaped the country's agriculture toward more livestock and livestock products; Spain, where increased consumption of food and fiber was being met in part by U.S. sales under Public Law 480 and where there were discussions about selling the country $20 million worth of cotton on credit, payable over five years; Portugal, where he foresaw growth for U.S. sales as industrialization increased; France, where sales of U.S. cotton were strong because price stabilization had made cotton more competitive with synthetics; and England, where he reached an understanding with the British on the Public Law 480 fruit program that, it was expected, would maintain America's traditional market there.

Throughout the tour, Elder Benson made an effort to contact members of the Church in the countries visited to help encourage and motivate them. In countries where the Church had organized missions, the Bensons stayed with the mission presidents and their families. This made it possible to hold informal gatherings with the missionaries where the Apostle was able to bear testimony to them, infusing them with his own faith and fervor. He also held meetings with local members along the way as his schedule allowed and with American servicemen stationed overseas.

Arriving in Washington, D.C., on November 16, the Bensons found Beth anxiously waiting for them, along with Dr. and Mrs. Edgar B. Brossard, with whom she had stayed in their absence. "When she saw us," her father wrote of the emotional occasion, "she began to run towards us and broke into tears. I swept her up in my arms. With all the wonders of the world, that moment was suddenly the best of the entire trip" (ibid., p. 371).

Secretary Benson's later assessment of the impact of his world tour was guardedly optimistic. "The trip, I thought, was worthwhile. Not once had I heard the word 'dumping.' Not once was a sour note injected. We returned proud and grateful for America, knowing that no nation under Heaven, past or present, had ever been so generous with its abundance as had our own blessed land" (ibid.). And when his critics complained about the expense of his taking members of his family with him, Ezra explained that

President Eisenhower had encouraged him to do so because of the goodwill value. He also answered his critics, who seemed to him to make a career of monitoring his activities and who were looking for something to complain about, by citing the statistics already mentioned, showing the marked increase in the quantity of American farm exports since the commencement of his initiatives to reduce the farm surpluses.

These explanations did not silence Secretary Benson's critics, whose voices came from both sides of the aisle. Loud demands for his resignation were made by Republican leaders when Democrat William Proxmire was elected to the Senate in Wisconsin, traditionally a Republican state, in a special election to fill the vacancy created by the death of Senator Joseph McCarthy. Especially troubling was the fact that Proxmire had made Ezra Benson's farm policies a key issue in his campaign.

In the forefront of the Republican leaders who sought Ezra's removal was powerful Senator Karl Mundt of South Dakota. The senator, who was on the stand at the meeting in Sioux Falls when eggs were thrown at Secretary Benson, was convinced the Republican party would lose heavily in farm states in the 1958 elections if Ezra remained in the cabinet. He wrote a strong letter to Sherman Adams to that effect in late October 1957. Any efforts the chief of staff made to persuade the president to drop his secretary of agriculture failed. Eisenhower continued to give Ezra unqualified support and turned a deaf ear to any efforts to remove him. Had the president shown any weakening of his support at this time, Ezra undoubtedly would have left the cabinet at the end of 1957. However, buoyed up by Ike's show of confidence and receiving a signal from President McKay that he should remain if Eisenhower needed him, Secretary Benson called a press conference in December to announce he was staying. He defended his decision by saying that no political party was ever hurt by telling the truth, and that he intended to continue telling the truth. This uncompromising announcement set the stage for the most bruising battle Ezra Benson would wage during his years in the cabinet.

President Eisenhower openly showed his support of Secretary Benson when he sent a message to Congress in January 1958 that included a call for lower price supports. The Democrats answered the next day at a meeting of the Senate Agricultural Committee. Called to testify, Secretary Benson began to read a lengthy prepared statement that elaborated on the items in the president's message pertaining to agriculture. Ordinarily the committee allowed a witness to read his statement, with clarifying questions to follow. Within minutes, it became obvious that the Democrats on the committee intended to embarrass and, if possible, to provoke Secretary Benson for political purposes. With Senators Allen J. Ellender, Hubert H. Humphrey, and Stuart Symington taking the lead, the secretary was interrupted repeatedly as he attempted to read the prepared statement. The grilling continued for more than seven hours. All semblance of collegial courtesy disappeared as the senators turned from questions to accusations. During the day Secretary Benson, in turn, was accused of being insincere, of lying, and of using "false advertising" to support his policies. Throughout the ordeal, Ezra displayed a characteristic for which he became noted during his years in Washington. Even under the heaviest provocation, he never lost his temper. He responded evenly and rationally to all questions. The accusations were brushed aside without comment, although occasional flushing at his shirt collar hinted at the anger bottled up inside. His poise under fire earned him the grudging admiration of his political opponents. And it also earned him the support, temporary though it was, of many political reporters and commentators who came to his defense against the bullying tactics of the senators.

In February, Secretary Benson faced a serious challenge from a group of Republican congressmen. Led by Walter H. Judd of Minnesota and Arthur L. Miller of Nebraska, thirty representatives from eleven midwestern farm states formally requested that the secretary resign. Knowing that he had the support of the one person who really counted, Dwight D. Eisenhower, Ezra held firm and politely rejected their request.

Caught in the cross fire between Democrats and Republicans, Secretary Benson became a heroic figure in the minds of many. He seemed like the lone marshall facing off against a wild gang of gunmen in Dodge City. That image soon translated into the idea that here was the kind of man who should lead the country as president. Comments of friends and the media planted the idea in Ezra's mind. It was nourished by favorable polls in the second quarter when farm prices rose. He mused about the fickleness of the public, how one's popularity rose and fell with price fluctuations. He was wary of the situation. He always believed one's greatest danger lay at the height of his greatest success. Then was a person most vulnerable to the wiles of the adversary, and then was the time he should exercise the greatest care. Yet, Ezra could not refrain from savoring what clearly was a personal victory. In the face of carping criticism and personal abuse, he had survived. But more, he had gained the grudging respect of his political enemies. And his conservative views were gaining wider public acceptance.

The November election confirmed Ezra's philosophy about the volatile nature of public opinion. The Republicans suffered an overwhelming defeat. They expected some losses in the off-year election, but not to the extent of fourteen seats in the Senate and fifty-one in the House. Devastated, the professional politicians looked for explanations—and scapegoats. By habit, many of them pointed the finger at Ezra Benson. Typical of these was Vice President Richard Nixon. "The farmer has never had it so good," wrote he. "But, someway, somehow, our Democratic friends have done such a job on Ezra Benson that they have the farmers thinking he and the Republican party are against them. We took the first shellackings in the farm states. That is where we lost the three Senate seats that I didn't think we would lose. That also denied us a couple of governorships and lost us two." Secretary Benson responded pointedly: "In this statement of the Vice President was hidden a key to our future relationship" (ibid., p. 415). In the 1960 presidential campaign, Mr. Nixon soft-pedaled his predecessor's agriculture policies. Understandably, Ezra was annoyed and would have preferred another candidate. However, when Nixon was nominated by his party, Ezra supported him, but not with noticeable enthusiasm.

Secretary Benson's disappointment over the 1958 election was eased somewhat by President Eisenhower's approval of a program proposed by the USDA called "Food for Peace." Ezra considered it the most creative proposal of his administration designed to reduce surpluses while promoting world peace. President Eisenhower included the proposal in his message to Congress in January 1959: "I am setting steps in motion to explore anew with other surplus-producing nations all practical means of utilizing the various agricultural surpluses of each in the interest of reinforcing peace and the well-being of friendly peoples throughout the world—in short, using food for peace" (ibid., p. 433).

After the proposal was approved by Congress, Secretary Benson and his department had the responsibility to implement it. After leaving office, he was pleased to report that during 1960 alone, more than twenty million U.S. citizens and sixty-two million people in ninety-two foreign countries received donations of surplus food under this program.

The Food for Peace program was part of an overall strategy of the Eisenhower administration to ease international tensions. The greatest source of global tension came from conflicts between the United States and the Soviet Union. As part of an effort to increase understanding and goodwill between the two countries, President Eisenhower invited Soviet leader Nikita S. Khrushchev to visit the United States. He arrived in mid-September 1959. Ezra was cool to the idea of the visit. He distrusted Khrushchev and loathed the communist system, considering it to be the embodiment of evil because of its atheism and its iron suppression of individual freedom. So it was with a notable lack of ardor that Ezra agreed to host the visitor and his party on a tour of the USDA Experimental Station at Beltsville, Maryland.

Before asking his specialists to conduct the tour, Secretary Benson made preliminary remarks. "Our farmers are free, efficient, creative and hard working," he told the visitors, giving special emphasis to the word *free*. He also explained how research was conducted "and how it is carried to the people through our free press; and how new ideas—the findings of agricultural research—are freely available to everyone interested" (ibid., pp. 468, 469).

Chairman Khrushchev was silent afterward, as he was during most of the tour, although occasionally he interjected brief statements about the superiority of certain aspects of Soviet agriculture. "Then he began to make comments," reported Secretary Benson. "There were about three hundred newspaper, TV, and radio personnel in attendance and suddenly with one of those mercurial changes so characteristic of him, Khrushchev began to show off before the photographers. From the strong, stolid, silent spectator, he became the hearty, blustering, effusive buffoon, joking and wisecracking, even lecturing" (ibid., p. 469). Later, Ezra left no doubt about his attitude toward the visitor and his associates and his convictions about the future of communism. "It is my faith that in the Lord's due time He will find a way to break down this murderous conspiracy and bring the truth and liberty to those Russians who are honest in heart" (ibid., p. 471).

Only a week later, Secretary Benson left on another international trip that would enable him to make a personal assessment of the differences between American and Soviet agriculture. Its purpose was to foster goodwill and to check on the development of foreign farm markets. The itinerary included visits to Yugoslavia, West Germany, Poland, the

Soviet Union, Finland, Sweden, and Norway. With him were Flora, Beverly, Bonnie, and four staff members.

The procedures were the same followed on previous trips. Meetings with government leaders were interspersed with inspections of farms and experimental stations. The Soviet Union's size, its importance, its competition with the United States, and the recent visit of Khrushchev made that country the most important stop on Secretary Benson's tour. He was most interested in its farming economy. "Compared with typical American country life, Soviet rural standards are almost primitive," he wrote. Few Soviet farms had electricity. Many families lived in wooden cabins or mud huts without running water or the "multitude of conveniences" found in most American farmhouses. Tractors and other farm implements were scarce, as were motorized vehicles. "The Soviet farm family rides in horse-drawn carts over roads to match" (ibid., p. 482).

Secretary Benson acknowledged that while Soviet agriculture lagged far behind America's, progress had been made. Yet, one Soviet farm worker still could produce only enough food to feed six, whereas the ratio in the United States of people fed per farmer was twenty-five to one. In the Soviet Union, the potential to compete was there, but missing were the tools, modern farm technology, and motivation. The incentive to increase farm production, created by the profit motive under capitalism, was stimulated in the Soviet Union by a desire to best the United States. "We saw hundreds of posters," Ezra wrote, "urging farmers to surpass the United States in per capita production, and forecasting the ultimate victory of the Communist system" (ibid., p. 480).

Ezra detected a similar mind-set in other facets of Soviet society, though not shown by conspicuous posters as found on the farms. The whole thrust of their government seemed geared to an effort to outdo the United States. It was a reflection of Khrushchev's attitude; he had boasted the Soviet

Union would "bury" the United States and that America's grandchildren would live under communism.

Ezra's revulsion for communism derived mainly from its atheistic dogmas. These were an affront to his role as an Apostle of Jesus Christ and a denial of everything he held sacred. There could be no compromise with such a system. He was willing to debate the political and the economic issues involved in the conflicts between capitalism and communism, but his mind was closed irrevocably against any concession to atheism. This accounts for his unyielding, implacable opposition to communism and communistic governments. Given this attitude, it is apparent that Secretary Benson's priorities in visiting the Soviet Union were different from those of other U.S. government officials who went there. He was constantly on the alert for evidences of a religious sentiment among the people. He had requested the opportunity to visit a church while he was there. But his requests had been adroitly evaded by his hosts. On the way to the airport his last night in Moscow, he expressed disappointment that he had not been able to attend a Russian church. One of his guides whispered to the chauffeur, who promptly made a U-turn in the boulevard and, after driving through side streets, stopped before an old stucco building that was the chapel of the Central Baptist Church, located not far from Red Square. Led by his guide, Elder Benson entered the chapel to find a worship service in progress. He and his party were ushered to pews in the front that had been vacated by some of the worshippers when they saw the visitors enter. The minister who was speaking abruptly ended his sermon and announced a hymn to be sung.

"Hearing a thousand to 1500 voices raised there became one of the most affecting experiences of my entire life," Ezra wrote later. "In our common faith as Christians, they reached out to us with a message of welcome that bridged all differences of language, of government, of history. And as I was trying to recover balance under this emotional impact, the minister asked me, through an interpreter who stood there, to address the congregation" (ibid., p. 486).

Regaining his composure, Elder Benson spoke briefly and movingly. He extended greetings from the American people, assured the audience of God's nearness and love, sketched the plan of salvation, urged them to pray regularly, and bore his testimony. As Elder Benson and his party left the chapel, the congregation sang "God Be with You Till We Meet Again." "As we walked down the aisle, they waved handkerchiefs in farewell—it seemed all 1,500 were waving at us as we left."

As he reflected on it, Elder Benson said the experience was almost indescribable. "I shall never forget that evening as long as I live." Others in his party shared his opinion. "The Communist plan," wrote a reporter who was not a member of the Mormon Church, "is that when these 'last believers' die off, religion will die with them. What the atheists don't know is that God can't be stamped out either by legislated atheism or firing squad. This Methodist backslider who occasionally grumbles about having to go to church, stood crying unashamedly, throat lumped and chills running from spine to toes. It was the most heart-rending and most inspiring scene I've ever witnessed" (ibid., pp. 487, 488).

Secretary Benson was heartened by editorial comments made after he returned home. One piece written by an Associated Press correspondent was especially gratifying. "Impressed by these farm trips were U.S. diplomatic representatives assigned to these countries. A number of them accompanied the Bensons. They came back saying their own missions would be helped immeasurably. The comment was heard that personal visits of this nature did much more good than some of the financial aid the United States extends to some of the countries" (ibid., p. 490).

Not everyone applauded Eisenhower's secretary of agriculture. As the presidential election year approached, many in his own party again were calling for his resignation. In

December, as Secretary Benson lay in the hospital convalescing from abdominal surgery, he read that members of the Republican National Committee were calling for him to step down. Inviting the committee chairman, Senator Thruston B. Morton, to visit him in the hospital, Ezra asked how many of the 155 committee members wanted him to leave. "Three" was the answer. Understandably irked, he lectured the senator about the efforts to get him out of office made repeatedly since 1953 by those who "favor a socialized agriculture with more government in farming." He then defended his policies, noted they had been endorsed in large measure by all competent agriculture groups, and said it would be folly for the Republican party to turn its back on them at this late hour. Afterward, he was quoted in the press as saying the only thing he was resigned to was "to continue working for a prosperous, expanding, free agriculture. . . . The question is not is it good politics, but is it right? Our program is right. If anything is right, it ought to be done— and it will prove to be good politics" (ibid., pp. 494–95).

Ezra saw confirmation for his views when at a special election in Iowa to replace a deceased congressman, the Republican candidate won handily. Afterward, Chairman Morton "urged fellow Republicans to 'sell' Benson in the farm belt, not sell him out." *Time* magazine for December 28, 1959, noted, "When Benson heard that news, an austere but unmistakable smile of victory spread across his face."

Because the Republican presidential candidate in 1960, Richard M. Nixon, continued to downplay the agricultural policies of the Eisenhower administration, Secretary Benson played a minor role in the campaign. Instead of going on the stump as he had done in 1956, he continued with his international selling tours. On July 30, 1960, the Saturday following the Republican National Convention where Nixon was nominated, Ezra left for an eighteen-day tour that took him to Belgium, West Germany, the Netherlands, France, Egypt, Jordan, and Israel. With him were Flora and Beth, eight newsmen, and three members of his staff. "We wanted to investigate the possibilities of increasing sales and by personal contact with government officials and trade representatives to encourage economic goodwill," he explained. "In particular, I wanted to explore the implications of the newly developing European Common Market for U.S. agriculture" (ibid., p. 543).

In Holland, Secretary Benson represented his government at an international horticultural show called "the Floriade." The United States had an exhibit on a three-and-a-half-acre tract. It included a middle-income U.S. home surrounded by gardens and landscaped lawns, a supermarket featuring U.S. garden supplies, and a prefabricated plastic greenhouse. The exhibit, which Ezra felt "did us proud," was seen by more than five million visitors during the six months the Floriade continued. In assessing the Floriade and the Netherlands' progress in agriculture, Ezra recalled his previous visits to Holland, the short vacation he had spent there following his mission in the early 1920s, visits during his 1946 European mission, and an official visit made earlier as secretary of Agriculture. "But nothing that I had seen then had prepared me for the glories of the magnificent Floriade," he told his Dutch hosts. "I spoke from my heart and it seemed I could feel between all of us in that room that bond of brotherhood of which Carlyle wrote. Having made these observations at considerable length, I then spoke in terms of free world hopes and aspirations toward trade and the strengthening of the whole free world community" (ibid., p. 536).

With variations, Secretary Benson repeated these latter remarks at other stops during this tour. He did the same during an October tour of South America when he visited Brazil, Uruguay, Argentina, Chile, and Peru. And following the election, in which John F. Kennedy defeated Vice President Nixon, he did the same during a tour of the Orient and the South Seas when he visited Japan, Formosa, the Philippines, Australia, and New Zealand.

Prompted in part, perhaps, by the global views he had

acquired through his service in the Twelve, Ezra Taft Benson was a confirmed internationalist in terms of free trade. It was his conviction that trade barriers between nations should be lifted to provide for the free flow of commodities and products across national boundaries. In such a free, global market, he anticipated the United States would compete aggressively yet fairly for its share of that market. It is a curious anomaly that the only other Latter-day Saint who simultaneously served as a member of the Twelve and in high position in the government of the United States, Senator Reed Smoot, held the opposite view. It was Senator Smoot who cosponsored the legislation known as the Smoot-Hawley act that erected high tariffs on imported commodities, legislation designed to protect United States producers and manufacturers. Some have credited this protectionist legislation with causing, or at least worsening, the Great Depression of the 1930s.

When Secretary Benson completed this last international tour, his official duties were essentially over. The remaining weeks were devoted to tying up the loose ends and preparing to vacate his office. He did take one other trip, to Chicago. It was for personal reasons, not business. There at the Saddle and Sirloin Club he was inducted into the Agricultural Hall of Fame. Ceremoniously, his oil portrait was added to the three hundred other notables of American agriculture. Then before responding, he was lauded by Harold B. Lee, Ernest L. Wilkinson, and William I. Meyers, dean of the Horticulture Department at Cornell University. Elder Lee put the occasion in proper perspective. He told the distinctive, diverse group that his boyhood friend, "T" Benson, would now leave the national limelight, at the pinnacle of U.S. agriculture, to return to a work of more surpassing importance. He then described and attested to the global significance of his role as a member of the Twelve. In his concluding remarks, Elder Benson endorsed his friend's comments, acknowledging with appreciation the honor conferred upon him while implying that his eight years in the

Ezra Taft Benson served with distinction as a member of President Eisenhower's cabinet from 1953 to 1961

cabinet, important as they were, were only a minor inter-lude in his real life's work as a leader of the Mormon Church. The evening took on the tone of a colossal cottage meeting, with Elder Lee and Elder Benson alternately attest-ing to the significance of the Church and its message. In ret-rospect, it also was a celebration of the miracle of American democracy as the elite of U.S. agriculture paid homage to a man whose roots grew from the fertile soil of remote Whitney, Idaho.

Other special events awaited Secretary Benson on his return to Washington. More than seven hundred colleagues from the Department of Agriculture honored him and Flora at a reception and banquet on January 9, 1961. There he was presented with tokens of his government service that he always cherished—his cabinet chair, an American flag that had flown over the USDA building, and a trophy case from his office. Later the chair was part of the furnishings of his offices at Church headquarters. Special visitors were always invited to be seated in that chair as they conferred with the Church leader.

Ezra served as master of ceremonies at a black-tie testimonial dinner hosted by the cabinet and their wives to honor President and Mrs. Eisenhower. During the evening, Secretary Benson presented the honored guests with two antique sterling-silver beverage coolers as a memento of admiration and friendship. In making the presentation, Ezra, known by all Washington for his abstemious habits, wryly suggested that the coolers would be ideal for the milk and other farm beverages the Eisenhowers would want to serve their guests. Two days later Secretary Benson attended his last cabinet meeting. Only two members of Eisenhower's original cabinet remained, Ezra and Postmaster General Arthur Summerfield. The final, perfunctory business matters having been disposed of, the meeting became a sort of valedictory for those present. Expressions of appreciation and goodwill predominated. The bruising battles and partisan enmities were swallowed up in a sort of euphoric remembrance of the past eight years. They had been tough years. But, overall, they had been good years.

Chapter 16

The Transition

Once he left the controversial environment of Washington, D.C., Ezra Taft Benson received widespread commendations for his government service. It was hard not to like him as a man. He usually displayed a genuine quality of cordial goodwill, even in the most contentious situations. So when he stepped down, the political rancor that had surrounded him for eight years dissipated and he was viewed in a more sympathetic light. The image he then projected was that of a wise, kindly parent who had endeavored to administer needed but distasteful medicine to the American farmer and the public. And while many continued to reject the medication, they nevertheless seemed to sense that his intentions were pure and that what he had done was for their own good.

The *Dallas Morning News* of February 20, 1961, accurately captured the general sentiment about former Secretary Benson: "What a man that old Mormon secretary of agriculture turned out to be," it editorialized. "Where Benson had a free hand, he showed intelligence, fidelity and results. It is only fair to say that, but for the stubborn old, honest old, dedicated old Ezra Benson, we would still be storing butter, eggs, cheese and heaven knows what all besides." Obviously the name "Old Ezra Benson" was used as a term of endearment, even as his friends in Newcastle had given him the affectionate title "Our Benson" as he left the mission field.

Once the Bensons had bid farewell to members of the Church at a Washington Stake conference, it was time to go home. Flora and the girls returned to Utah in mid-February. Ezra remained for a while to complete the sale of the home and to handle other personal affairs. He then drove to Salt Lake City alone in early March, robustly singing Mormon hymns as he traveled. En route he had planned to visit his sister Lera in Salem, Wisconsin, whose husband was ill. But at the junction, a strong spiritual impression prompted him to bypass Salem. He learned later that the road to Salem would have taken him into the path of a cyclone that blew cars off the highway and wrecked homes. His diary reflected deep gratitude for this spiritual prompting that was similar to others that had led him along safely through life. He would have further need of this monitor to help navigate the storms that lay ahead.

Of all the commendations he received for his service as secretary of agriculture, none was more appreciated and meaningful to Elder Benson than the one expressed by President David O. McKay at the April 1960 general conference. The prophet said that Ezra's service in the cabinet would "stand for all time as a credit to the Church and to the nation." Now that he had resumed his duties as a member of the Twelve, Elder Benson was anxious to enjoy regular association with this man whom he idolized and who had exerted such a profound influence upon his life since his days in the mission field in England. He also was eager to resume regular contact with the members of the Twelve, the other General Authorities, and the members of the Church.

There was no delay in taking up his official duties. The weekend after he arrived home found him at the conference of the Cottonwood Stake. "I have been looking forward to this for a long time," he told the reporter for the *Church News*. "I'm glad to be back in the full swing of the work that I love so much." He said that political activity was over for the present but added that he would always be interested in the progress of agriculture and other policies affecting the welfare of the country (*Church News*, March 18, 1961).

The Benson family was honored at a welcome-home banquet attended by a thousand guests; and at the April general conference, which followed soon after, Elder Benson was able to thank the members personally for the many expressions of kindness and support he and his family had received. Afterward, he and Flora spent a relaxing week in the Arizona sun. There, for the first time since leaving Washington, they were able to reflect at their leisure about the cabinet years and to plan ahead.

Despite his genuine happiness at resuming his duties as a member of the Twelve, Elder Benson found the transition more difficult than he had expected. For eight years he had been at the seat of national—indeed, world—power, exercising administrative control over a vast army of USDA employees and grappling with complex problems of international scope. During that time, he had had at his beck and call a large staff of professionals and numerous clerical workers to do his bidding, relieving him of every superfluous task and anxious to respond to his slightest wish.

Now at Church headquarters, he had to share secretaries with other General Authorities. This created a serious bottleneck, given his voluminous correspondence with former government associates, acquaintances around the world, and the numerous people who wrote to him seeking counsel or requesting favors. He received literally hundreds of invitations to speak at both Church and non-Church functions. All these had to be acknowledged, if only to express regret at his inability to accept. And his appointment to the board of directors of Corn Products International, and the correspondence that entailed, added to the clerical snarl. All this placed Elder Benson in an awkward position. He was embarrassed to ask for more help than that provided for other General Authorities, yet the work had to be handled. So he struggled as best he could, using whatever help was available, whether from members of his family or from his brethren who understood the problem and were willing to cooperate by making more secretarial help available to him.

For a while after his return, Elder Benson also had a sense that he was underused in the fulfillment of Church duties. This did not imply a demeaning attitude toward them; it only reflected the difference between being one of twelve and being the main figure among thousands of subordinates. This was an inevitable reaction to his changed status. In time these feelings disappeared as his focus altered.

As his remarks following the Cottonwood Stake conference implied, Elder Benson's greatest satisfaction in his apostolic calling came from direct contacts with the members of the Church. Not long after his return, he joined with Elders Spencer W. Kimball, Mark E. Petersen, and Delbert L. Stapley in visiting stakes and missions in the northern United States. This was challenging and enjoyable work as he counseled with local leaders, endeavored to uplift the members, and motivated the missionaries. It also was work that satisfied an inherent need to be part of something that had eternal significance. It was infinitely more rewarding than promoting the sale of butter and beans abroad, for instance.

Elder Benson's enjoyment of his apostolic work was clouded by a nagging concern about the dangerous drift of international affairs. While in the cabinet, he had witnessed from ringside the emergence of the cold war and the deterioration of relations between the United States and the Soviet Union. He also had seen the opening of the space age when, in the autumn of 1957, the Soviet Union launched *Sputnik*, the first earth satellite. This had frightening implications for the United States, given the ability of Soviet technology to proliferate nuclear weapons. He had then watched the "Race into Space," with the two nations vying with each other to demonstrate their ability to build and to launch ever more sophisticated space satellites.

Toward the end of the Eisenhower administration, Ezra had been privy to many confidential discussions in which President Eisenhower had mapped out to the cabinet his plans to bridge relations with the Soviet Union, thereby reducing the danger of nuclear war. The visit of Khrushchev to the United States had been part of those plans. Because of his deep distrust of the Soviets, and his conviction that communism was bent on world domination and would use any devious means to achieve its end, Ezra had little confidence in President Eisenhower's plans, which is why he was negative about Khrushchev's visit to the United States. He also was negative about plans for Eisenhower's visit to the Soviet Union in 1960 and about a scheduled summit meeting between the heads of the two governments during that year. These meetings were abruptly canceled in May 1960 amid much acrimony when the United States' U-2 reconnaissance plane, piloted by Gary Francis Powers, crashed in the Soviet Union. After that, relations between the two countries became progressively more distant, distrustful, and dangerous as Khrushchev denounced the United States for spying on the Soviet Union while making what he said were empty overtures for peace.

These events weighed heavily on Elder Benson. He was convinced that the goal of international communism was to dominate the United States, either by armed force or by subversion. He also was convinced that the American people were not conscious of the peril the country faced and that something had to be done to jolt them out of their lethargy. It was against this background, in the late summer of 1961, that he prepared what perhaps was the most significant of the many sermons he had delivered thus far at general conferences of the Church.

Elder Benson was the last speaker at the Saturday afternoon general conference session on September 30, 1961. At the outset, he told the Tabernacle audience that with the Lord's blessing he wanted to talk about "the American heritage of freedom—a plan of God." He began by citing fourteen scriptures or principles that he said underlay freedom in America or described dangers that threatened this freedom. Most of these were scriptures quoted from the Book of Mormon. After citing those that identify America as a land choice above all other lands and decree that its inhabitants must worship the God of the land, Jesus Christ, or be swept off, he cited number ten as follows: "Concerning the United States, the Lord revealed to his prophets that its greatest threat would be a vast, world-wide 'secret combination' which would not only threaten the United States but also seek to 'overthrow the freedom of all lands, nations, and countries' (Ether 8:25)." Referring to the Prophet Joseph Smith's prophecy about the Constitution of the United States hanging by a thread, he said: "It is my conviction that the elders of Israel, widely spread over the nation, will at that crucial time successfully rally the righteous of our country and provide the necessary balance of strength to save the institutions of constitutional government." After citing and discussing the fourteen scriptures and principles, he said: "In the light of these prophecies there should be no doubt in the mind of any priesthood holder that the human family is headed for trouble. There are rugged days ahead. It is time for every man who wishes to do his duty to get himself prepared—physically, spiritually, and psychologically—for the task which may come at any time, as suddenly as the whirlwind."

Elder Benson then identified "the socialist-communist conspiracy" as the primary danger threatening the United States, likening it to the Gadianton robbers told about in the Book of Mormon. He quoted at length from the sermons and writings of President David O. McKay and President J. Reuben Clark that warned about the dangers of international communism, after which he asked rhetorically, "What can priesthood holders do?" In answering, he listed six things: First, to become informed about communism. Second, to treat socialistic communism as the tool of Satan. Third, to help those who have been deceived find the truth. Fourth, to avoid branding as communists those who had unknowingly helped communism. "The remedy," he said, "is to avoid name calling, but point out clearly and persuasively how they are helping the communists." Fifth, to use personal influence in the community to resist the erosion process taking place in political and economic life. Sixth, to set one's personal house in order. (See Conference Report, Sept.–Oct. 1961, pp. 69–75.)

During the next nine years, thirteen of Elder Benson's eighteen general conference talks focused on one aspect or another of this subject. In addition, he gave hundreds of other talks, both inside and outside the Church, in which he dwelled on the perils of communism and the remedies to thwart it. During this period he also published three widely circulated books on the subject, *The Red Carpet* (Bookcraft, 1962), *Title of Liberty* (Deseret Book, 1964), and *An Enemy Hath Done This* (Parliament, 1969). And, of course, his book *Cross Fire* (Doubleday, 1962) contained many references to the perils of communism and his strong opposition to it. Meanwhile, seemingly following his own counsel, he set about to make himself better acquainted with economics, history, and the goals and strategies of communism. He read extensively on these subjects. He was assisted in this effort by Reed, who had become affiliated with the John Birch Society, an educational group that echoed Elder Benson's warnings about the threat of international communism. While he never joined the John Birch Society, Elder Benson endorsed its views and occasionally cited its literature with approval.

Many members, responsive to the suggestions of Elder Benson, became deeply immersed in the study of communism and active in speaking out against it. Some of these were dogmatic and militant and, contrary to the caution of Elder Benson in his "American Heritage of Freedom" speech, were inclined to brand as communists anyone who disagreed with them. And many of them joined the John Birch Society. At the same time, numerous inquiries were received at Church headquarters from members who were confused about the Church's stand on the John Birch Society and about the strong recommendations made by Elder Benson to study and to fight communism.

To help resolve any uncertainty created by this situation, the following announcement appeared in the March 16, 1963, edition of the *Church News:* "Elder Ezra Taft Benson of the Council of the Twelve issued the following statement this week in Sacramento after consultation with President David O. McKay: 'I have stated, as my personal opinion only, that the John Birch Society is the most effective non-church organization in our fight against creeping socialism and godless communism. Obviously only one man, President David O. McKay, speaks for the church on matters of policy. In response to many inquiries, the office of President McKay has stated "that members of the Church are free to join anti-communist organizations if they desire and their membership in the Church is not jeopardized by doing so. The Church is not opposing the John Birch Society or any other organization of like nature; however, it is definitely opposed to anyone using the Church for the purpose of increasing membership for private organizations sponsoring these various ideologies."'"

While the prophet did not endorse Elder Benson's specific recommendations for opposing communism, neither did he choose to restrain him in speaking out on the subject. Thus Elder Benson continued to do so.

On October 18, 1963, Elder Benson's ministry took a new turn when President McKay called him to serve as president of the European Mission, with headquarters in Frankfurt, Germany. The call came as a surprise; Elder Benson had received no prior hint of it. But he accepted the call without question. With Flora's dutiful help, plans were made immediately for still another move. It was decided to take Beth with them.

The Bensons arrived in Frankfurt on New Year's Eve. Before leaving the United States, Elder Benson called on the ambassadors or chargés d'affaires of the seven European countries that would be under his jurisdiction as European mission president. Within that area were twelve missions, including six in Germany (the Bavarian, Berlin, Central German, North German, South German, and West German Missions) and the Austrian, Danish, Finish, Swedish, Swiss, and Norwegian Missions.

The two years Elder Benson spent in Europe as president of the European Mission were productive and personally rewarding. His skills as a Church administrator, his high spirituality, and his buoyant enthusiasm had an elevating effect upon the leaders, the members, and the missionaries. Also, his numerous official contacts in these countries made during his tenure as secretary of agriculture opened many doors and helped to increase the stature and the influence of the Church throughout Europe.

In reporting the highlights of his mission in October 1965, Elder Benson emphasized the centralization of all European Mission and Church agencies in Frankfurt in a Church-owned office building; the setting up of an efficient distribution system for supplying English literature and supplies to LDS servicemen; the centralization of translation work in Frankfurt for missions whose native languages were French, Italian, Dutch, German, Finnish, Danish, Swedish, and Norwegian; the inauguration of missionary work in Italy; creation of a European Information Service to place Church literature in libraries, to prepare press releases, to cultivate good relations with the European media, to prepare lectures for presentation to various groups, to promote Church film showings, and to prepare special brochures, filmstrips, and other audiovisual aids. Concerning Church films, he reported that the New York World's Fair film,

Man's Search for Happiness, had been shown to 30,000 Europeans and that a million copies of a Mormon Pavilion brochure had been distributed. He also reported that a color brochure, *A Church for All the World,* had been developed to replace the World's Fair brochure. (See *Church News,* Oct. 2, 1965.)

It was a significant piece of work that perhaps none of the other Brethren had been better prepared to perform. His intimate contacts with Europeans during his mission following the war and while he served in the Eisenhower cabinet gave him insights that enabled him to focus his time and efforts in the most effective way. And perhaps the most significant aspect of his service never appeared in any report of the mission. This was the motivating influence he exerted on the members and missionaries who were directly exposed to his speaking and counseling. The mood created by the apostolic mantle he wore was intensified by the distinction of his government service. This added weight and a compelling impact to his words.

Chapter 17

Presidential Overtures

S hortly after Elder Benson's return from Europe in October 1965, he was told about the formation of a public-spirited group called the 1976 Committee. Its purpose was to influence political thought in the country toward patriotic, conservative themes looking to the bicentennial celebration in 1976. The committee also sought to encourage those whom it considered qualified to run for the presidency of the United States and other political offices.

Within days after he delivered the report of his European Mission to the general conference in early October, Elder Benson was contacted by the committee and asked if he would be a candidate for the presidency in 1968. Senator Strom Thurmond of South Carolina was suggested as his running mate. Ezra was overwhelmed. He had been out of government office for almost six years and out of the United States for two. He had no political base. He had no organization. He had no money. Indeed, he had none of the components ordinarily thought vital to success in a political contest. He did, however, have a recognizable name, a set of conservative political principles, a capacity for work, and a talent for campaigning. Still, these could not compensate for the deficiencies if there were any hope of success. And the odds against success were multiplied because his candidacy likely would have to be on a third-party ticket, an attempt that would be very difficult given the poor record of third-party movements in the United States.

Elder Benson was not a political amateur. It must be assumed, therefore, that he knew there was little chance of success were he to become a presidential candidate. Yet he was prepared to run. One wonders why. Lacking an answer from him, these assumptions may explain it: A campaign for the presidency would provide a national pulpit from which to expound his ideas of government and to warn about the dangers of communism. If he could persuade large numbers of people to accept his views, defeat at the polls could still be a polemic victory. Joseph Smith's campaign for the presidency would have been a persuasive precedent supporting this idea. Moreover, like Joseph's experience, the campaign also might provide the opportunity to present the Church and its teachings in a more favorable light. Finally, were he to enter the public arena again, the criticism about speaking out so often and so forcefully on secular issues could be muted.

Whatever personal reasons caused him to do so, Elder Benson decided to authorize the 1976 Committee to explore the prospects for his candidacy. Before doing so, however, he counseled with President McKay about it. The prophet told Ezra to allow the committee to proceed with its plans to put his name forward, but he also cautioned him not to help or hinder those plans.

While Elder Benson followed this counsel and refrained from becoming involved in the mechanics of the 1976 Committee, he began to accept numerous invitations to speak to secular groups. Typical of these was a talk he delivered on February 11, 1966, titled "Stand Up for Freedom," sponsored by the Utah Forum for the American Idea. The thrust of the talk, which coincided with the approach of the 1976 Committee in promoting Ezra Taft Benson's candidacy, was suggested in its opening paragraphs. "We have moved a long way," he began "and are now moving further and more rapidly down the soul-destroying road of socialism. The evidence is clear—shockingly clear—for all to see. . . . With the crass unconstitutional usurpation of powers by the Executive branch of the federal government, anti-spiritual decisions of the Supreme Court—all apparently approved by a weakly submissive rubber-stamp Congress—the days ahead are ominously frightening" (*An Enemy Hath Done This* [Salt Lake City: Parliament Publishers, 1969], pp. 30–31).

In assessing the reasons for this condition, the speaker said, "I am convinced that a major part of the cause can be justly laid at the door of the socialist-communist conspiracy which is led by masters of deceit who deceive the very elect." In defining this conspiracy, Elder Benson referred to a communist convention held in Moscow in December 1960, which, he said, "issued an edict that the rising tide of patriotism and anti-communism must be smashed—especially in the United States. All the tricks of the hate propaganda and smear tactics were to be unleashed on the heads of American patriots."

He went on to say, however, that the attack on the anti-communist movement in the United States did not come from Moscow. "It came in the name of influential Americans who espoused the socialist-communist line." He said that by 1962, "these American liberals had almost completely neutralized the resurgence of American patriotism. They had frightened uninformed citizens away from study groups and patriotic rallies. They had made it popular to call patriotism a 'controversial' subject which should not be discussed in school assemblies or churches." As to the motives of these so-called liberals, he acknowledged they might be sincere. "But sincerity or supposed benevolence or even cleverness is not the question. The question is: 'Are we going to save this country from the hands of the enemy and the deceived?'"

The remedy he proposed was clear: "I think it is time for every patriotic American to join with neighbors to study the Constitution and the conspiracy." He recommended several publications deemed suitable for this purpose and concluded with a call to action: "To the patriots I say this: Take that long eternal look. Stand up for freedom, no matter what the cost. . . . In this mighty struggle each of you has a part. Every person on the earth today chose the right side during the war in heaven. Be on the right side now. Stand up and be counted" (ibid., pp. 30–45).

In the months that followed, many similar talks were given in different parts of the country. "Elder Ezra Taft Benson of the Council of the Twelve was busy last week giving public addresses on the subject Stand Up For Freedom," reported the *Church News* on March 5, 1966. "On February 26 he addressed the American Academy of Dental Practice at Chicago, attended by delegates from all states and from several foreign countries. On February 28 he addressed a public meeting at St. Louis, Missouri, sponsored by the Wake Up America Committee and attended by more than five hundred people. He also was scheduled to give the same talk on May 16 at the National Association of Credit Management in Portland, Oregon." On July 4, 1966, he was the featured speaker at a God, Family, and Country rally in Boston. And at a rally in Oregon, he delivered a talk entitled "It Can Happen Here," in which he defined the issue as being between light and darkness, freedom and slavery, and the spirit of Christianity and the spirit of anti-Christ.

These talks attracted large, enthusiastic audiences. Behind the scenes, thousands of people became involved in studying the Constitution and communism. Meanwhile, the 1976 Committee was busy trying to drum up support for the candidacy of Elder Benson and Senator Thurmond. During the last half of 1966, there appeared to be what was called a "groundswell" of support. Later, however, this support dwindled as the candidates of the two major parties began to dominate the headlines. Later in 1967 the American Independent Party launched a movement to draft Elder Benson as their presidential candidate. It was done without his knowledge or consent. Nothing came of it.

In February 1968, Governor George Wallace of Alabama, a candidate for president, urged Elder Benson to join him as a vice presidential candidate on an independent, third-party ticket. Elder Benson and Reed traveled to Montgomery, Alabama, to discuss the matter with Governor Wallace. However, when President McKay was briefed about the discussion, the prophet suggested that Elder Benson not become involved. Contacts with the governor were then terminated, although as late as September 1968 Mr. Wallace was still making overtures. This ended any prospect of Elder Benson's becoming involved in politics as a candidate for the presidency. However, it did not end his vital interest in public affairs and especially in the conflict over communism. He continued to speak out on this subject, both in his general conference sermons and in talks delivered to groups outside the Church. But these talks were merely the expressions of a concerned private citizen and not those of a potential presidential candidate.

During the busy period from October 1965 to February 1968, while Elder Benson was involved with groups promoting his presidential candidacy, he continued to carry a full load as a member of the Twelve. Shortly after returning from Europe, he was appointed to the board of directors of Bonneville International Corporation and to the Expenditures Committee. These were key appointments that introduced him more intimately to the media outlets owned by the Church and to the procedures governing the disbursement of Church funds.

Bonneville International is an umbrella corporation that oversees the operation of Church-owned radio and television companies. Membership on its board of directors exposed Elder Benson to the intricacies of commercial radio and television and to the worldwide networking involved in arranging the international broadcasts of the Church's general conferences. The global insights and organizational know-how gained from his service in the Twelve and in the cabinet effectively equipped Elder Benson to make meaningful contributions in establishing policies and goals for the company. He was not a mere figurehead; his international reputation and contacts added distinction to the board.

From the time of his induction into the Twelve, Elder Benson served as a member of the Council on the Disposition of the Tithes. This council, comprising the First Presidency, the Twelve, and the Presiding Bishopric, is the equivalent of an appropriations committee. Traditionally it met only once annually, although in later years it also met to consider special budgets for education. On the other hand, the expenditures committee meets regularly throughout the year to process expenditures falling within the budgets approved by the Council on the Disposition of the Tithes. Service on the Expenditures Committee gave Elder Benson a wider view and a more persuasive voice in the financing of Church projects and programs around the world.

In addition to these and other headquarters duties, Elder Benson continued to fill many assignments in the field. After his release as European Mission president, he was assigned to oversee the work there. This entailed periodic trips to Europe. He and Flora traveled to the Continent on a July-August trip in 1966 and again in November of that year. He trained missionaries, met with servicemen, counseled local leaders, and held general meetings. He also inspected Church buildings and possible new sites or other acquisitions. Urgent matters he handled unilaterally; others were processed through normal channels. The apostolic authority he held enabled him to act immediately if deemed necessary. However, he was slow to act alone.

During the July-August trip he installed John Duns Jr. as president of the Italian Mission. In November he toured the new mission. The Church first attained a foothold in Italy in the early 1850s under the leadership of Elder Lorenzo Snow of the Twelve, who, on a mountain near Torre Pellice in northern Italy, dedicated the land for the preaching of the gospel. Afterward Elder Snow and his companions had success in that area among a Protestant group called the Waldenses. Some of their converts, including the Cardon and Toronto families, later immigrated to the United States. Those who remained dwindled and scattered due to the lack of priesthood direction. The neglect resulted from the pressures of colonizing Utah and surrounding areas and of the so-called Utah War in 1857. Because there had been no organized proselyting in Italy since then, the Brethren decided the land should be rededicated. Elder Benson was assigned to do it.

On November 10, 1966, Elder Benson and Flora, along with President and Sister Duns and a group of Church members and missionaries, gathered near the top of a mountain outside Torre Pellice. It was as near the site of Elder Snow's dedication as could be determined from the scanty records available. The occasion was solemn and impressive. Following a song, a prayer, and preliminary remarks, Elder Benson dedicated the land of Italy for the preaching of the gospel.

The dedication was a procedure peculiar to the apostolic calling, one that had been followed since the earliest days of the Church. Among the first and most widely publicized dedications of this kind was Orson Hyde's dedication of the land of Jerusalem in 1841. In the same year that Elder Benson rededicated Italy, his fellow Apostle Marion G. Romney dedicated the land of Venezuela high on a mountain overlooking the city of Caracas. Before and since then, many other similar dedications have been performed all around the world by members of the Twelve, whose duty it is to see that the gospel is preached everywhere. "We are to take the gospel to every person," Elder Benson said at a Regional Representatives' seminar on April 5, 1985, just a few months before he became President of the Church. "Without exception, without excuse, without rationalization, we are to go 'unto all the world and preach the gospel to every creature.'"

One of Elder Benson's chief satisfactions was to watch the growth of the Church. In view of the Catholic Church's dominant influence in Italy, it was a special source of satisfaction to see the growth of the LDS Church there following his rededication of the land. Within a few years the Italy Mission was divided to create the new Italy North Mission. Then followed new missions in Milan, Padova, and Catania. In the early 1980s stakes were organized in Milan and Venice, and by the end of 1991 there were 16,000 members of the Church in Italy.

During this period, Elder Benson continued to fill many assignments to attend conferences in stakes in the United States. In these meetings he never delivered talks prepared in advance, but spoke extemporaneously. His sincerity and spirituality shone through on these occasions. The topics were dictated by the needs of the people at the moment. Some were talks of solace and comfort, some were doctrinal, some were inspirational, and some warned against conditions threatening the youth—alcohol and drug abuse and sexual misconduct. He was like the proverbial "watchman on the tower," scanning the surroundings and giving counsel of warning or encouragement as the circumstances required.

Elder Benson usually stayed with local Church leaders on these occasions. Having received many General Authorities in his own home while he served in a stake presidency, he was conscious of the pressures exerted on a host by his visit and endeavored to alleviate them. He especially enjoyed staying in the home of a farmer where he would pitch in to help with the daily chores, milking, feeding the animals, or perhaps helping to take a water turn. Undoubtedly he gave counsel, requested or volunteered, about farm economics and government farm policies. To have such intimate contact with an Apostle and a former secretary of agriculture was an event long to be remembered by a Mormon farmer, talked about and perhaps recorded in a diary for descendants to read about.

Elder Benson's organizational and diplomatic skills developed in Washington, D.C., were put to good use by the Brethren. He was called on to give mission presidents going into the field tips about how to obtain and utilize the help of government officials. He also gave wise counsel about delegation. Because one of his first steps as the secretary of agriculture was to restructure his department in order to increase efficiency, he was very pleased with an action taken on September 27, 1967. On that day, sixty-nine men were called to serve as Regional Representatives of the Twelve. These men were to serve as trainers in the field to assist stake presidents and to see that instructions from the First Presidency and the Twelve were implemented. This historic change would help promote efficiency and unity in the Church as it expanded globally.

Amid the pressures exerted by these diverse activities, Elder Benson never allowed his priorities to become scrambled. Regardless of how busy or stressed he might be, he never failed to allocate time for family affairs. With the marriage of Beth in June 1966 to David Burton, the Bensons were without a child in the home for the first time in thirty-eight years. All six of the children had found companions of high caliber to whom they had been sealed in the temple. This opened a new phase in their lives—grandchildren. Ezra and Flora were as solicitous about the welfare and training of their grandchildren as they had been about their own children. They were like jewels in their crown. Repeatedly Elder Benson expressed the fond hope that there would be no empty chairs in the circle of what he and Flora projected to be an eternal family. They never missed an opportunity to have meaningful relationships with the children and grandchildren so they might imbue them with their values and goals.

Typical of their efforts at grandparenting was a month they spent in Europe with granddaughter Flora Walker, daughter of Barbara and Dr. Robert H. Walker. It was a working trip for Elder Benson, who spent much time counseling and teaching members, missionaries, and local leaders. As time allowed, however, he joined the two Floras in visiting museums, zoos, amusement parks, and places of historic interest. The grandfather, now nearing seventy, was exhausted when he returned home. The trip doubtless caused him to appreciate more the maxim that the training and entertainment of children are best left to young parents, except for intermittent, short interludes reserved for meaningful grandparenting.

Ezra and Flora soon adopted a plan to foster unity and love among their children and grandchildren without creating strain in the family. They purchased a cottage in Midway, Utah, located in the heart of Heber Valley, fifty miles southeast of Salt Lake City. The setting, high in the Wasatch Mountains, had attracted many Swiss-German immigrants whose love for their homeland was reflected in the alpine houses they built and decorated with quaint, Old World gingerbread. Enlarged and renovated, this cottage provided an ideal hideaway for the Benson clan where they could come together for holidays and other special occasions. Aside from the opportunity to visit, relax, and catch up on family news, the cottage was a home base for outdoor activities for every taste—hiking, horseback riding, horseshoes, fishing, swimming, and, in the winter season, skiing and snowmobiling. The cottage was close enough to Salt Lake City so that Ezra and Flora could steal away on a moment's notice to enjoy its comfort and seclusion, away from the constant and unremitting pressures at Church headquarters.

Once the Bensons had acquired the cottage, word of it spread quickly among the residents of the rural, predominantly Mormon community. They took pride in the fact that an Apostle and former secretary of agriculture had become

From his earliest years, Elder Benson was an avid horseman

their neighbor. They kept their eye on the place when the Bensons were not there; and when word spread that members of the family were there for a visit, neighbors, without intruding, would contact them to wish them well and to inquire if there was anything they could do to make their stay enjoyable. It was a relationship and an environment the Bensons treasured.

While this idyllic hideaway was the source of some of Elder Benson's most satisfying experiences, in later years it also reminded him of one of his greatest traumas. In July 1978, during the traditional summer break when the General Authorities usually are on a reduced schedule, he went to Midway for a few days of relaxation. While Ezra steadied a horse as one of his neighbors attempted to mount it, the animal became spooked and, rearing unexpectedly, threw Ezra to the ground. The violent impact caused four fractures of his right leg between the hip and knee. Extensive surgery was required. There followed a lengthy and painful convalescence during which he progressed from bed, to wheelchair, to crutches, to a cane, and finally back to walking, though gingerly. Three years later, further extensive surgery became necessary when an artificial hip was implanted. Another long period of recuperation followed. Through it all, he maintained a remarkably optimistic and jocular outlook. He regarded it merely as an unfortunate episode of life in a hazardous world. He took pride in showing visitors to his office a cartoon drawn by his grandson Steve Benson. With the caption "That's what I get for horsin' around," it depicted him lying placidly beneath the horse, with his head resting on one hand and a smile on his face.

The incident, of course, was no laughing matter, especially if someone said or suggested he had been thrown from the horse. It was an inexcusable affront to imply that one such as he could be thrown from any horse, he who had been raised on a farm and who had been around horses all his life. He took genuine pride in his horsemanship and wanted to scotch immediately any false rumors that he had been thrown from a horse, especially while it was in the corral.

The injury Elder Benson suffered was serious and debilitating given the fact he was seventy-nine when the accident occured and eighty-two when he received the implant. The light touch he gave to it, suggested by the pride he took in his grandson's clever cartoon, was not meant to trivialize the affair. Rather, it seems to have been merely a reflection of his native, positive attitude, which, because President Kimball was ill at the time, no doubt helped allay possible concern among Church members about the physical condition of the Apostle who was next in line to become President of the Church.

Major factors in President Benson's successful recovery from what could have been a tragic accident were the love and concern shown him by his family and others. In typical Benson character, the family immediately closed ranks to assist in any way possible. Especially noteworthy was the way in which Beth and her husband, Dr. David Burton, opened their home to care for both President and Sister Benson during the long period of convalescence.

It also seems clear that the injury and the long recovery that followed were factors that aggravated some of President Benson's later physical problems. At the time of the accident he was in robust good health. The powerful physique developed in his early years through work on the farm and in athletics, and which had been maintained since then, had helped provide immunity from serious illness and physical disability. However, the restrictions on his mobility caused by the injury, the long convalescence, and its aftermath tended to weaken his system and its resistance to physical ailments. It was a crucial incident that had long-range implications.

In 1968, however, while final efforts were being made to persuade Elder Benson to become involved in the presidential race, his health was excellent. Despite his withdrawal from the public arena, he continued to retain a keen interest in the development of national and international affairs. On January 30, 1968, he shared the dismay of most Americans when the Vietcong launched the massive Tet Offensive, during which thirty-six of forty-four provincial capitals were assaulted. The offensive came as a great surprise because during previous years of the Vietnam War, the Vietcong had reduced their military activity during Tet to celebrate the lunar new year. Of special concern was the breaching of the walls surrounding the U.S. Embassy in Saigon, allowing nineteen Vietcong soldiers to enter the compound, where they fought to the death. The surprise was compounded by optimistic reports preceding the Tet Offensive that announced that Hanoi was weakening and that the tide of battle had swung in favor of the South Vietnamese and their allies.

This swelled the loud chorus in the United States of those who called for an immediate, unilateral withdrawal of the United States from Southeast Asia. The crescendo increased daily as television clips on the nightly news showed bloody scenes of death among both combatants and the civilian population. Especially grisly and provocative were scenes of the attack upon the small village of My Lai in the spring of 1968.

Such was the furor this created that President Lyndon B. Johnson announced on March 31, 1968, that he would not be a candidate for reelection. Five days later the country suffered another wrenching blow when civil rights leader Martin Luther King was gunned down in Memphis, Tennessee. This touched off rioting in more than a hundred cities across the United States, reflecting the deep anguish of the black community.

The political void in the Democratic party created by President Johnson's announcement was soon filled when Vice President Hubert H. Humphrey, Eugene McCarthy, and Robert F. Kennedy began campaigning aggressively for their party's nomination. Meanwhile, on the Republican side, Richard Nixon was the front-runner, challenged for a while by Ezra's Mormon friend George Romney. The Romney campaign was stopped abruptly when, after returning from a trip to Vietnam, the candidate said he had been "brainwashed" by U.S. military leaders, meaning he had been misled by skewed military statistics and projections. The press jumped massively on the unfortunate statement, portraying candidate Romney as weak-minded and unstable. From that moment, he was politically dead.

Finally, the political picture became almost unimaginably complicated on June 5, 1968, when Robert F. Kennedy was assassinated in Los Angeles, California. This touched off more wild scenes around the country, generated by political activists, which came to a head in August at the Democratic National Convention in Chicago. The disruptive tactics of these activists created such turmoil in Chicago that President Johnson was dissuaded from even attending in person.

It was against this background that Elder Benson began to fulfill his new responsibilities as the member of the Twelve

257

chiefly responsible to monitor and to move along the work in the Far East. Elder Bruce R. McConkie of the First Council of Seventy was appointed to assist him. Their appointments came in June 1968, near the time of Robert F. Kennedy's assassination. Elder Benson's first trip to the Orient in his new capacity was begun in August, near the time of the blow-up in Chicago connected with the Democratic National Convention. It was a tense and traumatic time in the United States and even more so in the Far East, where the Vietnam War had reached the height of its intensity. By the end of 1968 there were more than a half million Americans under arms in Vietnam, fighting a war that had lost its focus. The Johnson administration had adopted a strategy of gradual escalation whose object was not to win the war by military victory but, rather, to bring Hanoi to the peace table for a negotiated settlement. This strategy had angered and alienated both conservatives and liberals—the conservatives who thought it folly to enter a war unless it were intended to take all steps necessary to win, and the liberals who were incensed by the absence of a compelling rationale to support U.S. involvement, by the drain on the country's human and physical resources, and by the death and destruction being inflicted upon the civilian population of Vietnam.

Elder Benson was acutely aware of all this as he left for the Orient in August. He had been critical of the U.S. strategy, especially during the time when it appeared he might be a presidential candidate. Now, however, his purpose was not to debate war strategies and objectives but to succor the Saints in the area and to nourish the growth of the Church.

During this first trip, which he made alone, Elder Benson had very limited objectives: to survey and encourage the work in the Far East generally, to hold a special youth conference and other meetings in Tokyo, to check on plans for the World's Fair (Expo '70), where the Church was to have a major exhibit, and to visit and to hold meetings in the Philippines. Any plans to visit Vietnam were postponed until November, when he would return with Elder McConkie.

The trip was successful. He was received with typical oriental warmth and deference in Tokyo. He genuinely loved these people, admired their work ethic, and had confidence the Church would thrive among them. He was amazed by the rapid growth both there and in the Philippines, which had occurred in less than twenty-five years following the end of World War II. Perhaps as astonishing as the growth was the vast change in Japanese attitudes toward the United States and its people, from militant hatred to friendly acceptance. It was this change, a change paralleled by changed American attitudes toward the Japanese, that had made possible the establishment and the growth of the Church in that land. War had given birth to peace and enlightenment.

It was after Ezra's return from this first trip to the Orient that Governor George Wallace made his final overture to Elder Benson to become his vice presidential running mate. Failing that, the governor turned to General Curtis LeMay. Capitalizing on divisions within the Democratic party and questions about Richard Nixon, they waged an aggressive campaign that Elder Benson watched with great interest, given the efforts Governor Wallace had made to induce him to run. The outcome was never much in doubt as Richard Nixon swept to victory. Elder Benson was not enthusiastic about the result, although he preferred Mr. Nixon to Hubert Humphrey, who regularly had opposed Ezra's agriculture policies.

Shortly after the November election, Elder Benson and Flora, accompanied by Elder McConkie and his wife, Amelia, left for the Orient, where they would remain for almost a month. So that necessary meetings could be held with missionaries, members, and local leaders throughout this vast area, it was decided to divide the work. Originally, it was planned that Elder Benson would include Vietnam in his itinerary. However, because of his high profile in American politics and his outspoken views on communism and the war in Southeast Asia, local observers strongly urged him not to go there at that time. Elder Benson acceded to this counsel, and Vietnam was included in Elder McConkie's itinerary instead.

Included in Elder Benson's schedule were visits to Taiwan, Japan, Korea, and Thailand, where he would hold numerous instructional and motivational meetings. Special attention was given to the missionaries, in whose hands rested the key to the future growth of the Church in the Orient. As he taught the missionaries, it was evident that Elder Benson had retained his zeal for missionary work, first generated almost fifty years before as a young man in England. His enthusiasm for missionary work was infectious. He knew the challenges faced by missionaries from the United States who were laboring in a foreign land. These missionaries were tested as he had never been because of the need to learn a new language. He never ceased to marvel at the ingenuity and skill shown by these young men and women in mastering the rudiments of complicated languages so they could teach the people in their own tongue.

Elder Benson sought to improve the conditions under which the missionaries worked by routinely seeking the friendship and support of high-ranking government officials. To this end he was able to meet with the governors of Taiwan and Okinawa and with the king of Thailand. When it seemed appropriate to do so, he always gave such dignitaries copies of Church literature, especially the Book of Mormon. He therefore was pleased when the king of Thailand graciously accepted a copy of the Book of Mormon that had been translated into the Thai language.

Elder and Sister Benson flew from Tokyo to Washington, D.C., in time to participate in ground-breaking ceremonies for the Washington Temple on December 7, 1968. Considering the promising conditions at that time for the growth of the Church in Japan, the immense changes that had occurred in the twenty-seven years since Pearl Harbor were astonishing to contemplate. The occasion undoubtedly caused the Bensons to reflect on the rapid growth of the

Church in their own nation's capital since they first moved to Washington, D.C., from Boise almost thirty years before.

Elder and Sister Benson returned to Washington, D.C., the following month to attend the inauguration of President Richard M. Nixon. They received special treatment because their friend Bill Marriott was the chairman of the inauguration committee. It was a joy to mingle with many of their old friends and to witness the pageantry of the inauguration. The event aroused exciting memories of similar happenings sixteen years before that had opened one of the most significant periods of their lives. The memories became more vivid and poignant at the end of March when Dwight D. Eisenhower passed away. The public statement Elder Benson issued lauded President Eisenhower as a man of faith, deep spirituality, and courage. It implied regret that any statement or conduct on his part might have hinted that President Eisenhower was anything other than a loyal, patriotic American.

Later, in the spring of 1969, Elder Benson and Flora returned to the Orient, where the Apostle dedicated Singapore for the preaching of the gospel and presided at the ground breaking for the Mormon Pavilion for Expo '70 in Osaka. As Ezra's meeting schedule was arranged, it was decided it would now be appropriate for him to visit Vietnam. He held several meetings with Mormon servicemen in the south-central and northern sectors not far from active combat zones and sometimes within earshot of the din of battle. In his remarks Elder Benson brought the men a blessing from the prophet; assured them of the love and support of Church members everywhere; and encouraged them to pray and to read the scriptures often, to seek spiritual direction, to observe the standards of the Church, and to endeavor to teach the gospel to their buddies. He was touched when he visited a wounded Mormon boy and learned the youth had been praying fervently that the Apostle would come to him.

Elder Benson returned from this tour confirmed in his

belief that the military strategy in Vietnam was wrong. His views on the "no-win war" were eloquently expressed in his book *An Enemy Hath Done This,* which was published later in the year. The book also elaborated on his views about the threat of communism and about the dangers of what he called "creeping socialism."

The Bensons and the McConkies returned to the Orient again following the October 1969 general conference to tour the missions in the area. While in Indonesia, Elder Benson dedicated the land for the preaching of the gospel. The site was a remote mountainside covered with a lush growth of banana trees and other indigenous plants and flowers. It afforded a sweeping view of the well-tilled valley below and the terraced cornfields that crept up the hills beyond. Among the small group assembled for the sacred service was a government leader whom Elder Benson had met years before. The day was made complete for the Apostle when, following the ceremony, this man asked to be baptized. The incident seemed to symbolize the act of planting the seeds of the gospel in a new land and to foreshadow the abundant growth the future would yield.

A few months later, during another visit to the Far East, Elder Benson dedicated the Mormon Pavilion at Expo '70. The next day he and Flora attended the formal ceremonies officially opening the fair. The event was dignified by the attendance of the emperor and other high Japanese officials. The pavilion proved to be a highly successful undertaking for the Church. Over three-quarters of a million visitors to the pavilion filled out referral cards that were used by missionaries afterward in follow-up contacts.

Elder Benson continued to serve as the first contact for the work in Asia for several months following the opening of the pavilion at Expo '70. It was a source of elation when he was able to participate in the creation of the first stake in Japan at Tokyo. He continued to work in the area and to make intermittent visits to the Far East until his assignment was changed to the intermountain area of the United States.

Chapter 18

Major Changes

On Sunday January 18, 1970, Elder Benson was presiding at a conference of the Virginia Stake. As he counseled with the stake presidency, word came that President David O. McKay had passed away that morning in his Salt Lake City apartment in the Hotel Utah. The prophet's death was not unexpected. He was in his ninety-seventh year and had been in poor health for some time. During recent years, he had suffered a series of minor strokes that had impaired his movements and slurred his speech. However, his mentality had remained intact. With the help of his counselors (Hugh B. Brown and N. Eldon Tanner), three additional counselors he had called (Joseph Fielding Smith, Thorpe B. Isaacson, and Alvin R. Dyer), the Twelve, members of his staff, and his family, he had been able to carry on effectively despite his advanced age.

Ironically, as it would later be with Elder Benson, the deterioration in President McKay's health began with an accident involving a horse. It occurred several years before his death while he was at the McKay family home in Huntsville, Utah. As the prophet began to saddle his favorite horse, Sonny Boy, for a ride, the animal spooked, dragging President McKay several hundred feet. The first of the several minor strokes he suffered occurred not long afterward. The prophet was never the same, in a physical sense.

The death of President McKay deeply saddened Elder Benson. He genuinely loved the great man and had done so ever since their first personal acquaintance in England almost fifty years before. From that time, Ezra had become President McKay's protégé, looking upon the older man as his principal mentor and confidant among the General Authorities. There would never be another one to fill that important role until he became President of the Church and called counselors to serve with him. Moreover, President McKay had been Elder Benson's chief supporter in his efforts to arouse people to the dangers of communism and socialism.

Elder Benson was honored to offer the benediction at President McKay's funeral, which was held on January 22, 1970. The following day he joined the other members of the Twelve in the upper room of the Salt Lake Temple. There, after all the Brethren had had opportunity to express their feelings, Joseph Fielding Smith was approved, ordained, and set apart as the tenth President of the Church. Approved and set apart as his counselors were Elders Harold B. Lee and N. Eldon Tanner. Because Elder Lee was second in apostolic seniority to President Smith, he also was set apart as President of the Twelve. And because Elder Lee's duties in the First Presidency would prevent him from handling the day-to-day work of the Twelve, Elder Spencer W. Kimball was set apart as Acting President of the Twelve. These significant changes had little immediate effect upon Elder Benson's status, except they moved him one step closer to the prophetic office.

Elder Benson traveled to Idaho Falls, Idaho, following

the reorganization meeting in the temple. There in the evening he spoke to an audience of twenty-five hundred at a gathering arranged prior to President McKay's death. His subject was "America at the Crossroads." The talk, which was enthusiastically received, elaborated on the themes he had developed over recent years, warning against the dangers facing the country.

At the solemn assembly held in connection with the April 1970 general conference, the January reorganization of the First Presidency was ratified by the members of the Church assembled in the Tabernacle on Temple Square. At the same time, the vacancy in the Twelve was filled by the call of Elder Boyd K. Packer.

The new First Presidency soon sought to utilize Elder Benson's special skills more fully. In May 1970 he was appointed to the board of directors of Deseret Ranches of Florida. This ranch, acquired by the Church in the 1940s and centered at Deer Park, Florida, near Orlando, is reputed to be one of the largest cattle and farming operations in the United States. It is operated as a commercial enterprise, using the most modern equipment and technology. Elder Benson's professional training, his practical experience in farming, and his intimate knowledge of government regulations and marketing strategies brought a new outlook and expertise to the operation. He encouraged a multiple-use concept that included timber, wildlife, and citrus projects in addition to cattle raising. Later he was appointed to the boards of the Deseret Farms of California and the Temple View Farms in New Zealand, other farms owned and operated by the Church. Few of his Church assignments brought more personal pleasure to Elder Benson than did these. They brought him near to the soil and in direct contact with the kind of honest, hard-working people with whom he had been raised. He enjoyed nothing more than to go to one of these operations, put on riding garb, and mount a good horse for a look around.

Meanwhile there were numerous other assignments that

claimed his attention. In addition to the farms, Corn Products International, and Bonneville International, he served on the boards of Olson Brothers, Beneficial Life Insurance Company, and Zions First National Bank. Also, he chaired the committees on ward and branch changes, stake conference and regional meetings, and the budget. As already indicated, he also supervised the work in the inter-mountain area after his release from the Asia assignment.

Following President Smith's ordination, the talks Elder Benson delivered at general conferences increasingly reflected the breadth of his apostolic ministry. For instance, his April 1970 conference talk highlighted missionary work, especially the work in the Asian lands. "There has never been a time until now when the Church has had the strength and means to reach out effectively to the Asian nations," he told the Tabernacle audience. "In the timetable of the Lord, the door is now open, and this is apparently the day for work in Asia" (in Conference Report, Apr. 1970, p. 130). Six months later, his conference address dwelled on the family. He stressed family prayer, family home evening, and scrip-ture reading, "particularly the Book of Mormon." He encouraged fathers at nighttime "to go to each child's bed-side, to talk with him, answer his questions and tell him how much he is loved" and ended by quoting from Charles Sprague's poem, a favorite of his: "We are all here: father, mother, sister, brother, all who hold each other dear. Each chair is filled, we are all at home" (in Conference Report, Oct. 1970, p. 25).

The poem reflected Elder Benson's tender feelings about his family and the earnest hope there would be no vacancies in the circle at the end. Nothing ever took precedence over this. Because Flora always occupied the seat of honor in that vision of the future, her serious injury suffered a few days before Christmas in 1970 evoked a painful response in her husband. She had slipped on ice on the front step of the home, splintering the bone of her left leg below the knee. Major surgery became necessary. Ezra gladly would have traded places with her. It was more excruciating to see her suffer than to endure pain himself. In this emergency they turned to President Harold B. Lee for solace and a blessing. It was Brother Lee who had blessed Flora in her illness while Ezra was in Europe twenty-five years before. The blessing, which reflected the special spiritual qualities of their friend, brought tears to their eyes. Not only did President Lee invoke blessings of comfort, peace, and healing upon Flora and blessings of competence upon her doctors, but he also brought before the Lord the fine qualities and the achievements of the Benson family. It was an elevating and unifying experience, bringing them closer together than ever before.

A few months later, Elder Benson and Flora left for assignments in the Pacific that would take them to Hawaii, Guam, and the Philippines. It proved to be one of their most arduous trips. It also proved to be the last lengthy trip they would take together. Leaving Salt Lake City in May 1973, they were gone for eighteen days. The weather was stifling in the islands, the long flights were tiring, and the crowded schedule of meetings afforded little opportunity for relaxation. It was not the kind of trip one would recommend for a couple in their seventy-fourth year, especially for Flora, who not too many months before had suffered the terrible fracture and endured the surgery and long convalescence that had followed.

The Bensons were physically spent when they returned from the Pacific. After a few days, Elder Benson snapped back to normal. Flora did not. Her vital energies seemed depleted, and her weariness was accompanied by vague feelings of apprehension and concern she could not explain or dispel. At first the doctors were baffled and unable to diagnose her problem. Later they concluded she had suffered a mild stroke, if not a series of mild strokes. The remedy prescribed, rest and relaxation, seemed not to ease but to fuel her problem. Flora had always been in the forefront of family initiatives when a crisis arose, providing solace and support to others. Now she had to play a subordinate part, being the recipient rather than the provider of assistance. This switch in status may have negatively affected her condition, given the leading role she had always played in family affairs.

The family rallied around in typical Benson fashion to provide assistance and encouragement. The children eased her load wherever possible. Beth, who now lived in Salt Lake City, was especially solicitous. When her father's duties required travel, Flora would be brought to the daughter's home to stay while Elder Benson was out of the city. The parting in these circumstances often was accompanied by tears of sorrow. It was a wrenching experience for all. In time Flora's condition improved to the point where she could accompany her husband on some trips, even trips abroad. So in 1976 they were included in the official party to attend an area conference in Glasgow, Scotland. But the lengthy, meeting-filled trips like the one to the Pacific in 1973 were out of the question.

In order to simplify their living arrangements, Elder and Sister Benson moved to a condominium in late 1973. It was easier to maintain, had good security, and seemed to ease Flora's conscience about housekeeping chores. It was an ideal arrangement under the circumstances, especially since the Midway hideaway was still available to provide a more traditional home atmosphere when they visited there periodically.

The Bensons spent a peaceful Christmas in their new home, made joyful by the spirit of the day and visits from members of the family and friends. They looked forward to a restful holiday, free from Church assignments and other commitments, so they could reflect on the past and lay plans for the future. It was a pattern they had followed throughout their married life. Any plans they had made were abruptly changed the night of December 26 when word came that President Harold B. Lee had passed away at LDS Hospital. Elder Benson was incredulous at the news. Like most of the Brethren, he had been unaware of President Lee's precarious health. Outwardly, President Lee had seemed strong and active. That and the longevity of his two immediate predecessors, Presidents David O. McKay and Joseph Fielding Smith, both of whom had lived beyond their mid-nineties, created the expectation that President Lee would live for many years. Indeed, Elder Benson confidently expected Harold B. Lee would be the last President of the Church under whom he would serve. Thus, the news that his boyhood friend was dead created a revolution in his thinking. Suddenly Ezra Taft Benson was set on a new and unexpected course of action, a happening with which he had had some familiarity. His life was dotted with these swift and unforeseen changes in direction.

After learning the news, he contacted President Spencer W. Kimball to express his support and the Lee family to offer his condolences. The next morning, a Thursday, Elder Benson met with his brethren of the Twelve so that action could be taken to handle necessary Church matters pending the installation of a new First Presidency and to appoint a committee to arrange for the funeral services on Saturday. It turned out to be a wet and dreary day on which to bury a prophet.

The Twelve gathered in the upper room of the Salt Lake Temple on Sunday December 30, 1973, at 3:00 P.M. to reorganize the First Presidency. It was the fifth time Elder Benson had participated in this solemn procedure. This time, however, he played a more active role. In addition to expressing his views about the reorganization, he also nominated Spencer W. Kimball as the twelfth President of the Church and acted as voice in ordaining him to the prophetic office. After President Kimball had selected and set apart his counselors, N. Eldon Tanner and Marion G. Romney, Elder Benson was approved and set apart as President of the Quorum of the Twelve Apostles.

Chapter 19

President of the Twelve

E zra Taft Benson's new position as President of the
Twelve vastly altered his status in the leading councils of the Church. It placed him next in line to
become President of the Church should he survive
President Kimball. Objectively, this seemed to be a likely
scenario since the prophet was four years older than he and
was fragile in health, while Ezra was robust and active. The
new position also gave him administrative supervision over
the Council of the Twelve, the second governing body of the
Church, whose main duty is to preach the gospel and to set
in order the affairs of the Church worldwide, subject to the
ultimate direction of the First Presidency.

In this capacity, President Benson would direct stake
conference, mission tour, and other assignments of the
Twelve; receive and analyze their reports, giving any necessary counsel about them; preside at weekly meetings of the
Twelve to oversee and coordinate the work; and supervise
the calling and ordination of patriarchs. He also would
direct the work of the Assistants to the Twelve and the

Regional Representatives of the Twelve; and he had certain supervisory responsibilities over the Seventy, the Presiding Bishopric, and the Patriarch to the Church. To aid him in discharging these heavy responsibilities, President Benson had an administrative staff of assistants and secretaries who helped track the work and performed clerical chores. Until this time, he had never had a headquarters assignment that gave him such administrative authority and responsibility and freedom of action. He was now in a position to control his travel schedule, taking such assignments as he wished and allotting himself the time he considered necessary to perform them.

In this new role President Benson adopted the administrative style he had developed as a stake president and as secretary of agriculture. It was a style that combined a genuine interest in the welfare of his associates and a penchant for delegation. The paternal quality so evident in his family relations carried over into this setting. Those who served directly under President Benson while he was President of the Twelve attested to the caring concern he showed toward them. They were his "official family," and he treated them as a family. Each occupied an honored place, and each was expected to share the load through broad delegations of authority and responsibility. This was a skill that Elder Benson had polished to the highest degree while serving as secretary of agriculture. Applying it there was a matter of survival. Had he not mastered it, he would have been swamped by the weight and complexity of administering the affairs of that sprawling department. He brought this skill into his service as President of the Twelve and, later, into his service as President of the Church. By delegating as much responsibility as possible to his associates, Elder Benson was left free to devote himself to doing the things he alone could do and to charting the course.

He encouraged the open expression of each member's opinions on subjects coming before the quorum, but he disapproved of lengthy discussion that had no useful purpose.

Ezra Taft Benson in 1975 as President of the Council of the Twelve

An adroit way to end a discussion that he felt had run its course was to tell the Brethren there was enough hay down and it was time to bale a little. He also disapproved of what he descriptively called "dog and pony shows," presentations that were long on visuals but short on substance.

Elder Benson always took the work and the mission of the Church seriously, but he never took himself too seriously. Occasionally, when it was appropriate in an informal setting, he allowed his native good humor to shine through. A typical anecdote involved the husband who boasted to his wife he had been promoted to vice president of his company. The wife was unimpressed, observing there was even a vice president in charge of prunes at the supermarket. Doubting her statement, the husband called the store and asked for the vice president in charge of prunes. "Packaged or bulk?" responded the voice on the phone. He also told

272

about the man who insisted his wife serve only margarine because butter was too expensive. Once when guests were treated to butter at the family table, one of the sons, weary of margarine, helped himself to the butter. Hoping to restrain him in the future, the father later told the boy that butter cost sixty cents a pound. Not phased, the boy answered, "For butter, I would say it's worth it." At a basketball game after hearing an irate fan seated in the row ahead berate the referee for a call, Ezra leaned forward to say those were his sentiments exactly. And many heard and quoted his amusing quip about communism: "You can't feed dialectical materialism to a hog." Instances such as this, which were not uncommon, reflected President Benson's humanity and his basic cheerful temperament.

The first general conference talk given by Elder Benson after he had been set apart as President of the Twelve broadly defined his new responsibilities. It was delivered on Sunday, April 7, 1974, the day following the solemn assembly in which he was sustained as President of the Twelve. He began by paying tribute to his boyhood friend Harold B. Lee, commending his achievements and his spiritual stature as a prophet of God. After lauding and expressing support for President Spencer W. Kimball, he said: "From the days of Father Adam to the days of the Prophet Joseph Smith whenever the priesthood has been on the earth, a major responsibility has been the preaching of the saving, eternal principles of the gospel—the plan of salvation" (in Conference Report, Apr. 1974, pp. 150–55).

As President of the Twelve, he would play the key role in supervising the Missionary Committee of the Church. In appraising the scope of this duty, he related the experiences of the first latter-day missionary, Samuel Harrison Smith, whose only proselyting tool was the Book of Mormon. He also referred to the army of missionaries who had followed Samuel, those whom he called "Ambassadors of the Lord," who had "trudged through mud and snow, swum rivers, and gone without the common necessities of food, shelter, and clothing in response to a call." He also talked about the blessings that come to those who serve faithfully and who thereby become partners with God. "We accept humbly, gratefully, this major responsibility placed upon the Church," he said. "We are happy to be engaged in a partnership with our Heavenly Father in the great work of the salvation and exaltation of his children. Willingly we give of our time and our means with which he may bless us to the establishment of his kingdom in the earth" (ibid).

As President Benson moved forward leading his brethren of the Twelve, he applied a simple test to determine the propriety of any proposed action: "What is best for the kingdom?" he would ask. That question, asked repeatedly during the years of his service as quorum president, became a standard criterion for action by the Twelve. He adopted the same criterion to govern his actions when he became President of the Church.

In his talk at the October 1974 general conference, President Benson developed a theme with universal application. "We live in an age when, as the Lord foretold, men's hearts are failing them, not only physically but in spirit," he began. He referred to the "despair, discouragement, despondency, and depression" that were rampant in the world (in Conference Report, Oct. 1974, pp. 90–94). One suspects this theme was chosen in part because of the bouts with discouragement and depression that Flora had during the previous year. These had been triggered by what was diagnosed as a stroke. As Ezra tried to help his companion work through these down periods, he developed a formula that he shared with the Tabernacle audience: "To lift our spirit and send us on our way rejoicing, the devil's designs of despair, discouragement, depression, and despondency can be defeated in a dozen ways, namely: repentance, prayer, service, work, health, reading, blessings, fasting, friends, music, endurance, and goals" (ibid.). As one reflects on these principles, they not only are devices to help lift one out of despondency, but also, added to faith, are the guiding principles that led Ezra Taft Benson throughout every phase of his life.

In the fall of 1974, President Benson joined the First Presidency and other General Authorities for the dedication of the Washington Temple. There were ten dedicatory sessions held from November 19 to November 22. The event was a milestone in the life of the Benson family. Thirty-five years earlier, when the Bensons arrived in the nation's capital, there were only a few scattered branches of the Church in the area. Now to see strong stakes dotting the region, capped by the magnificent temple, was a source of joy to the family and a testimonial to the vigorous growth of the Church. The dedicatory services, marked by the presence of divine beings, imbued President Benson with a new sense of direction and commitment.

The enthusiasm created by the temple dedication was soon reflected in the activities of President Benson and his associates. In January 1975 the Twelve recommended to the First Presidency the creation of five new missions and three new stakes. One of the missions, the Utah Mission, established a new pattern of missions functioning within areas covered by organized stakes. The effect was to accelerate the conversion process by a dedicated force of missionaries that would reach 20,000 strong before the end of the year.

On June 20 and 21, President Benson directed a seminar for new mission presidents at the Missionary Training Center adjacent to the campus of Brigham Young University in Provo, Utah. The center had state-of-the-art equipment and facilities to accommodate the thousands of missionaries who were trained there and sent to missions all over the world. During the preceding year twenty-two new missions had been created. Missionaries of the Church were then proselyting in fifty-five countries using twenty-three different languages. Using the skills of returned missionaries enrolled at Brigham Young University, an intensive language training program for new missionaries was carried on at the Missionary Training Center.

Among the new mission presidents attending the seminar was President Benson's son Reed, who had been called to preside over the Kentucky Louisville Mission. Indicative of the way President Benson and his brethren were pushing the global expansion of missionary work was the presence at the seminar of Gustav Salik, who had been called as president of a mission in Yugoslavia. Due to delays in obtaining a visa, President Salik would have to live temporarily in an Austrian border town, directing the work of six Austrian missionaries. The missionaries, trained in the Croatian language, would work with Yugoslavian people in Austria while making periodic visits to Yugoslavia.

The problem of missionary visas was complicated at the time by a backlog of two hundred visa applications for Brazilian missionaries. These applications were being held up in a Brazilian government office in Los Angeles, California. A few days before the seminar, the Hon. Oswaldo Castro Lobo, the Consul General for Brazil in Los Angeles, was invited to Utah to discuss the visa problem. The visitor was taken to Provo, where he was given a tour of the Missionary Training Center. In time the backlog was cleared up, although there were occasional delays in the future in securing Brazilian and other foreign visas.

A few days before the mission presidents' seminar, President Benson and the Twelve made three important recommendations to the First Presidency: that the infirm or aged Assistants to the Twelve be relieved of active service and given emeritus status, that Assistants to the Twelve be authorized to reorganize stake presidencies, and that stake presidents be authorized to ordain and set apart bishops. In time, all these recommendations were approved. Their purpose was to streamline and strengthen the work and to diffuse authority and responsibility both at Church headquarters and among the stakes. Until these changes were made, only members of the First Presidency and the Twelve had the authority to reorganize stake presidencies and to ordain and set apart bishops. Given the rapid growth of the Church and the resulting multiplication of stakes and wards, it became apparent that the Twelve alone could not continue to reorganize all stake presidencies and ordain and set apart all bishops. Nor was it reasonable to expect that Assistants to the Twelve who were slowed by age or physical problems could continue to travel week after week throughout the world on Church assignments.

The process by which these changes were made is revealing. It shows the cooperative relationship between the First Presidency and the Twelve. Because the members of the Twelve were constantly in the field, faced regularly with complicated scheduling problems created by stake and ward reorganizations, it was they who were in the best position to recommend changes in procedure. Still, the ultimate authority to approve the changes rested with the First Presidency. That the First Presidency approved the proposed changes also reveals the influence of President Benson in his penchant for delegation and sharing of authority and responsibility.

Two months after the mission presidents' seminar, President Benson joined President Kimball and others to attend area conferences in the Far East. Meetings were held in Japan, Hong Kong, Taiwan, Korea, and the Philippines. During these travels President Benson renewed acquaintances with many whom he had known while he supervised the work in those countries. He was impressed by the rapid growth that had occurred since then. Utilizing the distinction that his former role in the cabinet afforded, he also met with government officials to lay the groundwork for future contacts by representatives of the Church. President Benson never failed to use his status as a former high government official to advance the interests of the Church.

A few weeks after returning from the Far East, another distinction was added to President Benson's résumé. In September 1975 Brigham Young University named a new food and agricultural institute after him. Its purpose was to provide information and training to help countries around the world increase the quantity and quality of agricultural production. The aim to help emerging countries become self-sufficient in agriculture accorded with President Benson's deeply held convictions. Although he was pleased with the U.S. government's Food for Peace program developed while he was secretary of agriculture to help dispose of surpluses in a creative way, the Ezra Taft Benson Agriculture and Food Institute went far beyond that initiative. The difference in the two is seen in the adage "The gift of a fish feeds a man for a day while teaching a man to fish will feed him a lifetime." The teaching potential of the Benson Institute is shown by a contract it negotiated with Ecuador to teach farmers how to operate efficiently on small acreages.

The ceremony at Brigham Young University announcing the creation of the Benson Institute was an appreciated milestone for Elder Benson. It marked the beginning of a program that would forever associate his name with the university and with agriculture, two of his most esteemed institutions. Moreover, the international scope of the institute's work would help improve the image of the Church around the world and would be another door opener for Elder Benson and his brethren.

The ceremony inaugurating the institute was enlivened by a cow-milking contest between Elder Benson and the capable young president of BYU, Dallin H. Oaks. The Apostle showed he had lost none of the milking skills learned on the Whitney farm. He won the contest, having finished milking while his young friend was upended when trying to milk his cow from the wrong side. The obvious fact that Dallin Oaks was not farm bred did not diminish the regard for him when, nine years later, Elder Benson welcomed him as the junior member of the Quorum of the Twelve Apostles.

A month after the BYU ceremony, another distinction came to President Benson when President Kimball asked him to represent the Church on the White House Forum on

Domestic Policy. Ezra's contribution to this advisory group mirrored his often expressed views about the limited role of government and the need for maximum freedom and personal responsibility. A few weeks later, in November 1975, President Benson met with President Gerald Ford, renewing an earlier friendship. President Benson's personal acquaintance with U.S. presidents, extending back more than thirty years to the days of Franklin D. Roosevelt, enabled him to speak frankly with President Ford, offering his support and counsel.

President Benson struggled to balance his growing Church responsibilities with increased demands on his time at home. Flora's weakened condition required that he assume many household duties she had always performed. Some shoppers probably were surprised to see President Benson pushing a grocery cart at the supermarket. That a man of such distinction also was faced with the ordinary tasks of daily living was an eye-opener to some. It was a matter of routine for him. He never put on airs about his high status. He had risen from humble origins and could mingle with people of all classes with no semblance of superiority or inferiority while retaining his basic dignity and sense of self-worth.

A talk that President Benson delivered at a BYU fireside in March 1976 focused on an issue that troubled him. He questioned some Latter-day Saint historians whose writings he felt were distorted by an overemphasis on negative aspects of Church history or by playing up temporal matters above spiritual events. He saw an example of the latter in a current history that devoted more space to the development of cooperatives like ZCMI and other temporal pursuits than to some of the main spiritual events surrounding the Restoration. This bias, he believed, unduly secularized the Church, lowering it from a heaven-inspired institution to a mere earthly organization, subject to critical analysis and judgment of the authors. Later in the year, he also counseled Church instructors to avoid distortions and innovations in

President and Sister Benson celebrate their fiftieth wedding anniversary in Louisville, Kentucky, in September 1976

President Benson visits with LDS Boy Scouts at a 1977 national Scout Jamboree in Pennsylvania

their teaching that veered away from the scriptures and from interpretations given to them by the prophets. His position was clear: All were free to say or to write anything they wished about the Church and its leaders. But those who were employed by the Church, who acted under Church appointment, or who were restricted by Church covenants were obliged to adhere to prophetic direction.

Another honor came to President Benson on May 2, 1978, when he received a Freedom Foundation Award. It was given at a Salt Lake City Rotary luncheon in the Hotel Utah and was based upon a talk he had given praising the benefits of free enterprise. "The President handled himself very well and was a distinct credit to the church and to his apostolic calling. He is growing in stature day by day. More people are beginning to listen to the plea he has been making so earnestly and so constantly for so many years. And what is that plea? 'Wake up America—assert yourself—return to the principles that made you great.' Of late there has been a noticeable loss of stridency in President Benson's tone. He has not let up in his relentless battle. He seems only to have altered his approach and to be working at it more wisely and adroitly" (author's personal diary, May 2, 1978).

These were momentous days for the Church. For several months President Kimball had been praying earnestly for divine direction about the policy that withheld the priesthood from blacks. He had spent many hours in the temple alone imploring God for guidance and had discussed the matter at length with his counselors. President Kimball also had met privately with President Benson and with other members of the Twelve to learn their views and to seek their counsel. The issue President Kimball faced was resolved when on Thursday, June 8, 1978, he informed the Twelve that the Lord had heard his prayers and by revelation had "confirmed that the long-promised day has come when every faithful, worthy man in the Church may receive the holy priesthood, with power to exercise its divine authority, and enjoy with his loved ones every blessing that flows therefrom, including the blessings of the temple" (Doctrine and Covenants, Official Declaration—2). President Benson was present at this meeting as well as at a meeting in the temple a week earlier when a powerful, confirming feeling came to all that the time had come to lift the priesthood restrictions. With his brethren, he was grateful the Lord had spoken to bring about a result that for decades all had yearned and prayed for.

During the month following the announcement of the revelation on priesthood, President Benson broke his hip. By the end of the year it had healed sufficiently to enable him to travel away from home. In January 1979, during his eight-ieth year, he began a round of Church assignments, most of which were overseas, that would have been considered strenuous for a man half his age. It is suspected that he did this in part to demonstrate to the Church that he was fit and competent despite his advanced age, the recent fracture, and the long convalescence that had followed. Such a demon-stration by the Apostle second in seniority was reassuring, given the long series of physical ailments President Kimball had suffered.

President Benson's first lengthy trip in 1979 was to South America, where he visited Colombia, Ecuador, Peru, and Bolivia. Numerous meetings were held with missionar-ies and members in which he endeavored to train them and build them up. He also held press conferences and met with government leaders to help improve the public image of the Church and to pave the way for future cooperative treat-ment for the Church by government agencies. While in Santa Cruz, Bolivia, on January 14, 1979, he created the first stake of the Church in that country, the 993rd in the history of the Church. President Benson selected Noriharu Ishigaki Haraguichi as the stake president, a convert of Japanese descent. He had been surprised at the large number of Japanese who had migrated to South America in search of land and greater economic opportunity. He found the largest concentration of Japanese in South America at São

Paulo, Brazil, where more than a half million of them lived. Like the Japanese converts he met in the Far East while he supervised the work there, he found that President Haraguichi and other Japanese like him in South America to be dedicated to the Church and hardworking.

Back in the United States, President Benson created the one thousandth stake of the Church—at Nauvoo, Illinois, on February 18, 1979. The event was not only historically significant for the Church but also was personally rewarding for President Benson because of the involvement of his great-grandfather and namesake, Ezra Taft Benson, in the early development of the city.

The following weekend, President Benson returned to South America and on February 25 organized the first stake in Paraguay at Asunción. A convert of Spanish descent, Carlos Ramón Espinoia, was selected as the stake president.

In May President Benson traveled to the Middle East to visit Israel and Egypt, and he stopped in Greece on the way home. As there were no missions in these countries and not many members, he was unable to do the kind of work he ordinarily did while abroad. However, he did meet with the few Church members there to encourage and motivate them. A principal outcome of the trip was the positive reception he received from government leaders, contacts that would yield many benefits to the Church in the years ahead. In Israel he conferred with Prime Minister Menachem Begin and with Shimon Peres, who was the opposition leader in the Knesset. He also met Abba Eban, a personal acquaintance from the days when he had served as secretary of agriculture. All these men, and others in Israel, held President Benson in high regard, an attitude that redounded to the benefit of the Church in many subtle ways. Often it was as important to create a proper climate in which the Church could function as to promote its immediate growth. In Greece, for instance, he met with the acting minister of agriculture and minister of European affairs, Mr. Kontogiorgis, a man who once had worked under Secretary

Benson in the U.S. Department of Agriculture. This acquaintance and the admiration Mr. Kontogiorgis had for President Benson were important factors in the action taken a few months later by the Greek government in giving limited recognition to the Church.

Not long after returning from the Middle East, President Benson again traveled to South America to rededicate the country of Venezuela for the preaching of the gospel. During the balance of 1979, he participated in area conferences in Australia, New Zealand, and Mexico City and returned to Israel for the dedication of the Orson Hyde Park on the Mount of Olives.

At the October general conference in 1979, President Benson delivered a stirring address in which he repeated the themes he had been talking about fervently for the past thirty years. "Today, we are in a battle for the bodies and souls of man," he told the Tabernacle audience. "It is a battle between two opposing systems; freedom and slavery, Christ and anti-Christ. The struggle is more momentous than a decade ago" (in Conference Report, Oct. 1979, pp. 43–48). He repeated the admonitions he had given over the years, that Church members study the Constitution and become involved in the political process.

The following February, President Benson spoke at a meeting on the campus of Brigham Young University. There he said that the words of the living prophets are more important than the words of the deceased prophets and that the living prophets can give direction to the Saints in any aspect of life, including politics. As to the latter, he said, "Those who would take the prophet out of politics would take God out of government."

Shortly after April general conference in 1980, President Benson left Salt Lake City for Europe. Flora's condition had improved, so she was able to accompany him. Neither of them, however, was in robust health. Flora's stroke had slowed her perceptibly, and her husband suffered much discomfort from his fractured hip, especially after sitting in a cramped airplane for hours. Notwithstanding, they followed a vigorous schedule. During several weeks in Europe, President Benson created the first stake in Austria and visited the four missions in Italy. He and Flora also traveled to Finland, where son-in-law James Parker, Beverly's husband, was the mission president. The grandparents were surprised at the speed with which the Parker children had learned the difficult Finnish language and were pleased at the way their parents had trained them to do missionary work.

On May 12, 1980, shortly after returning home from Europe, President Benson blacked out while reading and was hospitalized. This had happened before and was the cause of great concern. He was given a battery of tests that revealed no basic dysfunction. It was, however, the beginning of a series of physical problems he would suffer over the next few months. He began at this time to receive regular physical therapy to ease the pain and discomfort in his hip. When this failed to give relief, he underwent an operation in October 1981 to implant an artificial hip. Two months later, just as he began to get around, he fell, fracturing his pelvis. This required two weeks of hospitalization. After release from the hospital, President Benson began to suffer spells of dizziness misdiagnosed as a stroke. He was placed in a wheelchair, and the doctors were pessimistic whether he would be able to return to full activity. Later the doctors decided it was not a stroke but that he had suffered a bad case of the flu. He lost sixty pounds during the ordeal.

President Benson's own physical problems were aggravated by his concern over the condition of President Spencer W. Kimball. In late 1979 President Kimball underwent two operations for subdural hematomas, and in September 1981 he underwent a third such operation. These had left the prophet weak and unable to perform his duties fully. This, coupled with the physical difficulties of his counselors, President N. Eldon Tanner and President Marion G. Romney, had prompted President Kimball to call Gordon B. Hinckley as a third counselor on July 23, 1981.

These events added a heavy psychological burden to the physical problems Elder Benson suffered. It took almost a year for him to recover fully and to return to his regular schedule of duties.

In October 1982, at age eighty-three, President Benson began again to shoulder a full load of activities. At the October general conference he delivered a thoughtful sermon about the family. He reminded the audience that family life was ordained of God, that family members must strive to attain a righteous unity, that children must be nurtured in love, and that parents have the responsibility to prepare children for gospel ordinances. "The most important teachings in the home are spiritual," he told the audience. "Parents are commanded to prepare their sons and daughters for the ordinances of the gospel: baptism, confirmation, priesthood ordinations, and temple marriage. They are to teach them to respect and honor the Sabbath day, to keep it holy. Most importantly, parents are to instill within their children a desire for eternal life and to earnestly seek that goal above all else" (in Conference Report, Oct. 1982, p. 87).

Later in the month, he traveled to Kirtland, Ohio. He seemed to be drawn magnetically to this and other sites of early Church history. Three years before, he had presided at ceremonies to break ground for a chapel in Kirtland. Now he had returned to dedicate the building. In his remarks, he reviewed the early history of the Church in the area and the location of the first organized ward and the first temple. It had been 145 years since the Prophet Joseph Smith and his followers had left the city. During that interval, Kirtland had dwindled in vitality and importance, the result of what President Benson saw as a predicted "scourge" that had rested on it (see D&C 124:83). Now with a thriving community of Latter-day Saints in the area and a beautiful new chapel, he foresaw a lifting of the scourge and a period of vigorous growth ahead. Not very long after that, President Benson's insight was confirmed when a stake and a mission

President Benson speaking at the Tabernacle pulpit in 1982

were created in the area and many descendants of early Latter-day Saints were converted.

During this visit, President Benson was given a tour of the Kirtland Temple by Sebe Morgan, the local stake president of the Reorganized Church. President Morgan graciously invited President Benson to offer a prayer. It was a touching moment for the Apostle to pray in that place where the Savior had appeared.

Shortly after President Benson returned from Kirtland, President N. Eldon Tanner passed away. The death of this able man, who had served in the First Presidency for almost twenty years as a counselor to four Presidents of the Church, necessitated a reorganization of the First Presidency. President Kimball selected President Marion G. Romney as his First Counselor and President Gordon B.

Hinckley as his Second Counselor. President Kimball, though mentally able to carry on, was weak from recent head surgeries and was further hindered by a weak heart and a bad back, by the inability to speak above a whisper, and by problems with his sight and his hearing. President Romney, who was almost blind, suffered from other problems of old age. Because President Hinckley was in good health though in his early seventies, President Kimball delegated full authority to him to administer the affairs of the Church in accordance with the existing guidelines. Any action beyond them was taken only with the express authorization of President Kimball.

This created a unique historical precedent—one counselor directing the worldwide affairs of the Church. It also provided a critical test for the flexibility of the First Presidency and for the adaptability of the Twelve and other General Authorities to a new, unprecedented situation. This was especially true in the relationship between President Hinckley and President Benson. President Hinckley was the younger of the two by eleven years and the junior in apostolic seniority by eighteen. When Elder Benson was called to the Twelve in 1943, Brother Hinckley was a young man of thirty-three, occupying a staff position as the secretary of the Radio, Publicity, and Literature Committee of the Church. He did not acquire General Authority status until 1958, when he was called as an Assistant to the Twelve. Before then he was little known outside the administrative headquarters of the Church, while Elder Benson was known worldwide as a member of the Twelve and as the secretary of agriculture.

Against this background, and human nature being what it is, those unacquainted with the operation of the Church might have expected that President Benson would dominate, or at least would have tried to dominate, the younger man. The opposite was true. From the beginning of their unusual relationship, President Benson completely subordinated himself to President Hinckley, both in word and in deed. Repeatedly he admonished the Twelve regarding the need to give unqualified support to President Hinckley in the delicate role he played. As for President Hinckley, he retained unfailing loyalty to President Kimball, following precisely the guidelines he had set, briefing him regularly about the work, and seeking his direction on any matters beyond the guidelines. As a result, the work of the Church continued unabated on a global scale despite the serious physical disabilities of two members of the First Presidency. It was possible because of the unity among the Brethren and the submersion of personal interests for the benefit of the work.

One of the most sensitive duties of the First Presidency is to make final decisions regarding applications for cancellation of temple sealings, restoration of blessings, and appeals of judgments from high council disciplinary proceedings. The volume of these cases is substantial and increases proportionately with the growth of the Church. Clerical staff sift through the details of these cases and prepare summaries to aid the First Presidency. Even then, the sheer number of cases and the weight of responsibility make it a formidable task even for three men. Accordingly, President Hinckley felt the need for assistance in deciding them. It was then he began to invite President Benson to meet with him regularly on Tuesday mornings for this purpose. This procedure continued regularly throughout the balance of President Kimball's administration. Meanwhile, President Hinckley briefed President Benson and the Twelve about other matters he was handling for President Kimball and often sought their counsel so that all were fully informed and moving in concert. The close rapport built between President Benson and President Hinckley during this critical period is suggested by President Benson's selection of President Hinckley as his first counselor when he became President of the Church.

In the spring of 1983, President Benson traveled to Europe and the Middle East again. Flora accompanied him.

Customary meetings with members, missionaries, and Church leaders were held in Europe. In Jerusalem, Ezra sought to move along plans for a Brigham Young University educational center near the Mount of Olives. Opposition from ultraconservative rabbis had slowed the process. President Benson's good relationship with government leaders helped remove some of the roadblocks. In time all obstacles were surmounted, and the center was completed.

Even before the center was completed, BYU maintained a presence in the Holy Land by conducting a study-abroad program for selected students. Reed was an instructor there at the time of his parents' visit. His wife, May, and their children had accompanied him. The Bensons' visit to some of the sacred sites in the ancient city were enhanced by the presence of Reed and his family. Before leaving for home, they enjoyed a typical Benson gabfest, bringing each other current on recent happenings of mutual interest.

Ezra and Flora returned in time to prepare for the dedication of the Atlanta Georgia Temple. The ceremonies were held from June 1 through June 4, 1983. In the absence of President Kimball, President Benson played a more prominent role than at previous temple dedications. He conducted five of the eleven sessions and spoke at five others, alternating with President Hinckley. The spiritual impact of the meetings was profound. The high point of each session was the Hosannah Shout, followed by the choir's rendition of the "Hosannah Anthem" and, at the end, by the choir and congregation singing "The Spirit of God Like a Fire Is Burning." Afterward there were few dry eyes in the audience.

The quiet reverence of a temple always awakened President Benson's deepest spiritual sense. It was there he felt at peace and more in tune with godly influences. These feelings always came as he counseled with his brethren in the upper room of the Salt Lake Temple. He sought to strengthen those feelings by attending weekly endowment sessions in the nearby Jordan River Temple. In these sacred precincts, away from all strife and turmoil, he felt more deeply, saw more distinctly, and understood more clearly. It was a refreshing and stimulating interlude that encouraged him to continue the course.

Independence Day 1983 found President Benson in Provo, Utah, where he served as grand marshal of the city's annual Freedom Festival. Wearing a Western-style shirt and an ornamented clutch tie topped by his trademark Stetson, he cut a fine figure, smiling and waving at the thousands gathered along the parade route as Flora sat demurely by his side. He loved it. And the watchers loved him. These were his kind of people. And this was his kind of celebration, a celebration of America's independence and freedom from foreign domination.

In November, President Benson was deeply touched when the Utah Farm Bureau and the Salt Lake Area Chamber of Commerce honored him at a banquet for distinguished service to people everywhere through his work in agriculture. It was gratifying to see he was honored by those at home who knew him best. He was moved by President Hinckley's eloquent tribute given in behalf of the Church. In it he sketched President Benson's pioneer heritage, traced his rise from the obscurity of the Whitney farm to the pinnacle of American agriculture, lauded his characteristics of faith and loyalty, and emphasized the gentle side of his nature.

Many who knew President Benson only from his public addresses and writings never really understood him or his core qualities. Some read into his unyielding, persistent views on politics and government an intellectual narrowness and a crotchety personality. His enemies and detractors sought to promote this view of him. It was a gross and misleading caricature. Actually, in discussing issues, no one was more open and interested than he or more desirous of hearing the views of all. And no one showed a greater restraint and self-control when the issues debated had emotional overtones. There were times when, because of sharp differences of opinion, he would maintain an aloofness and indifference toward someone who he felt had betrayed him or who had attacked him unfairly. But once all the facts were known and differences of opinion had been fully aired, he was the first to step forward to make amends and to bridge over any misunderstanding. A case in point is the well-known columnist Jack Anderson, who is a member of the Church. Following his days in the cabinet, Elder Benson had negative feelings toward Anderson because of an incident that had occurred while the young reporter was an associate of Drew Pearson, proprietor of the nationally syndicated column "Washington Merry-Go-Round," who was strongly oriented toward Democratic politics. Later, when the two met and found there had been a misunderstanding, Elder Benson took a surprised Jack Anderson in his arms to give him a fatherly hug. It may have been the only time Ezra Taft Benson hugged a Washington columnist. The exception illustrated one of his most endearing qualities of character.

There were many reminiscences of his Washington days when in July 1984 President Ronald Reagan invited President Benson and other former secretaries of agriculture to come to the White House to commemorate the thirtieth anniversary of the International Food for Peace program. Because President Reagan recognized him for having spearheaded this program, it was one of the most significant official accolades Ezra received for his years of work on the firing line in Washington. In terms of personal satisfaction, we gather it ranked alongside the honor accorded him by the Utah Farm Bureau and the Salt Lake Area Chamber of Commerce. It seemed to give him the sense that the years of strife, turmoil, and opposition were really worth it after all.

The touch that made this event complete was the generosity of Ezra's dear friend, Bill Marriott, who insisted that he and Flora occupy the luxurious presidential suite in the Marriott Hotel. When Beverly and Jim and their children came to visit, with the group singing to the accompaniment of the grand piano in the suite and talking about the old days in Washington, the past took on a rosy hue and the future looked as promising and fulfilling as the present.

Meanwhile, President Benson continued with his regular apostolic duties, attending stake conferences and other meetings and handling the administrative work at headquarters. On stake assignments he relied heavily on spiritual promptings in making decisions, especially when selecting a patriarch. At a Salt Lake Bonneville Stake conference, President Benson called on Harold H. Bennett to respond after he had been sustained as a patriarch. In his remarks, the speaker said that years before as he traveled home after work, a voice spoke to him to say that LeGrand Richards would be called as the new member of the Twelve. At home his wife, Emily, questioned that this would happen, because Elder Richards was then the Presiding Bishop. Harold's only response was that that was what the voice had said. This stroke of inspiration proved true. Harold also said that in the interval between when his phone had rung that morning and his answer, the same voice whispered he would be called as a patriarch. On the phone was the stake president, Russell M. Nelson, who invited Brother Bennett to the high council room at the stake center. There Elder Benson called him to be a patriarch. President Benson later told the author that the final decision to call Harold Bennett was not made until early that morning after fervent prayer when several candidates were being considered (author's personal diary).

The spiritual quality this incident suggests became more pronounced in President Benson as he aged and as he drew nearer to the prophetic office. So long had he relied on these whisperings that following them had become a way of life. He deferred action in any critical situation until he had received the spiritual confirmation of what to do. This procedure illustrates the subordinate role played by a prophet who is an agent, not a principal. The confidence he placed in the validity of personal revelation is revealed in the fervent testimonies he bore over the years, such as this: "I know that God is a personal being, the Father of our spirits, and that He loves His children and hears and answers their righteous prayers. I know that it is His will that His children be happy. It is His desire to bless us all. I know that Jesus Christ is the Son of God, our Elder Brother, the very Creator and Redeemer of the world. I know that God has again established His kingdom on the earth in fulfillment of prophecy and that it will never be overcome, but it shall ultimately hold universal dominion in the earth and Jesus Christ shall reign as its King forever" (*This Nation Shall Endure* [Salt Lake City: Deseret Book Co., 1977], pp. 112–13).

Chapter 20

President of the Church

T he last months of President Benson's service as President of the Twelve were arduous. He lived in a state of constant uncertainty. President Kimball's precarious health meant he could pass away at any moment, transferring instantly to President Benson the full weight of Church leadership. Yet, until that moment came there was nothing President Benson could do or wanted to do to assume that demanding role. He carried on in the usual way, directing the Twelve, fulfilling assignments in the field, and supporting and assisting President Hinckley.

The end came for President Kimball on Tuesday, November 5, 1985, at 10:08 P.M. when he passed away quietly in his Hotel Utah apartment. At that moment, upon President Benson fell the responsibility and authority of the prophetic office, which he would exercise de facto until he was formally ordained later. It was a role President Benson had realized might come to him because of President Kimball's age and infirmities. But it was a role he had never sought. He and Flora had prayed regularly for President

Kimball's health and continued service as President of the Church. President Benson would have been content to complete his earthly service as President of the Quorum of the Twelve Apostles.

President Kimball's funeral was held in the Tabernacle on Saturday, November 9, 1985. President Benson acknowledged President Hinckley's faithful service to President Kimball by asking him to conduct the services. President Benson was the main speaker, lauding his friend and recalling the many years they had sat side by side in the upper room of the temple.

A special meeting of the Council of the Twelve was held in the Temple on Sunday, November 10, at 3:00 P.M. There President Ezra Taft Benson was sustained and ordained as the thirteenth President of the Church. Elder Howard W. Hunter acted as voice in the ordination. President Benson selected and set apart Elders Gordon B. Hinckley and Thomas S. Monson as his counselors. Elder Hunter was sustained as Acting President of the Twelve (because of the illness of President Marion G. Romney) and, at President Benson's request, was set apart by President Hinckley.

The tone of President Benson's administration was set the next morning at an eight o'clock meeting in the temple. There a statement the prophet had prepared for a press conference to be held later that morning was read. He asked for comments and suggestions. Several amendments were made. Throughout his administration, he actively sought input from all his brethren regarding important matters.

The press conference was held at ten o'clock in the rotunda of the Church Administration Building. All the major television and radio networks and press outlets were represented. President Benson did not submit to questions. Had he done so, the media representatives likely would have focused on the recent bombings connected with the Mark Hoffman case or other things extraneous to the functions of the First Presidency. He wanted the focus to be on other things. "The President's statement was a judicious one which affirmed the three-fold mission of the Church, to preach the gospel, perfect the Saints, and redeem the dead; expressed love for people of every race, nationality, and religious and political persuasion; and testified of the divinity of the Savior and the divine mission of the Church" (author's personal diary).

The first full meeting of the new First Presidency was held on Wednesday, November 13, 1985. There the prophet demonstrated again the style that would characterize his administration when "the counselors were authorized to review and make recommendations about the headquarters assignments of members of the Twelve and about the division of responsibilities among the members of the First Presidency" (ibid.). Later at a temple meeting, "President Benson authorized the Twelve to develop suggestions and criteria as to the following principles and concepts which will be given special emphasis at the coming April General Conference: 1. The Book of Mormon. It is expected this will stimulate missionary work and will develop greater spirituality among the members. 2. Temple Attendance. Not only will this accelerate vicarious temple work, but it will also have the effect of encouraging the payment of tithes as tithing faithfulness is one of the conditions to receiving a temple recommend. 3. Strengthen Families, thereby helping to perfect the Saints. This will include a major emphasis on reactivation. 4. Reemphasize Welfare. Next year will be the fiftieth anniversary of the establishment of the Welfare Program, which will provide an important point of emphasis" (ibid.).

These steps, taken at the threshold of his presidency, show the administrative genius of President Benson. The key was to involve his brethren in the process of developing policies, programs, and procedures. This had the dual effect of causing them to feel an integral part of the finished product while relieving him of cumbersome detail. Moreover, it enriched the final product by the addition of the ideas of all. It is a notable example of the kind of cooperative administration that would mark President Benson's tenure as President of the Church.

The impact of his new role upon President Benson was clearly evident to his associates and his family. They saw a marked increase in the level of his energy, his alertness, and his enthusiasm. He seemed much younger than his eighty-six-plus years. He was brimming with ideas and plans for the future. At the same time, he seemed to be endowed with a greater sense of love and concern, not only for those about him but for everyone. This was reflected in the first major initiative of President Benson's administration. It was launched only a few weeks after his ordination and was embodied in a statement published in the December 22, 1985, issue of the *Church News:* "We encourage Church members to forgive those who may have wronged them," it read. "To those who have ceased activity and to those who have become critical, we say, 'Come back. Come back and feast at the table of the Lord.'" This corresponded with a special invitation proffered in the Christmas message of the First Presidency: "To those who are lonely, we extend the hand of friendship and fellowship. We invite you to become one with us in worship and in the service of the Master" (*Church News,* Dec. 22, 1985). These foreshadowed a major effort at reactivation undertaken during President Benson's administration.

The first public meeting President Benson attended after his ordination was Sunday evening, November 10, following the special meeting in the temple. The occasion was a Churchwide satellite broadcast from the Salt Lake Tabernacle honoring the young women of the Church. The audience was unaware of what had taken place earlier, yet stood in unison when he entered to honor him as the senior Apostle. Flora was at his side. This reception was the first tangible sign to the prophet of the adulation that would follow him the rest of his days. He was quite unprepared for it. And, we gather, he never quite adjusted to it. It was difficult afterward for him to comprehend that when the Saints sang the hymn "We Thank Thee, O God, for a Prophet" (*Hymns*, no. 19), they had him in mind. The reality of that was overwhelming and often brought tears to his eyes.

Although it was not intended as such, this first meeting had symbolic significance for the new prophet. What more appropriate way to inaugurate his administration than at a youth gathering with Flora beside him? Their Church service during the early years of their marriage had been devoted almost exclusively to work with the youth. It was a service they loved and for which they were eminently qualified. And though in later years other Church calls focused their attention on different aspects of the work, they never lost sight of their first love.

This first meeting also enabled President Benson to make a significant statement to the young women of the Church and, indeed, to the entire Church, expressed visually by Flora's presence at his side. Ezra and Flora Benson were at that time what they always had been since their marriage and always would be—a team, working together toward a common goal. It was a true partnership. Their roles were different but complementary and equally important—he as the head of the family, leading out and providing sustenance and patriarchal direction; she as the heart of the family, creating a loving home environment, nurturing and counseling all. He had priesthood authority; she had influence. And with that influence Flora was able to leave her imprint on the entire family, and especially on her husband. This was never done intrusively, but quietly with tact and wisdom. It was an ideal relationship, characterized by genuine love and devoid of all contention and bickering. Their relationship was an ideal for all Latter-day Saint couples, as well as for the young women at the fireside who looked forward to marriage and to helping create their own homes.

During the first weeks after his ordination, President Benson maintained a low public profile, declining all invitations to speak except at the First Presidency's Christmas devotional. Behind the scenes he was very busy, counseling and planning with his brethren, endeavoring to master the mechanics of his new office, and handling the flood of correspondence and requests for interviews and speeches. The sheer volume of these was bewildering, made manageable only with the aid of his expert staff. At the outset this consisted of D. Arthur Haycock, a veteran at Church headquarters who had served five previous Presidents, and several secretaries who worked under him. During this transitional period, President Benson also received valuable help from members of his family, especially sons Reed and Mark.

After a joyful Christmas holiday with his family, President Benson was prepared to make his first trip as the head of the Church. While he could have gone anywhere, he decided to go to Washington, D.C., the place that was so significant in the lives of the Benson family. Two matters of Church business awaited him there: the division of the Annandale Virginia Stake and the installation of a new presidency of the Washington Temple. There was, however, another purpose of the trip that was of deeper and more lasting significance. It was while President Benson was in the nation's capital on this occasion that he launched the initiative that would be the centerpiece of his administration and the thing for which he would be best remembered by posterity. This was the prophet's emphasis on the need for members of the Church to read the Book of Mormon daily and to adhere faithfully to its teachings.

The setting for this historic inaugural was the Sunday morning session of the Annandale stake conference on January 5, 1986. President Benson and Flora were hardly prepared for the throng in attendance and for the show of love and affection that greeted them when they mounted the stand that morning. The hall was crowded to capacity. Some were standing in the rear and in the foyer. Others were seated in rooms throughout the building where television or sound was provided. Still, hundreds were turned away for lack of space. It was reported that many came to the building hours before the service began and that some came from as far away as New York to attend.

After the prophet had expressed his love for the people and appreciation for the kindnesses shown to him and Sister Benson, he launched into an eloquent sermon about the Book of Mormon. He had studied this sacred record and had prayed and spoken often about it. The message of the book had woven itself into the fabric of his life. It had almost become an obsession with him. This was driven by two forces—the desire that all share in the blessings of the Book of Mormon and that the Church escape the condemnation incurred by the neglect of it. He said the Book of Mormon, though written centuries before, was intended for our day. It was written for us. It was like a message from the dust to motivate and inspire us and to help us avoid the pitfalls of the past. His vision was to "flood the earth" with the Book of Mormon, then to inspire the people to read it regularly and to follow its teachings. He was persistent in this quest. He never failed to talk about the Book of Mormon in any appropriate forum. And wherever he went, he talked to people individually about it—to airline flight attendants, to hotel employees, to nonmember acquaintances, to strangers whom he met, and indeed to anyone who would listen. Frequently he would give away copies of the Book of Mormon to strangers from the supply he always carried with him. Over the years, through missionaries around the world, he gave away thousands of them that contained pictures of him and Flora and their written testimony.

After launching his Book of Mormon initiative at the Annandale stake conference, the prophet elaborated on his message by emphasizing that the Book of Mormon is another testament of Jesus Christ, that it contains the fulness of the gospel, that it is the keystone of our religion, that a person can draw closer to God by reading and following its message than in any other way, and, finally, that it is the "great converter." He admonished the missionaries to use the Book of Mormon in preference to any other proselyting

301

tool. He stressed that there is an influence and a spirit about the Book of Mormon that will help lead an honest inquirer to accept it and to join the Church.

Following the meeting in the Annandale stake, President Benson wrote that the spirit of the meeting was "electric." That the audience shared this feeling is evidenced by what happened afterward. Later the stake presidency sent to President Benson a booklet containing several hundred names of people who had committed to read the Book of Mormon by a certain date. This was the forerunner of a virtual avalanche of projects around the Church to stimulate a commitment to the Book of Mormon. For instance, the *Church News* of October 22, 1988, carried this item: "President Ezra Taft Benson received visual evidence this week that his message concerning the Book of Mormon is getting through to the children of the Church. He visited the Museum of Church History and Art on October 16, and viewed many of the 6,500 drawings on display in the exhibit, 'Through a child's eye—scenes from the Book of Mormon.'" And this from the *Church News* of March 11, 1989: "The BYU 11th stake's relief society homemaking fair's theme was taken from President Benson's opening address at the October 1988 general conference, in which he urged members to 'flood the earth' with the Book of Mormon. Stake relief society president Susan Easton Black said, 'We, as women of the BYU 11th stake, decided we would do what President Benson asked. We wanted to follow the Prophet and thought that this homemaking fair would be one way that we could do that.' Each of the stake's 13 wards set up displays of items made in relation to teachings from the Book of Mormon. Originally, stake leaders planned to send samples of the items to President Benson's office, but ward representatives had the honor of presenting the samples to him and Sister Benson in person when they attended the fair."

While he was in the East on the occasion of the Annandale stake conference, the prophet also visited

President Benson and President Gordon B. Hinckley meet with George Bush, vice president of the United States, and Mrs. Barbara Bush

President Ronald Reagan in the White House. They had been friends for years. He told the President how the Church had raised millions of dollars to help alleviate world hunger through a special fast. He also gave the president a specially bound and autographed copy of the new Church hymn book.

Following a familiar pattern, the prophet also visited other government leaders as a means of enhancing the image of the Church: Vice President George Bush, Chief Justice Warren Burger, and FBI director William Webster. He also visited Richard Schubert of the American Red Cross to discuss the distribution of some of the relief funds the Church had gathered through the special fast.

On Saturday, January 11, 1986, after returning from Washington, D.C., President Benson had a fainting spell. He had stood up suddenly to answer the telephone and was talking with Reed when it occurred. Tests conducted at the hospital revealed no serious physical condition. It was merely a blip in the life of a man in his eighty-seventh year whose blood didn't circulate as fast as it did when he was younger. The prophet was irritated when a news item reported that his hospitalization was the first since the series of hospitalizations following the accident when he was thrown from a horse. This was an affront that never failed to raise his indignation.

As President Benson prepared for the April general conference and the three major addresses he would deliver, his main focus was upon the Book of Mormon and some of its principal teachings. This coincided with the instruction he had given to the Twelve to develop suggestions and criteria about the Book of Mormon for use at the conference. As a means of fixing their attention on this topic, he asked the General Authorities to read the Book of Mormon again before the conference. Being aware of the prophet's deep feelings about the subject, of the direction he had given to the Twelve to develop suggestions relative to the Book of Mormon, and of the stirring sermon he had delivered at the Annandale stake conference, President Gordon B. Hinckley predicted at one of the gatherings of the Brethren that President Benson would become the Church's greatest advocate of the Book of Mormon. His three talks at the April 1986 general conference gave strong credence to that prediction.

President Benson delivered the keynote address of the conference on Saturday morning, April 5, 1986. He warned against pride and sexual immorality. The remedy for these and other ills, he said, was to read the Book of Mormon and to heed its teachings. He cited relevant Book of Mormon scriptures about sexual immorality (see Alma 39:5) and pride (see Moroni 8:27), urging the Church to give heed to them. "Unless we read the Book of Mormon and give heed to its teachings," he warned, "the Lord has stated in section 84 of the Doctrine and Covenants that the whole Church is under condemnation. . . . 'And they shall remain under this condemnation until they repent and remember the new covenant, even the Book of Mormon and the former commandments which I have given them, not only to say, but to

President Benson during a general conference with his counselors in the First Presidency, Gordon B. Hinckley and Thomas S. Monson

do according to that which I have written' (D&C 84:57)" (in Conference Report, Apr. 1986, p. 4).

At the general priesthood meeting Saturday night, the prophet directed his remarks chiefly to the young men. He reminded them they had been born at that time for a sacred purpose. "It is not by chance that you have been reserved to come to earth in this last dispensation of the fulness of times," he told them. "Your birth at this particular time was foreordained in the eternities." He then gave them a key to guide them along: "Young men, the Book of Mormon will change your life. It will fortify you against the evils of our day. It will bring a spirituality into your life that no other book will. It will be the most important book you will read in preparation for a mission and for life. A young man who knows and loves the Book of Mormon, who has read it several times, who has an abiding testimony of its truthfulness, and who applies its teachings will be able to stand against the wiles of the devil and will be a mighty tool in the hands of the Lord" (ibid., p. 56).

At the concluding session of the conference, just after he had been sustained as President of the Church, President Benson delivered a message intended for the general membership of the Church: "There is a book we need to study daily, both as individuals and as families, namely the Book of Mormon. I love that book. It is the book that will get a person nearer to God by abiding by its precepts than any other book." He then indicated the predominant role the Book of Mormon would play in his prophetic ministry: "The Lord inspired His servant Lorenzo Snow to reemphasize the principle of tithing to redeem the Church from financial bondage. In those days the General Authorities took that message to the members of the Church. Now, in our day, the Lord has revealed the need to reemphasize the Book of Mormon to get the Church and all the children of Zion out from under condemnation—the scourge and judgment. (See D&C 84:54–58.) This message must be carried to the members of the Church throughout the world." Finally, the prophet gave a blessing and a promise and bore his testimony. "I bless you with increased discernment to judge between Christ and anti-Christ," he said. "I bless you with increased power to do good and to resist evil. I bless you with increased understanding of the Book of Mormon. I promise you that from this moment forward, if we will daily sup from its pages and abide by its precepts, God will pour out upon each child of Zion and the Church a blessing hitherto unknown—and we will plead to the Lord that He will begin to lift the condemnation—the scourge and judgment. Of this I bear solemn witness. I testify that the Book of Mormon is the word of God. Jesus is the Christ. Joseph Smith is His prophet. The Church of Jesus Christ of Latter-day Saints is true" (in Conference Report, Apr. 1986, pp. 99–100).

Thus was launched the initiative that would be the keystone of President Ezra Taft Benson's prophetic ministry. By his own admission, he expected he would be remembered for this in the annals of the Church above anything else he did, even as President Lorenzo Snow is remembered for his prophetic emphasis on the law of tithing.

Like President Snow, President Benson was not content merely to announce his prophetic vision as he did during this general conference. Afterward he began an intensive campaign to emphasize the need for members of the Church to read the Book of Mormon regularly—daily—and to follow its teachings. During the first year of his presidency, he delivered no less than twenty major addresses about the Book of Mormon. The basic message was always the same, although the point of emphasis varied with the circumstances. "I have done as Moroni exhorts," he declared at a regional meeting in Salt Lake City, "and I can testify to you that the Book of Mormon is from God and so is verily true." And he told an audience in Kirtland, Ohio, "The Lord is not pleased with us in the manner of attention we're giving the Book of Mormon, a new witness for Christ. We need it in our homes, we need it in our families. It was written for us today, not for our posterity, but for us, as parents and children of today. Sister Benson and I try to read from it at least once a day" (*Church News*, Nov. 9, 1986). Being aware of the flood of pornography, the widespread use of drugs, and the sexual permissiveness rampant in the world, President Benson looked upon daily readings in the Book of Mormon as an antidote to help stem the tide of evil.

President Benson was hospitalized overnight on June 19 for a virus infection but was sufficiently recovered to give the keynote address at the mission presidents' seminar on Wednesday, June 25, 1986. Predictably, the main focus of his talk was the Book of Mormon. He urged the mission presidents to give special emphasis to this sacred record in training missionaries. He called the book "the great converter," a means not only of converting investigators but of converting the missionaries to lives of achievement and spirituality. The prophet also gave sound counsel to the mission presidents, urging them "to enjoy their work, to be led always by the Spirit, to love their missionaries, to motivate and inspire those around them, to teach the missionaries correct principles and to accelerate the work through good correlation with stake presidents and bishops to promote member fellowshipping" (author's personal diary).

On the day of his hospitalization, President Benson was pleased to receive the Service-to-Freedom Award of the Freedoms Foundation at Valley Forge. It was the highest honor the foundation could give. President Ronald Reagan also received a similar award at the same time. A few weeks later, the prophet sought to emphasize the favored status of Americans when he spoke at a BYU assembly about the protections guaranteed by the U.S. Constitution. Later, in celebration of the bicentennial of the Constitution, President Benson and his counselors urged Church members to read the Constitution during the year.

In August 1986 President and Sister Benson traveled east. At the request of the mission president, the prophet spoke in the Sacred Grove to two hundred missionaries of the New York Rochester Mission. It was a solemn occasion none would forget—to be in the place where the Father and the Son appeared to young Joseph Smith in answer to his fervent prayer. The presence and the words of President Benson and the nearness of the Smith home where the angel Moroni first appeared to Joseph gave the occasion an almost heavenly aura. That evening the Bensons were honored guests at the Hill Cumorah Pageant, where they received a tumultuous welcome from the large audience. And the next morning, a Sunday, the prophet addressed several thousand Saints assembled at the hill, a site that added powerful emphasis to his now familiar call to read and ponder the words of the Book of Mormon on a daily basis. While they were in this area, President and Sister Benson also visited the Peter Whitmer farm and other places of importance to the early history of the Church.

Shortly after returning from the East, President Benson addressed a large assembly of BYU students. It was a preview of the bicentennial celebration of the U.S. Constitution

Sister Benson accompanies her husband to one of his many speaking engagements.

during 1987. Here the prophet extolled the virtues of the Constitution, affirmed the inspiration of those who drafted it, warned against the influences and ideas of those who would twist or eliminate it, and encouraged the students to become acquainted with it and to help preserve it by being active in civic affairs. In January 1987 the First Presidency issued to the entire Church a statement that embodied these ideas.

As President Benson looked forward to the general conference in October 1986, he prepared two major addresses, one that would keynote the conference and the other to wind it up. Both focused on the Book of Mormon and, added to the three he delivered at the previous April conference, provided the foundation for the extensive campaign he carried on to encourage Church members to read the Book of Mormon regularly and to follow its teachings.

The keynote address launched into the subject without any preliminaries or explanations: "My beloved brethren and sisters, today I would like to speak about one of the most significant gifts given to the world in modern times. . . . I speak of the gift of the Book of Mormon, given to mankind 156 years ago. . . . Perhaps there is nothing that testifies more clearly of the importance of this modern book of scripture than what the Lord Himself has said about it. By His own mouth He has borne witness (1) that it is true (D&C 17:6); (2) that it contains the truth and His words (D&C 19:26); (3) that it was translated by power from on high (D&C 20:8); (4) that it contains the fulness of the gospel of Jesus Christ (D&C 20:9, 42:12); (5) that it was given by inspiration and confirmed by the ministering of angels (D&C 20:10); (6) that it gives evidence that the holy scriptures are true (D&C 20:11); and (7) that those who receive it in faith shall receive eternal life (D&C 20:14)" (in Conference Report, Oct. 1986, p. 3).

The prophet went on to say there are three main reasons why Latter-day Saints should make the study of the Book of Mormon a lifetime pursuit—because it is the keystone of our religion, because it was written for our day, and because a person can get nearer to God by abiding by its precepts than by those of any other book. "Since the last general conference," he added, "I have received many letters from Saints, both young and old, from all over the world who accepted the challenge to read and study the Book of Mormon. I have been thrilled by their accounts of how their lives have been changed and how they have drawn closer to the Lord as a result of their commitment." He ended with the prayer "that the Book of Mormon may become the keystone of our lives" (ibid. p. 7).

By way of reemphasis, the prophet had this to say in his remarks ending the conference: "The Book of Mormon [was] written under the hand of inspiration for our day, preserved through the centuries to come forth in our time, translated by the gift and power of God. It is the keystone of our religion. It is the keystone of our doctrine. It is the keystone of our testimony. It is a keystone in the witness of Jesus Christ. It is a keystone in helping us avoid the deceptions of the evil one in these latter days. Satan rages in the hearts of men and has power over all of his dominions (see D&C 1:35). But the Book of Mormon has greater power—power to reveal false doctrine, power to help us overcome temptations, power to help us get closer to God than any other book (see Introduction to the Book of Mormon). The Book of Mormon must be re-enthroned in the minds and hearts of our people. We must honor it by reading it, by studying it, by taking its precepts into our lives and transforming them into lives required of the true followers of Christ" (in Conference Report, Oct. 1986, pp. 102–3).

As President Benson's first year in office ended, he could look back on these achievements and changes, in addition to those already mentioned: permitting worthy persons married to unendowed spouses to enter the temple to receive their own endowments; the discontinuance of stake seventies quorums; changes in stake conferences to enable stake presidents to preside over one of the two conferences in their stakes each year; the change of age groupings in the single adult program; reaching six million members of the Church on April 30, 1986; the formation of the sixteen hundredth stake, in Toronto, Ontario, on June 22; and the dedication of new temples in Lima, Peru; Buenos Aires, Argentina; and Denver, Colorado.

Following the October 1986 general conference, President Benson suffered several episodes when his heartbeat slowed perceptibly. This created dizziness and feelings of ennui. To remedy this it was decided to implant a pacemaker, which was done during a three-hour surgery on November 6. Five days later, President Benson was at his office early.

At the general conference in April 1987, the prophet again emphasized the Book of Mormon. He also stressed the importance of the Doctrine and Covenants, referring to it as the "capstone" of our religion. "The Book of Mormon brings men to Christ. The Doctrine and Covenants brings men to Christ's kingdom, even The Church of Jesus Christ of Latter-day Saints" (in Conference Report, Apr. 1987, p. 105). He admonished the members of the Church to obtain a personal witness of the truthfulness of the Book of Mormon through the Holy Ghost.

A few days after this conference, President Benson experienced chest pains and was hospitalized. Diagnostic tests indicated he had suffered a mild heart attack. He remained in the hospital for several days, and for some time afterward recuperated in his apartment. During this period, his counselors met with him regularly in his apartment to report on the work and to receive instructions. In time he began to attend his meetings regularly and to assume the direct supervision of the work. He also began to fulfill assignments outside Salt Lake City. On February 27, 1988, he traveled to California to break ground for the San Diego Temple, the forty-fifth temple in the Church.

President Benson's keynote address at the April 1988 general conference focused on the first and the great commandment as taught in the Book of Mormon: "It is the pure love of Christ, called charity, that the Book of Mormon testifies is the greatest of all—that never faileth, that endureth forever, that all men should have, and that without which they are nothing (see Moroni 7:44–47; 2 Nephi 26:30). . . . To love God with all your heart, soul, mind, and strength is all-consuming and all-encompassing. It is no lukewarm endeavor. It is total commitment of our very being—physically, mentally, emotionally, and spiritually—to a love of the Lord. The breadth, depth, and height of this love of God extend into every facet of one's life. Our desires, be they spiritual or temporal, should be rooted in a love of the Lord. Our thoughts and affections should be centered on the Lord. 'Let all thy thoughts be directed unto the Lord,' said Alma, 'yea, let the affections of thy heart be placed upon the Lord forever' (Alma 37:36)" (in Conference Report, Apr. 1988, p. 3).

All that President Ezra Taft Benson worked for, all that he stood for, and all that he hoped for—for himself, for his family, and for the Church—is embodied in this sermon. It defines the ideal of Christian devotion and service—that one be led and motivated constantly by the Spirit and example of Jesus Christ. This ideal, the attainment of which marks one as a true Saint, is taught regularly to the members of the Church through the sacramental prayers in which the worshippers covenant to take upon them the name of the Son, to remember Him always, and to keep His commandments, all to the end that they may always have His Spirit to be with them (see Moroni 4–5). The pure love of Christ referred to in the prophet's sermon is demonstrated by keeping the commandments, something the worshipper commits to do through the sacramental prayers.

If one seeks for the lodestar that guided Ezra Taft Benson through his life, this is it. From his earliest days of remembrance, tutored by the words and the example of his parents, he sought this state of constant obedience and spiritual attunement. In the rough and tumble of life, with its challenges, its distractions, and its pressures, this was not always possible. But the ideal was never lost, nor was the repeated striving to attain it. And toward the end, after the old battles had been fought and the old enmities had dissipated, there settled upon him a benign, loving aspect that to his associates seemed otherworldly in its quality. His demeanor and expressions were marked by attitudes of love, forgiveness, and brotherhood for all, whether members of the Church or not.

The keynote address and the concluding address President Benson gave at the October 1988 general conference were the last sermons he delivered at the pulpit of the Salt Lake Tabernacle. They are both significant. The keynote address was another rallying cry for the Book of Mormon. Said he: "The time is long overdue for a massive flooding of the earth with the Book of Mormon. . . . In this age of the electronic media and the mass distribution of the printed

313

word, God will hold us accountable if we do not now move the Book of Mormon in a monumental way." He then challenged the members of the Church to become active in this vast effort and shared his vision of the future: "I have a vision," said he, "of homes alerted, of classes alive, and of pulpits aflame with the spirit of Book of Mormon messages. I have a vision of home teachers and visiting teachers, ward and branch officers, and stake and mission leaders counseling our people out of the most correct of any book on earth—the Book of Mormon. I have a vision of artists putting into film, drama, literature, music, and paintings great themes and great characters from the Book of Mormon. I have a vision of thousands of missionaries going into the mission field with hundreds of passages memorized from the Book of Mormon so that they might feed the needs of a spiritually famished world. I have a vision of the whole Church getting nearer to God by abiding by the precepts of the Book of Mormon. Indeed, I have a vision of flooding the earth with the Book of Mormon" (in Conference Report, Oct. 1988, pp. 4–5).

Finally, the prophet expressed a sense of urgency about the work, the need for the entire Church to become involved in it, and his determination to pursue it diligently to the end: "I do not know fully why God has preserved my life to this age, but I do know this: That for the present hour He has revealed to me the absolute need for us to move the Book of Mormon forward now in a marvelous manner. You must help with this burden and with this blessing which He has placed on the whole Church, even all the children of Zion. Moses never entered the promised land. Joseph Smith never saw Zion redeemed. Some of us may not live long enough to see the day when the Book of Mormon floods the earth and when the Lord lifts His condemnation (see D&C 84:54–58). But, God willing, I intend to spend all my remaining days in that glorious effort" (in Conference Report, Oct. 1988, p. 5).

The prophet's concluding address is remarkable, not

314

only because it was the last time President Benson's voice would be heard in the Tabernacle, but also because of the content and the tone of the talk. It was devoted entirely to a series of testimonies about the Church and its doctrines: "As a special witness of Jesus Christ and as His humble servant," he began, "it is now my obligation and privilege, as the Spirit dictates, to bear pure testimony and witness to that which I know to be true (see Alma 4:19). This I will do." Then followed a series of nineteen declarations, each beginning with the words "I testify that." In these, the prophet bore solemn testimony about truths such as our premortal existence; the way God leads His children through revelation; the birth, ministry, and sacrifice of the Savior; the Apostasy and Restoration; the Book of Mormon; the favored status of America; the role of living prophets; the conflict between good and evil; the need for the Saints to be actively engaged in the work; and the final judgment and cleansing that will take place. He ended with these words: "I testify to you that a fulness of joy can only come through the atonement of Jesus Christ and by obedience to all of the laws and ordinances of the gospel, which are found only in The Church of Jesus Christ of Latter-day Saints. . . . To all these things I humbly testify and bear my solemn witness that they are true, and I do so in the name of Him who is the head of this church, even Jesus Christ, amen" (in Conference Report, Oct. 1988, pp. 101–4).

Following this conference, President Benson suffered a stroke that made it impossible for him to speak in public, although it did not impair his mentality. Through the April 1991 general conference, he attended the sessions in person, but his talks were read by his counselors. Later, as his physical problems increased, he discontinued going to the Tabernacle, instead watching the sessions on television. Behind the scenes, however, he continued to speak, though haltingly. It was then that he used means other than words to communicate to those around him. "The prophet attended our sacrament meeting today. I sat by him on the

315

President Benson demonstrates his buoyant enthusiasm at general conference

stand. He showed great love for everyone. He shook hands
with those who prayed, patted me on the knee during the
meeting, and stopped the young father who had just blessed
his baby to congratulate him and to admire the little girl.
There were tears in the father's eyes. It was an event which
will be talked about in this family for many years—perhaps
for generations. The prophet now has great difficulty in
expressing himself. It seems as if he may have suffered a
mild stroke" (author's personal diary, Oct. 8, 1989).

Behind the scenes, President Benson continued to attend
meetings and to speak to his brethren within the limits of his
reduced capacity: "The monthly meeting of all General
Authorities was held in the upper room of the temple this
morning. President Benson was present and spoke briefly at
the end. His speech has been impaired so that he can say
only a few words such as 'I love you all' and 'I know it's
true.' His infirmities have brought with them an aura of
peace and composure. He does not seem to be agitated
because of them. His expression is benign and smiling; and
he is easily touched as when someone compliments him or

extends love and best wishes to him from members around the world" (ibid., Dec. 7, 1989).

In the same vein is this from the meeting of all General Authorities on February 1, 1990: "President Benson was much stronger today and spoke more extensively than he has done in the last while. Instead of remaining behind the table which sits before the First Presidency, he walked alone out in front of it and spoke briefly, but effectively. The import of his message was that while he used to serve with 'vim and vigor,' he is no longer able to do so and that this responsibility now rested on the 'younger men.' He said as much with the gestures of his hands and arms as he did with his words. It was quite touching and symbolic to see the way in which his counselors and the Twelve sat forward expectantly to catch him if he had fallen. Although he is aged and weak and no longer speaks with the verve and facility he once did, he is providing powerful, prophetic leadership" (ibid.).

The loving and kindly quality now shown by the prophet was evident to all who were close to him: "President Monson mentioned the sweet, spiritual quality which now characterizes President Ezra Taft Benson. He told of a recent incident when President Monson performed the sealing for one of President Benson's grandchildren. As President Monson put his hand on the arm of the prophet to ask if he should proceed, President Benson lovingly patted his hand and arm. President Monson feels that his memories of this prophet will always be colored by that unplanned and tender show of affection" (ibid., Aug. 30, 1990).

President Benson was operated on September 19, 1990, for the removal of two subdural hematomas. Dr. Bruce Sorensen, who had performed similar surgeries on President Spencer W. Kimball, performed the surgery. The prophet recovered satisfactorily and was able to attend the First Presidency's Christmas devotional on Sunday, December 2. "He is quite strong and alert. He is unable, of course, to be involved in the day-to-day operation of the Church. But no new initiatives are taken without his knowledge and consent" (ibid., Dec. 2, 1990).

His counselors went forward under delegations of authority from the prophet and met with him regularly to brief him on the progress of the work and to seek his direction on any unusual matters. This procedure would continue throughout the remainder of his life. While the prophet's voice was no longer heard in public meetings of the Saints, his words, contained in recorded writings and sermons, remained alive and in effect. Through them he continued to remind the members of the Church about his special prophetic ministry and to admonish them to read the Book of Mormon regularly and to follow its teachings.

Epilogue

T he Benson apartment, located atop The Gateway apartment complex on State Street, commanded a striking view of the Salt Lake Temple a block to the west. In between was the fountain in the plaza separating the Church Administration Building and the highrise Church Office Building. Beyond the Administration Building on the left, looking from the Benson apartment toward the temple, was the Hotel Utah, which was later renovated and renamed the Joseph Smith Memorial Building. In this setting President Benson and Flora spent their last days in comfort and security, surrounded by those who loved them.

After Flora passed away, the prophet remained alone in his apartment except for security and domestic personnel who were constantly in attendance. There he received his counselors, who came regularly to visit with him personally and to report matters of Church business. Members of the Quorum of the Twelve Apostles came intermittently; family members visited on a regular basis. Occasionally, President

319

Benson left the apartment on special outings, such as a trip to a drive-in restaurant for a hamburger and shake, one of his favorite snacks, or to visit someone.

In September 1991, arrangements were made to take President Benson to the Cannon cabin in Emigration Canyon, the place where President Heber J. Grant called him to the Twelve. There, with members of the family, he went into the bedroom adjoining the living room where President Grant had extended the call to him. Closing the door, they spent some time together alone, reminiscing about the incident that had reshaped the prophet's life. A track of almost fifty years lay behind. Along that track were events of joy and sadness, trial and triumph, anxiety and tranquility. Amid the changing scenes, however, were the constants that never changed—his love for family, devotion to his apostolic calling, and loyalty to his country.

Ahead lay a track of unknown length with twists and turns hidden from view. Whatever the future held for him, Ezra Taft Benson was prepared to face it with faith and confidence, assured that whatever occurred was best for him and his family and for the church over which he presided.

The end came quietly for the prophet on May 30, 1994. There was no sadness among his family and associates, except that caused by the knowledge of a temporary separation. He had lived a long, productive, and distinguished life, the outlines of which were traced by those who spoke and eulogized him at the funeral in the Tabernacle. President Howard W. Hunter captured the essence of President Benson's years of apostolic leadership in his remarks. "He spoke to everyone and had concern for all," said President Hunter. "He spoke to the women of the Church and to the men. He spoke to the elderly. He spoke to those who were single, to those in their youth, and he loved speaking to the children in the Church. He gave wonderful, personalized counsel to the entire membership, whatever their personal circumstances. Those sermons will continue to sustain us and guide us as we reflect on them for many years to come" (*Ensign*, July 1994, p. 42).

When the funeral services ended, the prophet's casket was carried to the waiting hearse, passing through two lines formed by members of the Quorum of the Twelve. Then began the long drive from Salt Lake City to Whitney, Idaho. Long before either of them passed away, President and Sister Benson had decided they were to be interred in the small, quiet Whitney cemetery in the community where the prophet was born and where they had established their first family home. Following Sister Benson's death, a beautiful joint headstone had been put in place that contained key information about their lives, except the date of President Benson's death. That missing fact was added later. Reflecting the unity that always characterized their family, the names of the children had been etched on the back side of the headstone.

It is doubtful anyone had foreseen the extraordinary show of love and admiration for President Benson that was exhibited along the route to Whitney. At practically every overpass there were people waiting to pay their respects, waving their hands or handkerchiefs or small American flags, people of both sexes and of every age. There were Scouts in uniform. Some adults were seated in camp chairs and some in wheelchairs. As the cortege left the highway and entered the farming areas, workers left their machines and approached the dirt road, removing their hats in respect. Here and there were yellow ribbons attached to fence posts, welcoming home their friend and neighbor whom the old-timers affectionately called "T." He belonged to them and they to him. And now that he was buried in their midst, everyone in Whitney, and indeed, throughout Cache Valley, would have some proprietary claim upon this great man.

What made this display all the more remarkable is that no one knew just when President Benson's funeral cortege would pass any given point. Yet they were prepared to wait as long as necessary to salute their leader and friend.

President and Sister Benson undoubtedly knew they would feel comfortable in that small, rural cemetery, surrounded by the headstones of many of their family and friends and near the fields Ezra had tilled as a boy and as a man. Yet the remoteness of their burial place will never conceal the monumental labor they performed on an international stage in the service of their Lord and His Church and of the country they loved.

Bibliography

PRIMARY SOURCES

Benson, Ezra Taft. Manuscripts. Historical Department. The Church of Jesus Christ of Latter-day Saints.

Gibbons, Francis M. Diaries, 1970–94.

Official Reports of the General Conferences of The Church of Jesus Christ of Latter-day Saints, 1943–94.

NEWSPAPERS

Church News (Salt Lake City, Utah), 1943–94.

Deseret News (Salt Lake City, Utah), 1943–94.

Salt Lake Tribune (Salt Lake City, Utah), 1943–94.

PERIODICALS

Selected Articles by or about Ezra Taft Benson
(Listed Chronologically)

November 1943. "'The Least among You.'" *Improvement Era*, 679.

December 1943. "What I Read As a Boy." *Children's Friend*, 559.

May 1944. "Spirituality—A Safeguard Against Delinquency." *Improvement Era*, 287, 324–25.

Bibliography

November 1944. "America: A Choice Land." *Improvement Era*, 674–75, 726.

May 1945. "The Importance of Missionary Work." *Improvement Era*, 254, 307–8.

November 1945. "Principles of Cooperation." *Improvement Era*, 653, 710–11.

October 1946. Frederick W. Babbel. "Europe's Valiant Saints Forge Ahead." *Improvement Era*, 622–23, 664–67.

November 23, 1946. "'I'll Go Where You Want Me to Go.'" *Church News*.

February 1947. "A Child's Example." *Children's Friend*, 72.

May 1947. "Special Mission to Europe." *Improvement Era*, 293–94, 296.

November 1947. "Responsibilities of the Latter-day Saint Home." *Improvement Era*, 718, 754, 756.

May 1948. "America: Land of the Blessed." *Improvement Era*, 283, 342–43.

November 1949. "The Sunday School Now and Then." *Instructor*, 533–35.

February 1950. "Preservation of Our Blessings of Freedom." *Relief Society Magazine*, 75–82.

October 1950. "Our First Obligation." *Children's Friend*, 450–54.

November 9, 1953. "Benson Strikes Back at Critics." *Life*, 40, 43.

November 1954. "The Best Advice I Ever Had." *Reader's Digest*, 97–99.

November 1955. "The Twelfth Article of Faith." *Instructor*, 332–33.

January 1956. "Strengthening the Latter-day Saint Home." *Children's Friend*, 34, 36.

January 1956. "Farmers Can Prosper and Be Free." *Nation's Business*, 39–41.

January 1957. "For Security—Look beyond Materialism." *Instructor*, 8–9.

February 22, 1957. "The Farm Problem—Can It Be Solved?" *U.S. News & World Report*, 54–56.

April 1957. "Foundations for Family Solidarity." *Children's Friend*, 26.

May 1957. "The Balance of Government." *Improvement Era*, 304–6, 350–51.

March 1958. "We Saw the Church around the World." *Instructor*, 68–70.

February 1964. "Scouting: A Great American Partnership." *Improvement Era*, 100–103, 127.

January 1967. "The Greatest Work in the World." *Improvement Era*, 24–27.

April 1969. "How to Delegate Wisely (Part 1)." *Improvement Era*, 24–26.

May 1969. "How to Delegate Wisely (Part 2)." *Improvement Era*, 70–73.

March 1970. "The Future of the Church in Asia." *Improvement Era*, 14–15.

Bibliography

December 1970. "A Peculiar People." *Instructor,* 441–42.

May 1971. "Keeping the Sabbath Day Holy." *Ensign,* 4–7.

August 1971. "Missionary Memories." *Friend,* 14–15.

January 1973. "Family Joys." *New Era,* 4–6.

February 1975. "Scouting Builds Men." *New Era,* 14–18.

May 1975. "Jesus Christ—Gifts and Expectations." *New Era,* 16–21.

July 1975. "The Teachings of Parents." *Friend,* 6–7.

November 1976. "Receive All Things with Thankfulness." *New Era,* 4–9.

June 1978. "Respect for Standards." *New Era,* 11.

July 1978. "America at the Crossroads." *New Era,* 36–39.

September 1979. "Your Charge—To Increase in Wisdom and Favor with God and Man." *New Era,* 40–45.

December 1979. "Five Marks of the Divinity of Jesus Christ." *New Era,* 44–50.

September 1981. "The Honored Place of Woman." *Ensign,* 104–7.

May 1982. "Prepare Yourself for the Great Day of the Lord." *New Era,* 44–50.

January 1984. "Christ and the Constitution." *Jurisdiction Journal and Sovereign Review,* 1–5.

July 1984. "Honor." *New Era,* 4–6.

April 1985. "He Is Risen." *New Era,* 5–7.

August 1985. "What I Hope You Will Teach Your Children about the Temple." *Ensign,* 6–10.

November 17, 1985. "President Benson Expresses Feelings on First Presidency Reorganization." *Church News,* 3, 7.

February 1986. "The Power of Prayer." *Friend,* 1.

March 1986. "Joy in Christ." *Ensign,* 3–5.

April 1986. "He Lives." *New Era,* 4–7.

April 13, 1986. "Make Book of Mormon Study Lifelong Pursuit." *Church News,* 5, 23.

May 1986. "To 'The Rising Generation.'" *New Era,* 4–8.

July 1986. "A Voice of Warning." *Ensign,* 2–5.

October 1986. "Do Not Despair." *Ensign,* 2–5.

November 1986. "To the Young Women of the Church." *Ensign,* 81–85.

February 1987. "Valiant in the Testimony of Jesus." *Ensign,* 2–3.

June 1987. "'Pay Thy Debt, and Live.'" *Ensign,* 2–5.

Bibliography

June 27, 1987. John L. Hart. "President Benson Emphasizes the 'Miracle of Conversion.'" *Church News*, 3, 6.

July 4, 1987. Gerry Avant. "'Apply Savior's Teachings,' Says Prophet." *Church News*, 3.

September 1987. "'Feed My Sheep.'" *Ensign*, 2–5.

September 1987. "The Constitution—A Glorious Standard." *Ensign*, 6–11.

January 1988. "The Book of Mormon Is the Word of God." *Ensign*, 2–5.

January 1988. "The Law of Chastity." *New Era*, 4–7.

April 1988. "Seek the Spirit of the Lord." *Ensign*, 2–5.

April 1988. "Come unto Christ." *New Era*, 4–7.

June 4, 1988. "We Need to Raise Our Sights." *Church News*, 6.

September 1988. "In His Steps." *Ensign*, 2–6.

November 1988. "Flooding the Earth with the Book of Mormon." *Ensign*, 4–6.

November 1988. "I Testify." *Ensign*, 86–87.

December 1988. "Christmas Remembered: A Joyful Reunion." *New Era*, 21.

November 1989. "To the Elderly in the Church." *Ensign*, 4–8.

September 1990. "Keys to Successful Member-Missionary Work." *Ensign*, 2–7.

BOOKS

Allen, James B., and Glen M. Leonard. *The Story of the Latter-day Saints.* Salt Lake City: Deseret Book Co., 1976.

Anderson, Joseph. *Prophets I Have Known.* Salt Lake City: Deseret Book Co., 1973.

Arrington, Leonard J., and Davis Bitton. *The Mormon Experience: A History of the Latter-day Saints.* New York: Alfred A. Knopf, 1979.

Babbel, Frederick W. *On Wings of Faith.* Salt Lake City: Bookcraft, 1972.

Benson, Ezra Taft. *Come, Listen to a Prophet's Voice.* Salt Lake City: Deseret Book Co., 1990.

———. *Come unto Christ.* Salt Lake City: Deseret Book Co., 1983.

———. *The Constitution: A Heavenly Banner.* Salt Lake City: Deseret Book Co., 1986.

———. *Cross Fire: The Eight Years with Eisenhower.* Garden City, N.Y.: Doubleday & Co., 1962.

Bibliography

———. *An Enemy Hath Done This.* Compiled by Jerreld L. Newquist. Salt Lake City: Parliament Publishers, 1969.

———. *Farmers at the Crossroads.* New York: Devin-Adair, 1956.

———. *Freedom to Farm.* Garden City, N.Y.: Doubleday & Co., 1960.

———. *God, Family, Country: Our Three Great Loyalties.* Salt Lake City: Deseret Book Co., 1974.

———. *A Labor of Love: The 1946 European Mission of Ezra Taft Benson.* Salt Lake City: Deseret Book Co., 1989.

———. *The Red Carpet.* Salt Lake City: Bookcraft, 1962.

———. *So Shall Ye Reap.* Salt Lake City: Deseret Book Co., 1960.

———. *The Teachings of Ezra Taft Benson.* Salt Lake City: Bookcraft, 1988.

———. *This Nation Shall Endure.* Salt Lake City: Deseret Book Co., 1977.

———. *Title of Liberty.* Compiled by Mark A. Benson. Salt Lake City: Deseret Book Co., 1964.

———. *A Witness and a Warning: A Modern-day Prophet Testifies of the Book of Mormon.* Salt Lake City: Deseret Book Co., 1988.

Berrett, William E. *The Restored Church.* 12th ed. Salt Lake City: Deseret Book Co., 1965.

Cowan, Richard O. *The Church in the Twentieth Century.* Salt Lake City: Bookcraft, 1985.

Dew, Sheri L. *Ezra Taft Benson: A Biography.* Salt Lake City: Deseret Book Co., 1987.

Swinton, Heidi S. *In the Company of Prophets: Personal Experiences of D. Arthur Haycock.* Salt Lake City: Deseret Book Co., 1993.

Index

Abdominal surgery, 160, 229
Adams, Sherman, 194–95, 221
Advertizing. See Marketing
Agricultural Act of 1954, 197
Agricultural Adjustment Act,
94–95, 96, 99, 193
Agricultural Adjustment
Administration, 94–95, 99
Agricultural Conservation
Programs (ACP), 186
Agricultural Hall of Fame, 231
Agricultural Postwar Planning
Committee, 135, 139
Agricultural Trade Development
and Assistance Act (Public Law
480), 198, 203, 217–18, 220
Agriculture. See Ezra Taft
Benson—professional life
Alder, Louise, 18
Alger, Horatio, 23
America. See United States of
America

American Council of Churches,
179
American Farm Bureau
Federation, 178
American Institute of Cooperation
(AIC), 105, 142–43, 161, 164–65,
172
Ames, Iowa, 30, 71, 74–78
Amussen, Barbara Smith (mother
of Flora): ETB meets, 45; bears
seven children, 67; death of,
122; predicts ETB's apostleship,
123, 125, 126
Amussen, Carl Christian (father of
Flora): 45, 66–67, 122; ETB
visits birthplace of, 149, 207
Amussen, Flora. See Benson, Flora
Amussen
Amussen, Mabel, 122
Amussen, Martha, 67
Anderson, Jack, 292
Anderson, Joseph, 127

329

Andrus, Adeline. *See* Benson, Adeline Andrus

Andrus, Orrin C., 3

Andrus, Pamelia. *See* Benson, Pamelia Andrus

Annandale Virginia Stake conference, 300–303

Argentina, 230, 311

Assistants to the Twelve, 270, 276–77

Australia, 230, 284

Austria, 154, 242, 276, 285

Automobiles: ETB uses father's Dodge, 42–43; ETB's Model T breaks down, 73–74; Benson family embarrassed to ride in limousine, 98, 200; Benson family purchases Pontiac Six, 157; ETB travels on surfaced roads, 159

Babbel, Frederick W., 146, 148, 151, 156

Babcock, H. E., 113

Badger, Chaplain, 156

Ballard, Melvin J., 85, 97, 99, 104–5

Ballard, Melvin Russell, 105

Ballif, Louisa A. *See* Benson, Louisa A. Ballif

Ballif, Serge (uncle of ETB), 64

Ballif, Serge Louis (great-grandfather of ETB), 209

Baptism: of Ezra T. and Pamelia Andrus Benson, 7; for dead, 9; of converts, 53, 262

Basketball, 27–28, 38

Bear Lake, hike to, 40, 41

Beets, thinning, 23

Begin, Menachem, 283

Belgium, 63, 154, 229

Beneficial Life Insurance Corporation, 266

Ben-Gurion, David, 219

Bennett, Emily, 293

Bennett, Harold H., 293

Bennion, Adam S., 69

Bennion, Louise, 115

Bennion, Mervyn, 115

Benson, Adeline Andrus (great-grandmother of ETB), 10, 12

Benson, Barbara (daughter of ETB): birth of, 98; offers prayer, 114; increased responsibilities of, 119; family pictures of, *138, 141*; visits Church historical sites, 169–70; injured in car accident, 190; marriage of, 210–11; daughter of, 253

Benson, Beverly (daughter of ETB): naming of, 98; birth of, 10; increased responsibilities of, 119; family pictures of, *138, 141*; visits Church historical sites, 169–70; at marriage of Barbara Benson, 210; travels with ETB, 216–20, 226–28; lives in Finland, 285; visits ETB in Washington, 292

Benson, Bonnie (daughter of ETB): naming of, 98; birth of, 118; family pictures of, *138, 141*; travels with ETB, 164–65, 216–20, 226–28

Benson, Chloe Taft (great-great-grandmother of ETB), 2

Benson, Eliza Ann Perry, 12

Benson, Elizabeth Golliher, 12

Benson, Ezra T. (great-grandfather of ETB): ETB named after, 1, 13, 171; character traits of, 2; career of, 3–4; conversion of, 4–7, 169; moves to Nauvoo, 8–10, 169, 283; crosses plains to Salt Lake, 10, 164; settles Cache Valley, 11–12; family of, 12; reputation of, 16, 45, 127; great-grand-children of, 18; influences ETB, 18; serves as apostle, 74, 137, 170

Benson, Ezra Taft (ETB)

—childhood and youth: birth and naming of, 1, 14–15, 18–19; baby picture of, 19; considered special, 20; childhood home of, 20–21; early farming experiences of, 22–23; enjoys reading and music, 23–24; Christmas memories of, 24–25; youthful teasing and fighting of, 25–27; enjoys basketball, 27–28; family pictures of, 28, 32; schooling of, 29–30; spiritual growth of, 30; responsibilities of, while father serves mission, 32–34, 55; admires his father, 34–35; attends Oneida Stake Academy, 34–39, 42; uses family car, 42–43

—mission: serves under Orson F. Whitney, 14, 50–51; desires to serve, 30–31; called to Great Britain, 46, 49; prepares to serve, 46–47; travels to Great Britain, 47–49; serves in Carlisle, 51–54; overcomes discouragement, 54–56; serves as clerk and branch president, 56–59; as president of Newcastle Conference, 59–62; returns home, 62–65; growth of, 68, 78

—personal life: birth and heredity of, 1–2; marriage of, 14, 72–73; influence of Ezra T. Benson on, 18; youthful ambition of, 22; loves competition, 26–27; receives patriarchal blessings, 30–31, 64, 109; early love of Book of Mormon, 33; ambition of, to be a farmer, 33; involvement of, in WWI, 41–42; healed by priesthood blessing, 42; courts Flora Amussen, 43–46, 66–68; experiences car trouble during move to Ames, 73–75; moves home, 78–79; expects first child, 79; at birth of Reed, 83; relies on children for advice, 83–84; at birth of Mark, 87; moves family to Boise, 91; at deaths of parents,

96–98; at birth of Barbara, 98; at birth of Beverly, 104; moves to Washington, 108–9, 113–14; at birth of Bonnie, 118; persuasive ability of, 121; at death of Barbara Amussen, 122–23; travels to West Coast, 124, 126–27; character traits of, 125; financial concerns of, 130–31, 166; moves to Salt Lake City, 138–39; family pictures of, *138*, *141*; at birth of Beth, 140; moves to new home, 140–41; visits birthplace of father-in-law 149, 207; affection of, for America, 156; sings in K-Ration Quartet, 156; reunited with Flora and family, 157–58; takes vacation in Idaho, 159–60; burial place of, 160; takes vacation to Salt River Valley, 161; visits Church historical sites, 162, 167, 169–70; at farewell for Reed, 163; takes vacation to Yellowstone and Jackson Hole, 163–64; celebrates pioneer centennial, 163–64; at farewell for Mark, 165–66; suffers digestive problems, 168; visits sons in New York, 168; shares similar backgrounds with Dwight D. Eisenhower, 173–74; performs Mark's temple marriage, 180; receives blessing from Pres. McKay, 181; Flora cares for and helps, 183; settles family in Washington, 200; appears with family on television, 200–201; at marriage of Barbara, 210–11; has abdominal surgery, 229; moves back to Salt Lake, 235; protected by prompting of the Spirit, 235; welcome home party hosted for, 236; takes vacation in Arizona, 236; publishes books, 240; spends

time with grandchildren,
252–53; purchases cottage,
253–54; enjoys horseback
riding, 253, 254, 255; fractures
hip and knee, 254–56; shows
continued interest in political
affairs, 256, 259; opposes U. S.
strategies in Vietnam, 258, 262;
at death of Eisenhower, 261;
assists Flora during illness,
266–68, 279; moves to
condominium, 268; exhibits
sense of humor, 272–73; BYU
Agriculture and Food Institute
named after, 277–78; 50th
wedding anniversary of, 280;
receives Freedom Foundation
Award, 281; breaks hip, 282;
suffers from health problems,
284, 285–86, 303–4, 307; as
grand marshal of Provo's
Freedom Festival, 291; honored
at banquet, 291; temple
attendance by, 292; Ronald
Reagan honors, 292; receives
Service-to-Freedom Award,
308; suffers heart problems,
311, 312; suffers stroke, 315; has
subdural hematomas removed,
317; at death of Flora, 319;
visits Cannon cabin, 320;
passes away, 320–22
—professional life: graduate
studies of, 30; decides to
become farmer, 34–35; attends
BYU, 69–71; attends Iowa State
College, 71, 75–78; visits St.
Paul and local farms, 78–79;
improves Whitney farm, 80–82;
as county agent, 85–86, 88–90;
promotes cooperatives, 92–94;
opposes AAA, 94–95; as
agricultural economist and
specialist, 95–96; attends
University of California at
Berkeley, 102–4; works for
NCFC, 105–7, 110–13, 131;

serves on national committees,
119–21; opposes price ceilings,
121–22; leaves NCFC, 129–30,
135–36; works with AIC,
142–43, 161; speaks to AIC,
164–65; supports Thomas E.
Dewey, 166–67; watches
presidential campaign, 175;
appointed as U.S. secretary of
agriculture, 176–79; tours
United States, 179–80; at
confirmation hearing, 180;
attends Eisenhower
inauguration, 181; is sworn in
as secretary of agriculture,
181–83; inspects USDA office,
182–83; forms friendship with
Eisenhower, 183–84; suggests
cabinet meetings open with
prayer, 184–85; selects USDA
staff, 185; restructures USDA,
185; endures criticism, 185–86,
187–89, 194–95, 215–16, 223–24;
opposes price supports, 186–87,
194–98; inspects farmland, 189;
counters opposition, 191–92,
197–98; Eisenhower supports,
195; speaks to radio audience,
196; wins subsidy battle in
Congress, 198–99; considered a
political hero, 199, 223; agrees
to continue work as secretary
of agriculture, 199–200, 213–14,
221; works to liquidate farm
surpluses, 202–3, 205, 209–10,
216; sells surpluses to Latin
America, 203–5; sells surpluses
to Europe, 206–10; criticized for
policies about surpluses, 210;
campaigns for Eisenhower's
reelection, 214–16; sells
surpluses on world tour,
216–20; critics demand
resignation of, 221, 223, 228–29;
remains calm during political
abuse, 222; considers running
for president, 223; relationship

of, with Richard Nixon, 223–24, 229, 259; administers Food for Peace program, 224; meets Nikita Khrushchev, 224–25; visits Soviet Union and nearby countries, 225–28; travels throughout world, 229–30; promotes international free trade, 230–31; inducted into Agricultural Hall of Fame, 231; concludes service as secretary of agriculture, 231–33; leaves positive impression of cabinet service, 234–35; Pres. McKay commends cabinet service of, 235; serves on board of Corn Products International, 236–37; as possible candidate for president, 244–48, 259; speaks to secular groups, 245–47
—early Church service: Scout service of, 39–41, 88, 92; ordained as seventy, 85; YMMIA service of, 85, 92; as first counselor in Boise Stake, 98–102; high council service of, 102; as president of Boise Stake, 104–5, 107, 108–9; as part of "Mormon Colony," 115; as president of Washington D. C. Stake, 116–18, 122, 130, 131, 134–35; released as stake president, 136
—General Authority: teaches missionaries about prayer, 21–22; Scouting service of, 41, 140, 167, 169, *280*; shares ideas with colleagues, 84; called to the Twelve, 124–26, 127–31; sustained and ordained, 132–34, *133*; organizes Annapolis, MD branch, 134; attends stake conference in New York City, 135; attends first meeting with the Twelve, 137–38; fills first assignments as Apostle, 139–40; tours East Central States Mission, 142; speaks about America, 143; called to relieve Saints in Europe, 146–47; tours European continent, 147–49, 154; visits Germany, 150–54; gets supplies to Germany, 151–52, 154; as European Mission president, 154–55, 241–43; overcomes adversity in Europe, 155–56; returns from Europe, 156–58; serves on Church committees, 160; visits various stake conferences, 161–62; speaking assignments of, 162–63; opposes communism, 165, 166, 225, 227; visits President Truman, 167; at death of Pres. George Albert Smith, 170–71; at reorganization of First Presidency, 171–72, 264, 269; on problems confronting the nation, 172–73; discontinues regularly functioning as member of the Twelve, 180–81; Harold B. Lee praises name of, 189; speaks in general conference, 190–91; at dedication of Swiss Temple, 208–9, 211; warns Saints about liquor, 211–12; visits Church members throughout world, 220; speaks to religious congregation in Soviet Union, 227–28; resumes work with the Twelve, 235–36; experiences difficult transition, 236–37; visits Church members in northern United States, 237; feels concerned about Soviet Union and communism, 237–38; speaks out against communism, 239–41; fulfills responsibilities as Apostle, 248–52, 264–66; travels to Europe, 249–50, 284–85, 289–90;

dedicates land of Italy, 250; responsible for work in the Far East, 257–58; travels to Orient, 258–62; at death of David O. McKay, 263–64; travels to Pacific, 267; at death of Harold B. Lee, 268–69; ordains Spencer W. Kimball as prophet, 269; called as president of the Twelve, 269, 272; assumes new duties as pres. of Twelve, 270–71; administrative style of, 271–72; begins work as pres. of Twelve, 273–76; on world conditions, 274; recommends policy changes to First Presidency, 276–77; travels to Far East, 277; serves on forum for domestic policy, 278–79; on Church history, 279, 281; at revelation on blacks holding priesthood, 281–82; travels to South America, 282–83, 284; creates stake in Nauvoo, 283; travels to Middle East, 283–84, 289–90; on prophets, 284; on family, 286; travels to Kirtland, 286–87; political controversy surrounding, 287; Gordon B. Hinckley's relationship with, 288–89; promotes BYU Jerusalem Center, 290; attends Atlanta Temple dedication, 290; loves the temple, 290–91; prompted in choosing stake patriarch, 293; testimony of, 293–94
—prophet: becomes president of the Church, 1, 134; promotes Book of Mormon, 34, 58, 297; at death of Pres. Kimball, 295–96; ordained as pres. of Church, 296; asks Twelve for input, 296–98; holds press conference, 296–97; develops themes for general conference, 297; promotes reactivation, 298;

speaks to young women, 298–99; travels to Washington D.C., 300–303; speaks on Book of Mormon, 300–302, 304–7, 309–11, 313–14; visits government leaders, 303; meets with George Bush, 303; at general conference, 305, 309, 316; speaks on Constitution, 308–9; visits Church history sites, 308; institutes Church changes, 311; travels to San Diego Temple ground-breaking, 312; on loving God, 312–13; bears final testimony to Church, 315; physical incapacity of, 315–18
Benson, Flora Amussen (wife of ETB): marriage of, 14, 72–73, 72; lives in Preston, Idaho, 41, 86–88; ETB receives impression he will marry, 43, 71, 72; meets ETB, 43–44; courted by ETB, 45–46, 66–68; bids farewell to ETB as he leaves for mission, 47; writes to ETB, 54–55, 71; decides to serve mission, 68–69; returns home, 71; survives honeymoon drive to Ames, 74; learns to live meagerly, 75–76; enjoys life in Ames, Iowa, 76–77; moves home, 78–79; expects first child, 79; contributes to Whitney farm, 80; gives birth to Reed, 83; as partner with ETB, 84–85, 114; serves in YWMIA, 85, 88, 92; supports ETB, 86, 90, 102, 155, 183; gives birth to Mark, 87; moves to Boise, 91; gives birth to Barbara, 98; acts as hostess, 99–100, 200; endures difficulties at Berkeley, 102–4; gives birth to Beverly, 104; prompted that family will move to Washington, 107; remains with children in Boise, 109; moves to

Index

Washington, 113–14; as part of "Mormon Colony," 115; gives birth to Bonnie, 118; teaches Reed to box, 119; at death of mother, 122–23; learns of ETB's call to Twelve, 129; announces sixth pregnancy, 130; attends general conference, 131; unable to attend conference, 136–37; family pictures of, *138, 141*; moves to Salt Lake City, 138–39; gives birth to Beth, 140; moves to new home, 140–41; bids ETB farewell to war-torn Europe, 147; corresponds with ETB, 149, 155–56; reunited with ETB, 157–58; spends vacation in Idaho, 159–60; has abdominal surgery, 160, 161; burial place of, 160; spends vacation in Salt River Valley, 161; visits Washington and Church historical sites, 162, 167; praised for raising good family, 163; ETB spends time with, 168; visits sons in New York, 168; undergoes additional surgery, 169; calls ETB about Eisenhower appointment, 176; expresses confidence in ETB, 177; attends inauguration and ETB's swearing in, 181–83; cares for ETB before returning to Salt Lake, 183; stands by ETB during criticism, 188; injured in car accident, 190; fasts with ETB about farm legislation, 197; manages simple home in Washington, 200; appears with family on television, 200–201; tours Latin America with ETB, 204; travels to Europe with ETB, 206–9, 249–50, 284–85; visits birthplace of father, 207; attends Barbara's marriage, 210; campaigns for

Eisenhower's reelection, 214; accompanies ETB on world tour, 216–20, 229–30; travels to Soviet Union with ETB, 226–28; attends USDA reception for ETB, 232; moves back to Salt Lake, 235; vacations in Arizona, 236; moves to Germany, 242; spends time with grandchildren, 252–53; travels to Orient with ETB, 259–62; injures leg, 266–67; travels to Pacific, 267; suffers stroke, 267–68; moves to condominium, 268; suffers from depression, 274; weakened from illness, 279, 284; 50th wedding anniversary of, *280*; visits Reed in Israel, 290; attends Atlanta Temple dedication, 290; prays for Pres. Kimball's health, 295–96; as partner with ETB, 298–99; travels to Washington D.C. with ETB, 300; adds picture and testimony to Books of Mormon, 301; attends homemaking fair, 302; reads from Book of Mormon daily, 307; visits Church history sites, 308; photograph of, with ETB, *309*; passes away, 319, 321

Benson, Flora Beth (daughter of ETB): naming of, 98; birth of, 140; family picture of, *141*; suffers from health problems, 155–56; misses family, 220; travels with ETB, 229–30, 289–90; moves to Germany, 242; marriage of, 252; helps ETB recover from surgery, 256; helps mother during illness, 268

Benson, George Taft (grandfather of ETB): birth of, 10, 75, 170; settles in Cache Valley, 12; as bishop of Whitney Ward, 14, 16

335

Benson, George Taft, (brother of ETB), 33, 96–97

Benson, George Taft Jr. (father of ETB): 12–13; heritage of, 15–16; marriage of, 17–18; teaches ETB, 21–22; sings in choir, 24; enjoys basketball, 27–28; picture of, with sons, 28; serves mission, 31–34, 75; ETB's admiration for, 34–35; owns Dodge car, 42; ordains ETB an elder, 47; writes to ETB, 54; ETB purchases farm from, 70, 78, 80; death of, 97

Benson Institute, 277–78

Benson, Isabella, 10

Benson, Joe (brother of ETB), 26

Benson, John (great-great-grandfather of ETB), 2–3, 35

Benson, Lela Wing (daughter-in-law of ETB), 180

Benson, Lera (sister of ETB), 235

Benson, Louisa A. Ballif (grandmother of ETB), 12, 20, 44, 56

Benson, Margaret (sister of ETB), 41, 44–45

Benson, Mark Amussen (son of ETB): birth of, 87; increased responsibilities of, 119; family pictures of, 138, 141; reunited with ETB, 158; watches younger siblings, 159; travels with ETB, 164; serves in Eastern States Mission, 165–66, 169; sings in Utah Centennial Chorus, 168; reports on mission, 170; marriage of, 180; attends school at Stanford, 181; assists ETB, 300

Benson, Mary Larsen, 12

Benson, Mathias J., 104, 109

Benson, May (daughter-in-law of ETB), 290

Benson, Olive Mary Knight, 12

Benson, Orval (brother of ETB), 70, 78, 80, 90, 160

Benson, Pamelia Andrus, 3, 5–7, 10, 12

Benson, Reed Amussen (son of ETB): birth of, 83–84; learns boxing, 119; travels with ETB, 124, 126–27; learns of ETB's call to Twelve, 129; family pictures of, 138, 141; reunited with ETB, 158; watches younger siblings, 159; serves mission to Great Britain, 163, 168; and John Birch Society, 168, 240–41; serves in Eastern States Mission, 169; reports on mission, 170; attends inauguration and ETB's swearing in, 181–83; assists mother after car accident, 190; supports family television opportunity, 201; campaigns for Eisenhower's reelection, 214; meets George Wallace, 248; called as mission president, 276; teaches in Holy Land, 290; assists ETB, 300; ETB faints while talking with, 303

Benson, Sarah Dunkley (mother of ETB): marriage of, 12, 17–18; family of, 13; ancestry of, 16–17; character traits of, 17; gives birth to ETB, 18–19; bears eleven children, 20; home of, 21; loves the temple, 24; curtails ETB's fighting, 26; separated from George during mission, 31; picture of, with children, 32; insists George remain in mission field, 33; accompanies ETB to receive temple endowment, 47; writes to ETB, 54; death of, 96–97; predicts ETB's apostleship, 125

Benson, Serge (uncle of ETB), 20, 125

Benson, Steve (grandson of ETB), 255

Benson, Valdo (brother of ETB), 81

Berkeley, California, 102–4
Bethesda, Maryland, 114
Black, Susan Easton, 302
Blacks, priesthood given to, 281–82
Blessings: prenatal, 18; patriarchal, 30–31, 64, 109; healing, 42, 156, 267; ordination, 47, 85, 134, 269, 296; to ETB before trip to war-torn Europe, 146–47; father's, 147; to ETB as secretary of agriculture, 181
Boggs, Lilburn W., 4
Boise, Idaho: Benson family moves to, 91; ETB in stake presidency in, 98, 104; temple in, 100–101; stakes created in, 104; Benson family leaves, 108–9
Bolivia, 282
Bonneville International Corporation, 248–49, 266
Book of Mormon: ETB's early love of, 23, 34; ETB teaches discourse on, 57–58; ETB and Flora study, 77; history of, 162; ETB's interest in archaeological sites of, 204–5; ETB quotes from, 239; given to king of Thailand, 260; families should study, 266; as proselyting tool, 273; used as conference theme, 297; ETB emphasizes, as prophet, 300–302, 304–7, 309–11, 313–14, 318 ; ETB's final testimony of, 313–14
Bowen, Albert E., 116, 137
Boy Scout(s) of America: ETB shaves head with, 39–41; ETB works with, 88, 92, 140, 167, 169; Reed's achievements as, 124; ETB promotes, 204; picture of ETB with, 280
Brazil, 230, 276, 283
Bridger, Jim, 15
Brigham Young University: ETB attends, 30, 69–71; Ernest L.

Wilkinson president of, 115; Benson children attend, 158, 163, 210; Missionary Training Center near, 275; names food and agricultural institute after ETB, 277–78; ETB speaks at, 279, 284, 308; builds center in Jerusalem, 290; 11th Stake promotes Book of Mormon, 302
British Mission, 46, 48–49, 147–48, 163, 168
Brossard, Edgar B., 115, 136, 220
Brossard, Laura, 115, 200
Brown, Hugh B., 147–48, 263
Brown, Scott S., 98, 104
Brown, Zina, 147, 148
Burger, Warren, 303
Burton, David (son-in-law of ETB), 252, 256
Bunyan, John, 23
Bush, Barbara, 303
Bush, George, 303

Cache Valley: Ezra T. Benson called to colonize, 11–12; history of, 14–15; Bensons' influence farming in, 22; ETB known in, 127; ETB vacations in, 159–60; stake created in, 162
Cairns, Elder, 6
Callis, Charles A., 137, 162
Cannon, Abe, 115
Cannon cabin, 127–28, 320
Cannon, George J., 128, 129
Cannon, Hugh J., 58
Cannon, Sylvester Q., 125
Carlisle, England, 51–54, 206
Carpenter, Sam, 116
Central Baptist Church in Soviet Union, 227–28
Central Livestock Association, 187
Chadwick, James, 32
Charity, ETB on, 312
Cheating, ETB accused of, 38–39
Chile, 230
Christmas: in ETB's childhood home, 24–25, 64–65; in Benson home, 141, 268, 300

Church for All the World, A, 243

Church of Jesus Christ of Latter-day Saints, The: is not a "Sunday only" religion, 15; standards and doctrines of, 37–38; resistance to, in Great Britain, 52–53, 54, 60–61; resistance to, in Boise, 101; smooth operation of, 139–40; still functioning after WWII, 149, 152, 153, 154; historical sites of, 162, 167, 169–70, 286–87, 308; films and brochures of, 242–43; growth of, 251, 260–61, 275, 276–77, 311; ETB advises, historians, 279, 281; 1,000 stake of, created, 283; mission of, 297; under condemnation for neglecting Book of Mormon, 301, 304, 306, 314; members fast to reduce world hunger, 303; ETB bears testimony of, 306, 315; changes in, 311

Church Security Program, 99. *See also* Church Welfare Program

Church Welfare Program: beginnings of, 99; ETB's agricultural experience helpful to, 125; ETB promotes, 105; sends supplies to war-torn Europe, 149, 151–52, 154; emphasized at conference, 297

Clark, J. Reuben: daughter of, 115; writes to ETB, 116, 125; calls Spencer W. Kimball as apostle, 126; called to First Presidency, 144, 171–72; ETB reports on European Mission to, 158; ETB quotes, 239–40

Clawson, Rudger, 116, 124–25

Clay, Lucius D., 154

Cold war, 164, 237

Coleridge, Samuel Taylor, 51

Colombia, 204, 282

Coke, J. Earl, 185

Commodity Credit Corporation, 185

Communism: ETB opposes, 165, 225, 227–28; ETB speaks on, 166, 238–41, 245–47; John Birch Society opposed to,169; ETB writes about, 262; joke about, 273

Constitution, the; inspired men write, 143, 190–91, 309; ETB supports, 166; rights guaranteed by, 181; will hang by a thread, 239; Saints should study, 247, 284; bicentennial celebration of, 308–9

Cooperative Digest, 110, 111

Cooperatives, 88, 92–94. *See also* American Institute of Cooperation (AIC); National Council of Farmer Cooperatives (NCFC); Ezra Taft Benson—professional life

Corn Products International, 237, 266

Costa Rica, 204

Cottage, ETB's, 253–54, 268

Council Bluffs, 10, 170

Council on the Disposition of the Tithes, 249

Cowdery, Oliver, 169

Cowley, Matthew, 115, 144, 147

Cow-milking contest, 278

Cross Fire, 240

Cuba, 204

Czechoslovakia, 154

Dalley, John Edward, 30

Davis, John H., 185

De Gaulle, 219

de la Paz, Osvaldo Valdes, 204

Death: of ETB's grandmother, 56; of ETB's parents, 96–98; of Barbara Amussen, 122–23; of Pres. George Albert Smith, 170–71; of Pres. Eisenhower, 261; of Pres. McKay, 263–64; of Pres. Lee, 268–69; of Pres.

Kimball, 295–96; of Flora
Benson, 319; of ETB, 320–22
Dedication: of land of Israel, 7,
219, 250; of Swiss Temple,
208–9, 211; of land of Italy, 250;
of Venezuela, 250, 284; of land
of Indonesia, 262; of Mormon
Pavilion, 262; of Washington
Temple, 275; of Orson Hyde
Park, 284; of Kirtland chapel,
286; of Atlanta Temple, 290; of
temples, 311
Delta Cotton Council, 191
Democratic Party: members
oppose ETB, 178–79, 186, 195,
213, 222–23; presidential
candidates from, 257, 259
Denmark, 148–49, 206–7, 242
Denver Colorado Temple, 311
Depression, ETB on mental, 274
Depression, Great, 83, 88, 92, 193,
231
Deseret Farms of California, 265
Deseret Ranches of Florida, 265
Dewey, Thomas E., 136, 166–67,
176
Digestive problems, 168
Doctrine and Covenants, 311–12
Dunkley, Ann (cousin of ETB),
43–44
Dunkley, Joseph (grandfather of
ETB), 16, 17
Dunkley, Joseph Jr., (uncle of
ETB), 44
Dunkley, Margaret Leach, 16
Dunkley, Margaret Wright
(grandmother of ETB), 16–17,
25
Dunkley, Mary Ann Hobbs, 16
Dunkley, Sarah. See Benson, Sarah
Dunkley
Duns, John Jr., 249–50
Durham House, 49, 58, 63
Dyer, Alvin R., 263

Eagle Scout, 124
East Central States Mission, 142
Eastern States Mission, 165, 168

Eastland, James, 191–92
Eban, Abba, 283
Ecuador, 282
Eggs thrown at ETB, 216, 221
Egypt, 229, 283
Eisenhower, Dwight D.: selects
ETB as cabinet member, 83,
175–78, 180; counsels ETB to
soften approach, 95; commands
attack on Normandy, 144;
similarities between ETB and,
173–74, 184; inauguration
ceremonies for, 181; at ETB's
oath of office, 182; works with
ETB, 183; begins cabinet
meetings with prayer, 184;
supports ETB during
controversy, 188, 195–99, 213,
221–23; Church to pray for, 190,
211; campaign promises of, 194;
on character traits of ETB, 195;
asks ETB to continue work as
cabinet member, 199–200,
213–14; sends ETB to Latin
America, 203–4; is pleased with
ETB's Latin America tour, 205;
suffers heart attack, 210, 211;
ends first presidential term,
213; reelection campaign of,
214–16; begins second
presidential term, 216;
encourages ETB to travel with
family, 221; supports Food for
Peace program, 224; dinner to
honor, 233; expresses concerns
about Soviet Union, 238; passes
away, 261
Eisenhower, Mamie, 214, 233
Eisenhower, Milton S., 177
Ellender, Allen J., 180, 222
Ells, Doctor, 5, 6
Emigration Canyon, monument
in, 163
Enemy Hath Done This, An, 240,
262
England. See Great Britain
"Epistles of the Apostle," 191

Espinoia, Carlos Ramón, 283
Europe: ETB visits, after mission, 63–64; ETB called to help war-torn, 146–47; ETB travels to, 147; ETB tours continent of, 148–49, 154; ETB returns from, 156–57; ETB tours, as sec. of agriculture, 206–10; ETB travels as Apostle to, 249–50, 284–85, 289–90; ETB visits, with granddaughter in, 253
European Common Market, 230
European Information Service, 242
European Mission: presidents of, 50, 145; ETB as president of, 146–47, 148, 154–55, 241–43; ETB oversees work in, 249–50
Everett, Edward, 179
Expenditures Committee, 248–49
Expo '70, 258, 261, 262
Ezra Taft Benson Agriculture and Food Institute (Benson Institute), 277–78

Families: ETB speaks on, 266, 286; emphasized at conference, 297
Far East: ETB travels to, 230, 258–62, 277; ETB responsible for, 257–58
Farm Credit Association, 111
Farming: ETB's heritage of, 2, 35; ETB's early experiences with, 22–23; ETB chooses, as career, 34–35; ETB visits people involved in, 74, 79, 88; ETB improves family, 80–82; problems in U.S., 82–83; ETB gives up practicing, 86, 90; similarities between U.S. and European, 206–7; in Soviet Union, 226. See also Ezra Taft Benson—professional life
Ferguson, Clarence M., 185
Finland, 154, 226, 285, 242
Flood, Francis, 206
Floriade, the, 230
Flu epidemic, 42
Food for Peace, 224, 278, 292

Ford, Gerald, 279
Formosa, 230
4–H programs, 89, 204
France: ETB visits, as missionary, 63; ETB visits, after WWII, 148, 154: ETB visits as sec. of agriculture, 207–8, 216, 220, 229
Frankfurt, Germany, 241–42
Franklin County, 85, 89, 90, 93, 97
Franklin County Grain Growers' Association, 88
Freedom, 186–87, 225, 239, 247; ETB celebrates, 291
Freedom Festival, 291
Freedom Foundation Award, 281
Freedoms Foundation at Valley Forge, 308

Gateway apartment, 319
Geddes, Joseph A., 36
Germany: ETB visits, as missionary, 63; after WWII, 148, 150–54; ETB lives in, 241–42
Giannini Foundation for Agricultural Economics, 102, 104
Gibson, Walter Murray, 12
Golliher, Elizabeth. See Benson, Elizabeth Golliher
Gordon, Thomas, 5
Graham, Winifred, 52, 54, 55, 60
Grant, Heber J.: calls ETB on mission, 46; serves mission in Great Britain, 48; calls Flora Amussen on mission, 68; library named after, 69–70; visits Benson home, 100–101; calls ETB to Twelve, 102, 127–28, 320; ETB's relationship with, 116, 125; considers ETB for Twelve, 126; on ETB's employment, 130, 135–36; ordains ETB an Apostle, 133–34; death of, 144; J. Reuben Clark serves with, 171
Gray, Ralph S., 53–54
Great Britain: ETB called to serve in, 46; prophets who served in,

48–49; Church historical landmarks in, 51; Saints to remain in, 62; raises stock discount rate, 83; ETB returns to, after WWII, 147–48, 154; Reed called to serve mission to, 163, 168; ETB visits, as sec. of agriculture, 206, 216, 220

Great Depression, 83, 88, 92, 193, 231

Greece, 216, 219, 283–84

Guam, 267

Guatemala, possible Book of Mormon sites in, 205

Haircuts, Scouts get, 40

Hall, Leness, 204

Hanoi, 256, 258

Haraguichi, Noriharu Ishigaki, 282–83

Harris, Martin, 162

Hawaiian Islands: Ezra T. Benson travels to, 12, 267; Flora Amussen serves mission to, 68–69, 71; Pres. George Albert Smith visits, 170

Haycock, D. Arthur, 185, 300

Heart problems, 311, 312

"He-Coons," 197

High Cross of the Order of Merit of the Italian Republic, 210

Hill, Isaac, 3

Hill Cumorah, 162; pageant at, 308

Hinckley, Gordon B.: as counselor to Pres. Kimball, 285, 287–88; ETB's relationship with, 288–89; ETB assists, 289, 295; conducts at Atlanta Temple dedication, 290; pays tribute to ETB, 291; conducts Pres. Kimball's funeral, 296; as counselor to ETB, 296; meets with George Bush, 303; sees ETB as great promoter of Book of Mormon, 304; at general conference, 305

Hip problems, 254–56, 282, 285

Hiroshima, 144

Hodgson, Russell, 51

Hobbs, Mary Ann. See Dunkley, Mary Ann Hobbs

Hoffman, Mark, 296

Holland, 148–49, 230

Holmes, C. L., 76, 78

Holy Land. See Israel

Hong Kong, 216, 217, 277

Hoopes, Lorenzo, 185

Hoover, Herbert, 180, 185

Horse accidents, 254–56, 263–64

Hotel Utah: wedding breakfasts held in, 73, 210; ETB stays in, 131–32; prophets live in, 263, 295; honorary luncheon held in, 281; renamed, 319

House Agriculture Committee, 197

Humphrey, Hubert H., 222, 257, 259

Hunter, Howard W., 296, 320–21

Hyde, Orson, 7, 11, 219, 250, 284

Idaho Cooperative Council (ICC), 93–94, 105–6

Idaho Potato Growers' Association, 93–94

Illinois. See Nauvoo, Illinois, Quincy, Illinois

Imperious Mandate, 137

India, 216, 217–18

Indian trouble, 16–17

Indonesia, 262

Intermountain area of United States, 262, 266

International Federation of Agricultural Producers, 208

Iowa State College, 30, 71, 75–78

Isaacson, Thorpe B., 263

Israel: mission to dedicate, 7, 219, 250; ETB visits, as sec. of agriculture, 216, 218–19, 229; ETB visits, as Apostle, 283, 284, 290

Italy: ETB visits, as sec. of agriculture, 208, 216, 219; honors ETB, 210; missionary work in, 242; dedicated for preaching gospel, 249–50; growth of Church in, 251; ETB visits, as Apostle, 285

Jackson, H. Nelson, 73
Jackson Hole, Wyoming, 163
Jacksonville, Florida, 161–62
Japan: ETB visits, as sec. of agriculture, 216, 217, 230; ETB visits, as Apostle, 258–59, 260, 277; creation of stake in, 262; people from, in South America, 282–83
Jefferson, Thomas, 197–98
Jensen, Belle, 142
Jensen, James P., 142
Jerusalem. *See* Israel
Jesus Christ: ETB likened to, 20; Orson F. Whitney sees, in vision, 51; appears in Kirtland Temple, 287; ETB's testimony of, 294, 306, 315; appears to Joseph Smith, 308; ETB on being motivated by example of, 313
John Birch Society, 83–84, 168, 240–41
Johnson, Lindon B., 257; administration of, 258
Johnson, Peter E., 104
Jordan, nation of, 216, 229
Joseph Smith Memorial Building, 73, 319. *See also* Hotel Utah
Joy, Henry, 73–74
Judd, Walter H., 222

Kennedy, David M., 115
Kennedy, John F., 230
Kennedy, Leonora, 115
Kennedy, Robert F., 257, 258
Kentucky Louisville Mission, 276
Khrushchev, Nikita S., 224–26, 238
Kimball, Camilla, 136
Kimball, Heber C., 10, 50
Kimball, Spencer W.: called to the Twelve, 125–26, 132, *133*; ordained an Apostle, 134; reorganizes Washington Stake,

136; as member of the Twelve, 137; bids ETB farewell, 147; visits northern United States, 237; suffers from illness, 255; called as Acting President of the Twelve, 264; as President of the Church, 269; fragile health of, 270, 282, 285, 288; ETB supports, 273; travels to Far East, 277; asks ETB to serve on forum for domestic policy, 278; receives revelation on the priesthood, 281; reorganizes First Presidency, 287; delegates Church responsibility to Gordon B. Hinckley, 288–89; unable to attend Atlanta Temple dedication, 290; death of, 295–96; surgeries performed on, 317
King, Martin Luther, 257
Kiplinger Letter, 198–99
Kirtland, Ohio, 169, 286–87
Knight, Martha McBride, 8
Knight, Olive Mary. *See* Benson, Olive Mary Knight
Knight, Vinson, 8, 169
Koge, Denmark, 149, 207
Kontogiorgis, Mr., 283–84
Korea, 260, 277
K-Ration Quartet, 156

Larsen, Mary. *See* Benson, Mary Larsen
Latin America, ETB tours, 203–5, 230, 282–83, 284
Lava Hot Springs, trip to, 44
Leach, Margaret. *See* Dunkley, Margaret Leach
Leadership training, 117–18, 161, 252
Lee, Fern, 147
Lee, Harold B.: as friend of ETB at Oneida Academy, 37–39; on Church Security Program, 99; ETB works with, on welfare, 105; at general conference, 132; as member of the Twelve, 137;

drives ETB to airport, 147;
conducts funeral of Elder
Callis, 162; supports ETB
during controversy, 188–89;
attends ETB's induction into
Agricultural Hall of Fame,
231–32; as counselor to Joseph
Fielding Smith, 264; blesses
Flora, 267; passes away, 268–69;
ETB pays tribute to, 273
LeMay, Curtis, 259
Lincoln, Abraham, 23, 197
Liquor, 211
Little Visits with Great Americans,
24
Liverpool, 48–49, 58
Lobo, Oswaldo Castro, 276
Logan, Utah: ETB lives in, during
WWI, 41–42; ETB enrolls in
agricultural college in, 43; ETB
lives with grandmother in, 44;
Flora raised in, 67
London Philharmonic Orchestra,
148
Luce, Clare Boothe, 208

MacArthur, Douglas, 180
Man's Search for Happiness, 243
Marden, Orison, 24
Marketing, ETB skilled in, 93–94,
215
Marriott, Alice, 115
Marriott, Bill, *See* Marriott, J.
Willard
Marriott, J. Willard "Bill," 115, 190,
261, 292
Massachusetts, ETB's ancestors
from, 2–3, 11, 33
Maughan, Harold, 40
McCarthy, Eugene, 188, 257
McCarthy, Joseph, 221
McConkie, Amelia, 259
McConkie, Bruce R., 258–60, 262
McKay, David O.: serves mission
in Great Britain, 48; on
Winifred Graham, 52–53; as
president of British Mission,
58–59, 60, 61, 62–63, 142;

advises Saints to remain in
own countries, 62; as mentor to
ETB, 66, 101, 116, 125, 264;
counsel of, 68, 73; opposes
closure of BYU, 60; at funeral of
Sarah Benson, 96–97; ETB
visits, 126; congratulates ETB
on call to Twelve, 129; fails to
mention stipend, 130; called to
first presidency, 144; passes
away, 147, 263–64; opposes
communism, 165, 239–40, 264;
as president of Quorum of the
Twelve, 170; called as President
of the Church, 171–72; advises
ETB to accept cabinet position,
176–77, 180; blesses ETB, 181;
attends Swiss Temple
dedication, 208; encourages
ETB to continue as sec. of
agriculture, 213–14, 221;
commends ETB for cabinet
service, 235; ETB quotes,
239–40; does not restrain ETB's
opposition to communism, 241;
calls ETB as European Mission
president, 241; counsels ETB on
presidential candidacy, 245,
248; horse accident of, 263–64;
longevity of, 269
McKay, Emma Ray, 59
McKay, Thomas E., 145
McNarney, Joseph T., 151
Melchizedek Priesthood
Committee, 139, 160
Melchizedek Priesthood Handbook,
160
Mendon Memorial Park, 2
Menzies, Robert G., 205
Merrill, Harrison R., 37
Merrill, Joseph F., 137
Mexico, 204, 284
Meyers, William I., 231
Middle East, ETB travels to, 283,
289–90. *See also* Israel
Midway, Utah, 253–54
Millar, Z. Reed, 104

Index

Miller, Arthur L., 222
Miller, John D. (Judge), 105, 106, 107, 113, 114
Miller, Raymond W., 105, 106
Millennial Star, 53
Missionary Committee of the Church, 273
Missionary Training Center, 275–76
Missionary work, 117, 260, 275–76; ETB speaks on, 266, 273–74
Missions: to dedicate Holy Land, 7, 219; of Ezra T. Benson, 10; of George Benson, 31–34; of Flora Amussen, 68–69, 71; of Reed Benson, 163, 168–69; of Mark Benson, 165–66, 168–69
Missouri: Ezra T. Benson moves to, 3; trouble in, 4
Monson, Thomas S., 40, 296, *305*, 317
Morgan, Sebe, 287
"Mormon Colony," 115
"Mormon Mafia," 185
Mormon Pavilion, 243, 261, 262
Morse, True D., 185
Morton, Thruston B., 229
Moyle, Henry D., 162
Mundt, Karl, 221
Murrow, Edward R., 200–201
Museum of Church History and Art, 302
Music: ETB sings and plays trombone, 24, 37; ETB organizes Scout chorus, 39–40; Benson girls and, 98, 201; positive effects of, 148, 156; Utah Centennial Chorus, 168
Muskrat trapping, 36

Nagasaki, 144
National Agricultural Advisory Committee, 120
National Association of Manufacturers, 168
National Committee for Farm Production Supplies, 119
National Council of Farmers

Cooperatives (NCFC): offers ETB a job, 105–7; functions of, 109–10; ETB works for, 110–13, 120–21, 131, 177, 182; keeps ETB very busy, 118; Charles C. Teague president of, 124; offers ETB wage increase, 126; ETB leaves, 129–30, 135, 138; ETB's continued association with, 135–36, 139; ETB selects new exec. secretary for, 185
National Farm Credit Committee, 120
National Farmers' Union, 178, 196
National Republican Congressional Committee, 214
Nauvoo Illinois: Ezra T. Benson in, 8–10, 169; stake created in, 283
Nehru, Jawaharlal, 217–18
Nelson, Doctor, 6
Nelson, Russell M., 293
Netherlands, 154, 206, 229–30
New Deal, 94, 96, 120, 193, 202
New York, 135, 168–69; World's Fair in, 242–43
New Zealand, 230, 265, 284
Newcastle Conference: ETB as clerk in, 56–59; ETB as president of, 59–62; ETB returns to, 154
Nicaragua, 204–5
Nickname of ETB, 18
1976 Committee, 244–46
Nixon, Richard M.: cabinet of, 115; ETB's relationship with, 223–24; campaigns of, 229, 230, 257, 259; inauguration of, 261
North Atlantic Treaty Organization (NATO), 173, 175
Norway, 148–49, 226, 242

Oaks, Dallin H., 278
Obedience, ETB learns, 61–62
Olson Brothers, 266
Olverson, Kenneth, 86
Oneida Stake Academy: ETB plays basketball for, 27–28; ETB attends, 29, 35–39; ETB

temporarily withdraws from, 41; ETB graduates from, 42
Orient: ETB travels to, 230, 258–62, 277; ETB responsible for, 257–58
Orson Hyde Park, dedication of, 284

Paarlberg, Don, 185
Packer, Boyd K., 265
Page, John E., 7, 219
Pakistan, 216, 217
Palmer, James T., 56–57
Palmyra, New York, 162
Panama, 204
Paraguay, 283
Parker, James (Jim) (son-in-law of ETB), 285, 292
Parkinson, George B. (cousin of ETB), 26–27, 42
Parkinson, Lulu (aunt of ETB), 18, 26
Patriotism: of ETB, 133, 157, 177, 180, 188; ETB speaks on, 143, 164–65, 166, 172–73, 246–47; promoted by John Birch Society, 168–69. See also Constitution, the; Freedom; United States of America
Pearl Harbor, 115, 121–22, 260
Pearson, Drew, 292
Peres, Shimon, 283
Perry, Eliza Ann. See Benson, Eliza Ann Perry
Person to Person, Benson family appears on, 200–201
Peru, 230, 282, 311
Petersen, Mark E., 138, 147, 176, 177, 237
Philippines, 230, 258–59, 267, 288
Pilgrim's Progress, 23
Pioneer: trail, 74–75; celebrations, 163–64
Poland, 154, 225
Polygamy, 9, 10, 12, 67
Portugal, 216, 220
Powers, Gary Francis, 238
Pratt, Parley P., 53

Prayer: ETB on, 21–22; overcoming discouragement through, 55–56; Benson family and, 84–85, 114; ETB prompted through, 155; about cabinet appointment, 176–77; ETB begins political meetings with, 184–85; ETB on family, 266; sacramental, 313
Preston, Idaho: George Taft Benson lives near, 12; Oneida Academy located in, 36; ETB and Flora live in, 41, 86–90; ETB visits, 127, 160
Price ceilings, 121
Price supports. See Subsidies, farm
Priesthood given to blacks, 281–82
Promised Valley, 164
Provo, Utah, 69, 291
Proxmire, William, 221
Public Law 480 (Agricultural Trade Development and Assistance Act), 198, 203, 217–18, 220
Puerto Rico, 204

Quincy, Illinois: Ezra T. Benson moves to, 4; Pamelia Andrus Benson arrives in, 5; Church meetings held in, 6–7; stake created in, 7; ETB visits, 169
Quorum of Twelve: demands on, 58; history of, 137; ETB's fellow members of, 137–38; to attend stake conferences semi-annually, 168; duties of, 270

Rawson, Calvin, 3
Reactivation, 298
Reagan, Ronald, 292, 303, 308
Red Carpet, The, 240
Red Cross, American 303
Refugees, 217
Regional Representatives of the Twelve, 252, 271
Reorganized Church of Jesus Christ of Latter Day Saints, 287

Republican National Committee, 229

Republican party: members oppose ETB, 195, 213, 221–23, 228–29; loses power, 223; nominates Richard Nixon, 229, 257, 259

Rich, Charles C., 11

Richards, Franklin D., 11

Richards, George F., 137, 170

Richards, LeGrand, 97–98, 293

Richards, Stephen L, 137, 171

Rigdon, Sidney, 6

Robinson, J. Robert, 36

Romney, George, 257

Romney, Marion G.: ETB's basketball victory over, 28; dedicates Venezuela, 250; as counselor to Spencer W. Kimball, 269, 287; suffers from health problems, 285, 288, 296

Roosevelt, Franklin D., 94, 120–21, 131, 193, 279

Royal Albert Hall, 148

Russia. See Soviet Union

Sacred Grove, 162, 167, 308

Salik, Gustav, 276

Salt Lake Area Chamber of Commerce honors ETB, 291, 292

Salt Lake City, Utah: Ezra T. Benson moves to, 10–11; ETB visits, 126, 127; ETB moves to, 183–39; Benson home in, 140–41; Flora and girls stay in, until school ends, 183; ETB moves back to, 235; ETB spends final years in, 319

Salt Lake Tabernacle: ETB's first speech in, 132–33; funerals held in, 171, 296, 320; solemn assembly held in, 265; photographs of ETB in, 305, 309, 315; ETB's last speech in, 315

Salt River Valley, 161

San Diego California Temple, 312

San Francisco, California, 103–4

Schubert, Richard, 303

Scotland, 206, 268

Scottish Cooperative Wholesale, 206

Scouting. See Boy Scouts of America

Sea gulls, 163–64

Senate Agricultural Committee, 222

Service-to-Freedom Award, 308

Shakespeare, William, 67

Singapore, 261

Smallpox, 33

Smith, George A., 11, 171

Smith, George Albert: serves mission in Great Britain, 48; advises ETB on NCFC association, 135–36; as member of the Twelve, 137; ETB's friendship with, 140; tours East Central States Mission, 142; ordained as prophet, 144; works to relieve Saints in war-torn Europe, 145; calls ETB as president of European Mission, 146–47, 148; gives healing blessing to Beth, 156; ETB reports on European Mission to, 158; attends Reed's farewell, 163; extends greetings to Pres. Truman, 167; calls Reed on short mission, 169; travels of, 170; death of, 170–71; D. Arthur Haycock's association with, 185

Smith, Hyrum, 4, 7, 169

Smith, Hyrum Gibbs, 64

Smith, Joseph Jr.: in Liberty jail, 4; first vision of, 4–5, 55, 162, 167, 308; remains composed when character is attacked, 6; Ezra T. Benson is drawn to, 8; takes plural wife, 9; conspiracy against, 9; runs for U.S. president, 10, 245; martyrdom of, 10, 169; did not serve mission in Great Britain, 48;

receives gold plates, 162; street named after, 169; on U. S. Constitution, 239; responsible to preach, 273; leaves Kirtland, 286; ETB's testimony of, 306; never saw Zion redeemed, 314

Smith, Joseph Sr., 162

Smith, Joseph F., 31, 48

Smith, Joseph Fielding: serves mission in Great Britain, 48; as member of the Twelve, 138; as Acting President of the Twelve, 170; as counselor to David O. McKay, 263; called as President of the Church, 263; longevity of, 269

Smith, Milan, 185

Smith, Samuel Harrison, 273

Smoot, Reed, 231

Smoot-Hawley Act, 231

Snow, Erastus, 11

Snow, Lorenzo, 11, 12, 48, 250, 306–7

Socialism, 246, 262

Soil Bank, 203

Sonne, Alma, 156

Sonny Boy, 264

Sorenson, Bruce, 317

Sousa, John Philip, 47

South America. See Latin America

South Seas, 230

Southey, Robert, 51

Soviet Union, 224–28, 237–38

Space, race into, 237–38

Spain, 216, 219–20

Speech problems, 315–18

Spirit, the: influence of, 57–58; ETB protected by prompting of, 235; prompts ETB in selection of stake patriarch, 293; ETB on being motivated by, 313

Sprague, Charles, poem, 266

Sputnik, 237

St. Paul, Minnesota, 78–79, 187, 188

St. Peter's (Cathedral), 208

Stanton, Daniel, 7

Stapley, Delbert L., 170, 237

Stevenson, Adlai, 215

Stock market crash, 83

Stover, Walter, 156

Street meetings banned, 61

Stroke: Flora suffers, 267–68, 274; ETB suffers, 315

Subdural hematomas, 317

Subsidies, farm: ETB opposes, 179, 186–87, 194–98, 214–15; history of, 193; cripple U.S. trade, 203; Eisenhower supports lower, 222

Summerfield, Arthur, 233

Sunderland, England, mission experiences in, 56–58, 62

Surpluses, farm: New Deal creates, 202; ETB works to liquidate, 202–3, 205, 209–10, 216; ETB sells, to Latin America, 203–5; ETB sells, to Europe, 206–10; ETB criticized for policies about, 210; ETB sells, on world tour, 216–20; reduced by Food for Peace program, 224

Sweden, 148–49, 226, 242

Switzerland: ETB visits, as missionary, 64; ETB visits, after WWII, 150; ETB purchases supplies in, 151; temple dedicated in, 208–9, 211; as part of European Mission, 242

Symington, Stuart, 222

Taft, Chloe. See Benson, Chloe Taft

Taft, Robert, 2, 175, 177

Taiwan, 260, 277

Tanner, N. Eldon, 263, 264, 269, 285, 287

Taylor, John, 48, 51

Taylor, Ralph, 106

Teague, Charles C.: offers ETB position with NCFC, 106, 107; ETB works with, 113; ETB's visit with, 124, 126; ETB tells, of call to Twelve, 129–30

Television, Benson family on, 77, 200–201

Temple: Nauvoo, 8–9; Logan, 18, 24, 47, 159; Sarah Benson's love for, 24; ETB endowed in, 47; ETB's marriage in Salt Lake, 73; Boise, 100–101; ETB performs sealings in, 163, 180; Kirtland, 169, 287; Swiss, 208–9, 211; Barbara's marriage in Salt Lake, 210; all ETB's children sealed in, 252; Washington D.C., 260, 275, 300; Brethren meet in Salt Lake, 264, 269, 290; Atlanta, 290; ETB's love for, 290–91; Jordan River, 290; attendance emphasized at conference, 297; all worthy can receive endowment in, 311; Lima Peru, 311; Buenos Aires, Argentina, 311; Denver, 311; San Diego, 312; Salt Lake, 319

Temple View Farms, 265

Tet Offensive, 256

Thailand, 260

Thurmond, Strom, 244, 247

Titanic, 48

Tithing, 117–18, 306–7

Title of Liberty, 240

Tolstoy, Leo, 23

Trinidad, 204

Truman, Harry E., 167

Turkey, 216, 219

Twelfth Night, 67

United States Department of Agriculture (USDA), 110, 111, 191, 207, 225; ETB's office at, 182–83; ETB selects staff for, 185; ETB restructures, 185–86; Food for Peace program, 224; honors ETB, 232–33

United States of America: ETB speaks about, 143, 164–65, 166, 190–91; problems facing, 172–74, 265; dependent on God, 184; a blessed land, 220; relationship of Soviet Union with, 224–28, 237–38; communism could destroy, 239–40; involvement in Vietnam, 256–58; Japanese attitude toward, 259; favored status of, 315

United States Secretary of Agriculture. *See* Ezra Taft Benson—professional life

University of California at Berkeley, 30, 102–4, 124

University of Idaho, 86, 89; offers ETB position, 90; ETB censored by, 95; denies ETB continued leave of absence, 104; ETB leaves, 107–8

Uruguay, 230

Utah, colonization of, 11

Utah Agricultural College, 41, 43, 66, 69

Utah Centennial Chorus, 168

Utah Farm Bureau honors ETB, 291, 292

Utah Mission, 275

Utah War, 11, 250

Venezuela, 204, 250, 284

Victorian (a ship), 47–48

Vietcong, 256

Vietnam, 257, 259–60, 261

Vietnam War, 256, 258, 262

Vinson, Fred M., 181, *182*

Virgin Islands, 204

Visa problems, 276

Waldenses, the, 250

Walker, Flora (granddaughter of ETB), 253

Walker, Robert H. (son-in-law of ETB), 210

Wallace, George, 248, 259

Washington, D.C.: ETB moves to, 109–10, 113–16; ETB leaves, 138–39, 235; ETB visits, 106–7, 142–43, 162, 292–93, 300–303; monument honoring Brigham Young in, 170; ETB moves back to, 183, 200; Harold B. Lee visits, 188–89; temple in, 260–61, 275

Washington, George, 23

"Washington Merry-Go-Round" (syndicated column), 292

Washington Stake: ETB as president of, 116–18, 122, 130, 131, 134–35; reorganization of, 136; bids ETB farewell, 138, 235; ETB visits, 162; shows concern for ETB, 190

Watermelon patch, 26

Watkins, Arthur V., 176

Webster, William, 303

Wells, Daniel H., 11

West Germany, 225, 229

What Men Live By, 23

White House Forum on Domestic Policy, 278–79

Whitmer, Peter Sr., 162, 308

Whitney, Newell K., 50

Whitney, Orson F., 14; as pres. of British Mission, 50–51, 142; edits *Millennial Star*, 53; released as mission president, 58; ETB's relationship with, 66; performs ETB's marriage, 73

Whitney, Idaho: description of, 14–15; school in, 29, 37; smallpox epidemic in, 33; Scout troop from, 39–40; master's degree unique in, 78; ETB and Flora move back to, 80; ETB visits, 127, 160; ETB's burial in, 321–22

Widtsoe, John A., 137, 145–46

Wilkinson, Alice, 115

Wilkinson, Ernest L., 115, 116–17, 231

Wing, Lela. *See* Benson, Lela Wing

Women, role of, in marriage, 299

Woodruff, Wilford, 48

Wordsworth, William, 51

World War I, 41–42, 63

World War II: destruction caused by, 63, 148, 150–53; effect of, on agriculture, 119–22; rationing during, 142; end of, 144; Church offers relief after, 145–46; Church survives during, 149; Eisenhower commands forces during, 175; reconstruction after, 207, 211; Church growth after, 259

World's Fair, 242–43, 258, 261, 262

Wright, Margaret. *See* Dunkley, Margaret Wright

Yale Ward, 140–41, 163, 165, 170

Yearbook of Agriculture, 177

Yellowstone National Park, 163

Young, Brigham: leads Saints into Illinois, 4; home of, 8, 169; leads Saints to Utah, 10, 164; colonizes Utah, 11, 16; policy of, about Indians, 16; serves mission in Great Britain, 48; Orson F. Whitney serves as bishop over, 50; ordains Ezra T. Benson to apostleship, 74; monuments to honor, 170

Young, Milton R., 180

Young, Seymour B., 47

Young Men Mutual Improvement Association (YMMIA), 85, 92, 139, 160

Young Women Mutual Improvement Association (YWMIA), 85, 88, 92, 139, 160

Yugoslavia, 225, 276

ZCMI, 279

Zimmer, Max, 156

Zions First National Bank, 266